GOD



To: Irene
From: Karen
With love in our Lord

# CALLED *for the* VERY LAST *of* DAYS

GOD SPEAKS -2

# CALLED *for the* VERY LAST *of* DAYS

## VOLUME 2

LEE LEE

XULON PRESS

Xulon Press
2301 Lucien Way #415
Maitland, FL 32751
407.339.4217
www.xulonpress.com

Printed in the United States of America.

ISBN-13: 978-1-54564-852-0

***Please read this book through thoroughly, so that you will not miss out on the sequence and the importance of the messages that the beloved Lord Jesus is sending to His Church, through this and the other books that are to follow. You will therefore not understand what He is saying to His church, by partially reading any of them.***

THIS BOOK IS WRITTEN FOR AND DEDICATED TO
THE BRIDE OF THE LORD JESUS CHRIST

***"NOW THIS IS ETERNAL LIFE:
THAT THEY MAY KNOW YOU, THE ONLY TRUE GOD,
AND JESUS CHRIST, WHOM YOU HAVE SENT."
JOHN 17:3 NIV***

# TABLE OF CONTENTS

# INTRODUCTION

This Book is the continuation of Book 1 – "Called For the Very Last of Days" – Volume 1. The purpose of both Books is to introduce the Church of the Lord Jesus Christ to Lee Lee – His chosen servant – called to His Church to reveal the darkness that is over it and the plan of the beloved Lord Jesus to cleanse it, in preparation of her to become the spotless, holy Bride that He will be Coming for.

In this Book, Lee Lee begins to reveal what our Lord has given him in depth of knowledge and understanding of the work of the enemy of the human race – satan, using the lives of the students that the Lord had placed with him. It gives real learning specifics and is an exposé of the cause of the darkness over the church, as manifested in and through the lives of the students, who were professed Christians and seen as a part of the church. It shows how the devil robs us of the grace of God; of His many and continuous blessings and deliverances, through the deceitful beliefs and heart attitudes that everyone comes to the Lord Jesus with (due to the fall and the reality of us all being born in sin and shaped in iniquity). Hence our desperate need for this knowledge so that we no longer are easy prey and so permit the enemy of our souls to rob us through our ignorance of him and his evil work against us.

The following is taken from Chapter 15 – THE HEART OF THE CHURCH BEING REVEALED: "Notwithstanding, the Lord Jesus has used all that has happened to now begin to open my eyes, as He uncovers and reveals the working of satan and his demons against the church. This is now ongoing. "Thank You beloved Lord Jesus.""

Through what the Lord Jesus has revealed in the lives of the students and what He taught and permitted Lee Lee to personally know and experience, and to see and understand as the state of His church, he lists a total of 15 causes under the title: "SOME OF THE REASONS WHY THE CHURCH IS IN DARKNESS." All are pertinent to every church body and to every individual believer.

This Book documents the beginning of our Lord Jesus removing the shroud from over satan, exposing him through shining His Light of Truth in Knowledge, to free His Church, preparing His Bride for His Second Coming. This He continues in deeper and greater dimensions in the 12 Books that follow.

# FOREWORD

It could be that we do not believe there is an abundant life, one that is free from the worries, cares, the concerns and anxieties of life, where there are no more weights or burdens to carry. For the weight of life will be finally surrendered to the Lord Jesus to whom it belongs, and to Him alone. He is the only One who can carry it. It is only then that we will be free to clothe ourselves with, and to enjoy our dearest and beloved Lord, God and Father, looking to Him and receiving Him in all that we need to live this life. We are now able to walk in the abundant life of faith and love which He brought, and enjoy it because the focus will no longer be on self. This abundant life of faith and love gives true liberty and joy in the Lord Jesus to enjoy the life, which He, the beloved Lord Jesus bought and paid for with His own shed blood on Calvary's Cross.

Indeed, we need to look no further than our lack of faith to see that our all is not fully trusted into the hands of the Lord Jesus. This should help us to realize how much darkness we are in. Look how slow we are in every area of our lives to first put our trust in the Lord Jesus, and to wait upon Him because we truly believe His Word. This lack results in our picking up the life and carrying it, suffering under its burden, while at the same time worrying about it day and night. This is because we have not totally trusted the Lord Jesus with the life, and for some, it is the whole life they are carrying, and not trusting the Lord Jesus with any part of it.

# ACKNOWLEDGEMENT

We hereby acknowledge our Lord and Savior Jesus Christ for all that is written herein and in the Books to follow.

# CHAPTER 1

# LOVE

My Love reached out and touched me, and I was instantly drawn to Him. He then cleansed me and imparted life to me, and when He did, faith and love rose up in me and I desired Him greatly. I was drawn to His bosom, and there He embraced me. I was delighted! Then He showed me that His love for me is unconditional, and that He loves me far beyond that which I can comprehend. It is a love that is pure; a love that does not compel, though it firmly disciplines – all to keep me in His truth. It is a love that invites obedience; a love that seeks after my highest good in all situations and circumstances; a love that does not give up, but rather suffers long; a love that is always wooing me away from sin and into His loving arms; a love that continues cleansing me to bring me closer to Him; a love that is patient; a love that shelters and protects me there in His will; a love that watches over me and warns me of the danger of the old ways – sin. It is a love that gives me inner liberty, peace and joy. It enlightens me, and by His grace enables me to choose that which is pure, upright and good, over that which is evil, corrupt and wrong. It does not stifle or threaten; yet it gives me a reverent fear for my Father that keeps me from going astray. With His gentle breath He breathes on me, to strengthen and encourage me on the path of peace.

He understands all my ways, my desires, dreams, thoughts and fears – how wrong they are, and out of His love for me He chooses to transform me, and with His strong arm He lifts me up, holds me close to His bosom, and comforts me there. His love is so strong yet so gentle and tender towards me; a love that fails not; a love that keeps my head up high, and keeps my thoughts pure towards my Beloved. This love – God's love, keeps me strong in faith in Him. It makes me lean evermore on Him, desire Him more, love Him more, and put all my trust in Him even more.

For many years, I withheld myself from Him, until my Beloved showed me how great and tender His love for me really is, and how wonderful it is to have His strong, yet warm and tender arms to daily lead and guide me along life's path. While the world watches with envy, and at times with hate, my Beloved opens His truth to me, and lets me learn of Him: His inestimable goodness, His great and tender love, His mercies, His precious grace, His forgiving nature, His just ways, His faithfulness, His trustworthiness, His willingness to forgive, His pure and loving thoughts towards me, His always choosing for my highest good, and His warm embrace.

> For I know the plans I have for you," declares the LORD, "plans to prosper you and not to harm you, plans to give you hope and a future. [12]Then you will call upon me and come and pray to me, and I will listen to you. [13]You will seek me and find me when you seek me with all your heart. [14]I will be found by you,". . . Jer. 29:11-14

I have learnt to trust Him more each day, and have given all my love to Him. He rules over my life and affairs, and has placed many treasures in my heart that are pure. I am secure in Him, and my future is as bright as His light. No one can rob me of Him, and no one can take me from Him. I am at peace in Him and with Him; I am secure and am at rest in Him. I am now free because I have found my true Love. There is no more pain, tears, sorrow, fears, loneliness, grief, emptiness or death, all because my Beloved has taken me unto Himself and made me His child. Said my Beloved to me: "My heart yearned after you for many years, but now that you have decided to come to Me, My Heart is glad, for now you are safe with Me." Here He gives me hope and a bright future in Him for evermore. I love Him so. Amen.

The Lord appeared to us in the past, saying: "I have loved you with an everlasting love; I have drawn you with loving–kindness. Jer. 31:3

"When he came to his senses, he said, 'How many of my father's hired men have food to spare, and here I am starving to death! [18]I will set out and go back to my father and say to him: Father, I have sinned against heaven and against you. [19]I am no longer worthy to be called your son; make me like one of your hired men.' [20]So he got up and went to his father. "But while he was still a long way off, his father saw him and was filled with compassion for him; he ran to his son, threw his arms around him and kissed him. [21]"The son said to him, 'Father, I have sinned against heaven and against you. I am no longer worthy to be called your son.' [22]"But the father said to his servants, 'Quick! Bring the best robe and put it on him. Put a ring on his finger and sandals on his feet. [23]Bring the fattened calf and kill it. Let's have a feast and celebrate. [24]For this son of mine was dead and is alive again; he was lost and is found.' So they began to celebrate. Luke 15:17-24

**You can also come to that Everlasting Fountain and drink of the Waters. There you too can find this Great, Beloved God, Lord and Father, for He awaits you there.**

## CHAPTER 2

# VISIONS OF THE OLD MAN * THE TOMBSTONES * THE BLACKNESS OF THE HEAVENS

One day, while I was at home sitting in the living room and reading my Bible, a vision appeared before me. In it, I saw an old man who was bent over by the weight of a very long and large sack, filled with all his worldly possessions. He was carrying it all on his back while walking up a very winding and steep road, which went up a very high mountain – on his way to heaven – so he thought. I watched him as he stopped, took off his load, and rested. Then, after resting a while, he again picked up his load with a groan, and continued on his way up the mountain.

In his beliefs he is making his way to heaven, but it is hard work. It is very trying, for it is a hard road to walk and a rough and tough mountain to climb. Indeed, it is impossible. Nevertheless, many souls in the church do this very thing by picking up the weight of their lives every day, trying to carry it all by themselves, while murmuring and accusing their Lord and God every step of the way as this man was doing, rather than trusting it all to the Lord Jesus.

As with the vision of the little boy recorded in Volume 1 of this book, the beloved Lord Jesus was showing me, through this vision, the rejection of His Sacrificial Atonement on Calvary's Cross, along with His grace, by many in the church. He was also showing me how determined some are to make their own way through self-efforts and their own sacrifices, instead of receiving the sacrifice that the Lord Jesus made for us all on Calvary's Cross.

Many would rather offer the Lord Jesus self-efforts, sacrifices and works of all kinds, rather than to receive His Atoning Sacrifice on Calvary's Cross for themselves, and so to surrender to Him and trust Him with their lives. This, in reality, is making their own way and going their own way, which is away from the Lord Jesus Christ.

Again, the Lord Jesus was showing me a large part of the church that is working and making their own way, rather than embracing the way He has already made for them, and so from then on, to accuse the Lord Jesus for the hard and rough road that they themselves choose to walk. They do all this instead of looking to the Lord Jesus and putting their trust in Him, for Him to guide them along the way He has made for them to walk.

> Jesus answered, "I am the way and the truth and the life. No one comes to the Father except through me. John 14:6

In my few years of walking with the Lord Jesus, He has shown me many such persons, whom dishonesty and pride will not permit to humble themselves to ask Him for the help they so desperately need to be able to embrace Him, submit their lives to Him in obedience, and so be able to walk with Him. So, instead, they carry the weight of their own lives, and they are laden down with it. Yet, they are determined to carry it all by themselves, as if to ask the Lord Jesus for help is too much for them, too humiliating and belittling for them. There are many such souls in the church.

Works, works, works! For many, works and service are substitutes for a life and a walk of faith with the Lord Jesus, and if they are not striving and working, they feel as if there is no purpose for their lives. Some are restless and weighted down with the worries of life. Some are even condemned, and have no peace; at least not the sweet peace that our beloved Lord Jesus gives, because the desire to serve the church and different types of ministries outweighs the desire to surrender their lives to the Lord Jesus, and sincerely live for Him. This is the church we were brought into, and this is what we were taught, and so we just toed the line.

Yes, there is darkness over the church – thick darkness. But glory be to His holy name, our beloved and holy Lord Jesus, is going to deliver His church with a mighty hand! He is going to move across His church in every country in the entire world, cleansing it from all the selfish motivations, the self-will, and from all the filth of the flesh and this world that contaminates it. He is going to do this in order to bring us back to first base, where there will be a delightful preoccupation with loving the Lord our God with all our heart, soul, mind and strength.

The zeal for doing what some call "good works," has helped to dampen, or might even have eroded much of the sincere love that the church has had for our God and Lord. Nevertheless, I believe that there are individuals in the church who love the Lord Jesus, to the extent that we/they understand love for God, since we are all under darkness.

Because of our ignorance of satan's work against the church, this pitch darkness has been over the church throughout these many generations. Therefore, there has been a selfish neglect to submit in obedience and faithfulness, to be able to draw close to the Lord

Jesus to: **"'Love the Lord your God with all your heart and with all your soul and with all your mind and with all your strength.'"** (Mark 12:30) and therefore, to love our neighbor as ourselves and walk in obedience to our Lord and God.

> . . .I will bring him near and he will come close to me, for who is he who will devote himself to be close to me?' declares the Lord. [22]"'So you will be my people, and I will be your God.'" Jer. 30:21-22

Yet, at this point, there is nothing we can do to change this situation, apart from acknowledging our state of darkness individually, and also as a body. If we each did this, that would then be the basis for our individual, as well as our corporate repentance. The only thing that the church can do now is to acknowledge and repent. Then, after we have done so, we must stop making plans to fix things ourselves. Rather, we must pray and put our faith in our beloved Lord Jesus, and trust Him to move as He wills, and according to how He wills, when He wills, to cleanse our hearts and to bring us out of this thick darkness that we are in.

I would suggest however, that we all should have an attitude of surrender, and a willingness to yield all that we are to our beloved Lord Jesus. There are those who will want to hang on to the status quo in the church, along with the world and its ways, and will not be willing to let go of them, but I do warn you against such chosen positions.

> "To the angel of the church in Laodicea write:
> These are the words of the Amen, the faithful and
> true witness, the ruler of God's creation. [15]I know
> your deeds, that you are neither cold nor hot. I wish
> you were either one or the other! [16]So, because you
> are lukewarm – neither hot nor cold – I am about to
> spit you out of my mouth. [17]You say, 'I am rich; I
> have acquired wealth and do not need a thing.' But
> you do not realize that you are wretched, pitiful,
> poor, blind and naked. [18]I counsel you to buy from
> me gold refined in the fire, so you can become rich;
> and white clothes to wear, so you can cover your
> shameful nakedness; and salve to put on your eyes,
> so you can see. [19]Those whom I love I rebuke and
> discipline. So be earnest, and repent. [20]Here I am!
> I stand at the door and knock. If anyone hears my
> voice and opens the door, I will come in and eat with
> him, and he with me. [21]To him who overcomes, I
> will give the right to sit with me on my throne, just
> as I overcame and sat down with my Father on his
> throne. [22]He who has an ear, let him hear what the
> Spirit says to the churches." Rev.3:14-22

## VISION OF TOMBSTONES

One Sunday morning, I happened to visit a church, and after I sat for a while, the Lord Jesus gave me a vision of the church. In the vision, I saw a very beautiful, green and lush hillside, dotted throughout with tombstones. It was as if these tombstones were strategically placed within the beautifully manicured garden on this hillside. They were all lily white. Everything was spotlessly clean and orderly, and the grass was perfectly manicured.

Then, the beloved Lord Jesus impressed me in my spirit with these words: "Within are dead men's bones." The knowledge He gave me was that this whole church was like those whitewashed tombstones in the vision which looked beautiful on the outside, yet on the inside, there were dead men's bones. He also impressed me with this Scripture from Matthew Chapter 23.

> "Woe to you, teachers of the law and Pharisees, you hypocrites! You are like whitewashed tombs, which look beautiful on the outside but on the inside are full of dead men's bones and everything unclean.
> **28**In the same way, on the outside you appear to people as righteous but on the inside you are full of hypocrisy and wickedness. Matt. 23:27-28

## VISION OF DARKNESS OVER US

One day, my beloved Lord Jesus gave me a vision of what seemed to be the whole earth under a covering of thick darkness. All I could see was complete blackness over us – the darkness was so thick that I could not see the sky. He then opened up a small part of that blackness over the House of Life, just long enough for me to see a doubled-headed snake looking down on us, and then He closed it back again. He gave me no understanding at the time of what this meant, apart from showing me the extent of the blackness, which seemed to have covered the whole earth, or it could be the whole church, or both. Beyond this, its meaning has not yet been revealed. However, the context of this vision is darkness that does not allow the sky to come into view.

This is similar to the vision of the pitch dark jungle and the filthy stagnant dark water, which are speaking to the darkness over the church. This represents and reveals its condition at the same time. I therefore believe that this vision is another sign confirming the darkness that is over the church.

## CHAPTER 3

# WHAT IS HOUSE OF LIFE?

One day as I was driving along the highway, a question came to me deep within my spirit from my beloved Lord Jesus. The question was, "What is House of Life?" This is the name of the property which houses the ministry in Mexico. I did not know how to respond to this question from my Lord. So, I searched my mind, but there was no answer with which to respond to my beloved Lord Jesus. This was simply because neither the church nor the school were in operation any longer. I therefore had no understanding of what the present status of the House of Life was, because for many years there has been no visible movement or activity there, apart from the very few live-in students. I was therefore at a loss as to how to respond. This was before the Lord began to write the books through me.

I also realized in that moment, that I had never given a thought to the subject. This surprised me, because one would expect that I should have known what the present status of the House of Life is, and what its purpose is. But no, to my surprise and shame, I did not know. Eventually I gave up and responded with, "Lord, I do not know what House of Life is." With that response, I thought that the matter had ended, although I continued in a state of perplexity that I did not know what House of Life is. This was simply because the question had never come up before, and even if it had, I still would not have had an answer.

However, approximately ten minutes had gone by, and to my surprise, the question was repeated: "What is House of Life?" I was now even more perplexed, and again I searched my mind for an answer, but found none. I simply had no answer to give my Lord, and so with some surprise, dismay and embarrassment that I did not know, I said, "Lord, I do not know what House of Life is." So once more, I thought that the matter had ended. But no! About another ten minutes went by, when the question came again, just as it had on the two previous occasions. The fact that this question, "What is House of Life?" was repeated a third time astonished me very much; I believe that I could easily say I was shocked by it. Now my thoughts were, I must know the answer to this, because the question had now been asked a third time. At this point, I became very concerned.

Once again I searched my mind, and the more I searched, the more confounded I became. I thought, "I have searched my mind, but I found no answer, yet this must be a very important thing for me to know, as the question was asked three times." I was baffled, because I still was unable to find an answer to something that I should know at all times. But then I realized that I had never thought about it, and I also realized that even if I had, I still would not have known, and therefore would not have had an answer. So, I again said to the beloved Lord that I really did not know what House of Life is. Then I waited to see what would happen. For approximately another ten minutes, there was no response.

At the end of the ten minutes, these words came from our beloved Father and Lord: "House of Life is where God will be loved; where God will be desired; where God will be admired." That was the end of His communication. God will be loved, desired and admired; this was the most beautiful combination of words I have ever heard. These words were so delightful to my hearing; they brought tremendous joy to my heart. I was delighted to have heard them. "Thank You beloved Lord Jesus."

I will now look forward to that day, along with those who the beloved Lord Jesus will bring together with the singular purpose of loving, desiring and admiring our beloved God and Lord. What a delight and joy that will be to come together with faithful brothers and sisters in the Lord.

Here was yet another one of those many things that had been placed before me that the Lord Jesus requires me to trust Him for, and to wait upon Him for its fulfillment. After these many years had passed, I am still looking forward to that day when our wonderful and beloved God and Lord, will be so blessed by all His children, when these three beautiful words – Love, Desire and Admire, will become the reality from the pure hearts of all God's children towards Him. When this happens, the abundant life would be on its way to the church.

## CHAPTER 4

# THE ATTACKS AND AFFLICTIONS OF SATAN

Problems had developed around me that just could not be explained. My legal status in Mexico was gone, although I had spent a lot of money to obtain it, and the annual fees I paid were quite hefty. This happened during the ongoing devaluation of the Mexican currency. In addition, people who hated me seemed to be all around and multiplying. My health also began to fail.

Every night as I entered my apartment, a heavy state of demonic fear would come over me. The presence of the devil just seemed to be there, day and night. At nights, when I got awake to go to the bathroom, my head felt as if it was enlarged many times its size. My body was also covered with goose pimples, and I felt swollen and heavy with fear. This would happen although I no longer submitted to the fear of the devil, but that did not stop him from hitting me with fear.

In addition to this, whenever I heard the sirens of police cars, ambulances, etc., which was quite often, another type of fear would hit me, with a strong impression that said, "They are coming for you." This was because of the removal by my Lord of my legal status to be in the country. This would happen several times during the days and nights.

The enemy would torment my mind with the sounds of the sirens, along with many types of negative thoughts. At the same time, I had clear knowledge that it was God's will for me to be in this place that I was, and my beloved Lord Jesus was going to use this situation to push me further on in faith in Him, drawing me closer to Him, which He did, and continues to do to this very day.

In those days, while the fear of the devil was upon me and many enemies surrounded me, I was frequently very ill, and each illness that I had seemed to be terminal. I believed that I would certainly be going home to be with my Lord, as it seemed impossible that I would ever again regain my health. However, I used these times of severe illnesses to draw even closer to my Lord.

Then one day, I discovered a tumor inside my scrotum (the pouch that holds the testicles). As the days, months and years went by, I also noticed that my testicles were diminishing; they were gradually being eaten away. One day, as I examined, I found only the remnants of them – some string-like tissue. My testicles were finally eaten away, I assumed, by cancer. For many years, that area was painful, and even more so when touched. In all of this, the beloved Lord Jesus permitted me to trust Him with the situation, along with this life. My beloved Lord was putting me to the test that asks: How much do you trust Me, and will you endure going the distance I have called you to go, or will you stumble and give up?

The Lord Jesus permitted these things for the purpose of helping me to lay down this life and abandon it totally into His hands, without any reservation. This included those areas, which were, and are yet to be revealed. This went on for fifteen years. Then ten years ago, at the time of writing, I began to feel my testicles forming again. Today, they seem to be normal, although they are still slightly tender when touched. Glory to the name of our great and awesome God to whom we belong. "Thank You dearest beloved Lord Jesus, for sustaining me throughout this period."

Many times, I would ask the beloved Lord to take me home. The headaches I had were excruciating, and my body was so weak that at times I had difficulty moving around. I would have to use all the energy I had to accomplish the simplest task – it was a struggle. I also had all the symptoms of cancer throughout my whole body. My bones would ache with a tormenting type of pain within, and my entire body was racked with pain. I was uncomfortable in all positions. Sometimes, I would bleed when I had bowel movements and occasionally when I urinated. I also had urinal blockage a few times. My rectum and anus would itch, and I had flu very often; as often as twice per month. A day has not gone by without my being afflicted in my body by the enemy in one way or another.

The enemy would also afflict my eyes, doing his best to convince me that I was going blind. My whole body itched, yet with all that I was experiencing, I had no liberty to go to the doctor. And neither did I want to, by the grace the beloved Lord Jesus gave me, because I knew that this was not the Lord's will for me. So I never went, nor did I take any medication for any of the illnesses.

I felt according to the flesh that I was abandoned, and even though I never embraced or believed those lying feelings of the enemy, yet those feelings persisted. These afflictions went on for many years, although at times I would be given short periods of rest from the pain of some of them. Yet, by the grace of the beloved Lord Jesus, He sustained me strong in faith in Him, loving Him as always. That never changed – the sicker I became, the more I would love my Lord.

> How great is your goodness, which you have stored up for those who fear you, which you bestow in the sight of men on those who take refuge in you. [20]In the shelter of your presence you hide them from the intrigues of men; in your dwelling you keep them safe from accusing tongues. [21]Praise be to the LORD, for he showed his wonderful love to me when I was in a besieged city. Psa. 31:19-21

The beloved Lord Jesus gave me the confidence to stand firm against these afflictions of the enemy, and He used them to help me to grow in faith, trusting Him through all these difficulties, instead of allowing them to discourage me. Glory to the gracious and wonderful Lord to whom I belong.

> To keep me from becoming conceited because of these surpassingly great revelations, there was given me a thorn in my flesh, a messenger of Satan, to torment me. [8]Three times I pleaded with the Lord to take it away from me. [9]But he said to me, "My grace is sufficient for you, for my power is made perfect in weakness." Therefore I will boast all the more gladly about my weaknesses, so that Christ's power may rest on me. [10]That is why, for Christ's sake, I delight in weaknesses, in insults, in

> hardships, in persecutions, in difficulties. For when I am weak, then I am strong. 2 Cor. 12:7-10

There were great challenges coming at me daily from these afflictions, and from various other sources, which I cannot share now. It was either I succumb to them, or in dependency on my Lord, rise up in faith and confront those challenges head-on. These were the alternatives placed before me. I would either have to confront those challenges and overcome them in faith, or lie down and give up, permitting the devil to have his way through his many afflictions.

By the grace of God, which was given to me, I refused to submit to the enemy's tricks and demands. Yes, I wanted to die, but only if it was the will of the Lord Jesus. Therefore, I was not about to surrender to the will of the devil, and that is why I would not stop carrying out all my responsibilities. The fact is, as weak as I was, by the grace given to me, I was enabled to carry out all the responsibilities that my Lord had assigned to me in every area. Today, when I look back on all that was accomplished, it seems to me to be totally impossible from the standpoint of the natural. Indeed, when I do look back, I often wonder how all those things that were done were accomplished – by the Lord Jesus, of course!

Through all that was happening, the beloved Lord Jesus was putting me through the paces to make me into the man of God He has called me to be. Remember, He had made me an apostle of the Lord Jesus Christ, and the servant and a witness of the living God, for the very last of days. These must be the reality of my daily life, and there must be no excuses, and no escape from this reality. Rather, in faith, I must take my stand where He has placed me.

> In this you greatly rejoice, though now for a little while you may have had to suffer grief in all kinds of trials. [7]These have come so that your faith – of greater worth than gold, which perishes even though refined by fire – may be proved genuine and may result in praise, glory and honor when Jesus Christ is revealed. 1 Peter 1:6-7

Another thing that I realized was happening to me, was the devil was pushing me to disobey the Lord's will for my life, which is to trust Him only for all my needs, and therefore not to go to the doctor. So, the enemy would afflict me on every side with all kinds of sicknesses, with terrible feelings, along with fear of the consequences. In this way, he believed he could push me to disobey my Lord and go to the doctor. However, glory to the beloved Lord Jesus, for in spite of all the devil's efforts, he failed, because the glorious Lord sustained me by His grace. The Lord Jesus kept me strong in faith, looking to Him and only to Him, every day, all day long, as He carried me through all these afflictions without my ever seeing a doctor, in obedience to Him. Glory to His holy name!

These afflictions went on for many years, and to this very day I have not ceased being under attack on a daily basis, in one way or another. Nevertheless, my beloved Lord uses these attacks to continue to draw me closer to Him, and to build perseverance, faith, character, etc., in me. He does work all things for good for those who love Him. Thanksgiving to His glorious and holy name.

> Though an army besiege me, my heart will not fear; though war break out against me, even then will I be confident. 4One thing I ask of the LORD, this is what I seek: that I may dwell in the house of the LORD all the days of my life, to gaze upon the beauty of the LORD and to seek him in his temple. Psa. 27:3-4

I am also afflicted with extreme heat or cold in my body. At times, my hands and feet feel as if they are freezing, and at other times, as if they are on fire. There are times when my whole body is extremely hot, to the point where I would perspire heavily, and then suddenly, I would be extremely cold.

The devil torments me in this way to frustrate me, and in the beginning I was, until I understood what was happening. When I did, by the grace the Lord Jesus gave me, I began to use all these afflictions to trust this life more and more into the hands of my beloved Lord Jesus, and to find rest in Him at deeper levels. I also chose to be contented in the midst of all that was happening, accepting His will for my life. Through it all, He gave me His grace to stand.

> This is what the Sovereign LORD, the Holy One of Israel, says: "In repentance and rest is your salvation, in quietness and trust is your strength,. . .
> Isa. 30:15

There are growths or tumors in several areas of my body, but I have trusted them into the hands of the Lord Jesus. Now another very large tumor has developed in my groin that moves in and out of my body at will in a cavity of its own, and continues to grow, causing pain at times. There is also a constant pain in my neck. In addition, there is also a slight, continual pain in the general area of my lower stomach and crotch that continues to increase, while attacks of gas in the stomach continue to be ongoing, and cause much pain at times. My beloved Lord Jesus has not permitted, apart from the gas, any of these afflictions to hinder or interfere with any of my movements or activities. Indeed, I can say that in spite of them, I am very strong, and I feel healthy. "Thank You Lord Jesus."

> You are my hiding place; you will protect me from trouble and surround me with songs of deliverance. Selah Psa. 32:7

I have come to understand that without sicknesses, afflictions, persecution, insults, rejection from various sources and problems of all kinds, there is no proof or certainty that your surrender to the Lord Jesus is genuine. This is so because no matter how much you believe that you have surrendered all to the Lord Jesus, these problems can easily prove you to be a liar, if the surrender is not genuine and total. For these problems test every area of your surrender, to see if it is truly genuine or not.

I recently saw on the news, where a pastor had lost their daughter. As a result, they shared that they had lost their faith and therefore could not continue ministering. In fact, they shared that they could not forgive the killers of their daughter, and neither did they want to. This was their response, although they said they had counseled many souls through similar losses. So, the Lord Jesus can use even the loss of a loved one to test our heart.

There is no way that you can fake a surrender to the Lord Jesus under afflictions. When you are being tested in ways that are difficult, many give up and renounce their faith. The beloved Lord Jesus therefore permits these difficulties in our lives to test our heart commitment to Him, and to purify us. He also uses them to get us to know the extent of our commitment to Him. This will help us to choose whether or not we are willing to go all the way with Him – through the pain, the uncertainty, the sicknesses, the afflictions, and even unto death. While going through difficulties, many have chosen to give up along the way, and as a result of these difficulties, they fall by the wayside.

> Be strong and take heart, all you who hope in the LORD. Psa. 31:24

At this point, the blessed Holy Spirit brought Abraham to my mind, when God tested him with Isaac, as recorded in Genesis Chapter 22.

> [2]Then God said, "Take your son, your only son, Isaac, whom you love, and go to the region of Moriah. Sacrifice him there as a burnt offering on one of the mountains I will tell you about."
> [9]When they reached the place God had told him about, Abraham built an altar there and arranged

> the wood on it. He bound his son Isaac and laid
> him on the altar, on top of the wood. [10]Then he
> reached out his hand and took the knife to slay
> his son. [11]But the angel of the LORD called out
> to him from heaven, "Abraham! Abraham!"
> "Here I am," he replied. [12]"Do not lay a hand on
> the boy," he said. "Do not do anything to him.
> Now I know that you fear God, because you have
> not withheld from me your son, your only son."
> Gen. 22:2, 9-12

God has good reasons for testing our hearts. He already knows our limits, as well as the distance to which we will go with Him in whatever He has called us to. This is to see what we will do and what we will not do. A depth of sanctification might be needed for the purpose of cleansing us, where we will have to go through tremendous difficulties and suffering, or through something other, to reveal those things that can hinder us from doing the things the Lord Jesus has called us to do.

I believe God tests our commitment to Him, not because He does not already know what our responses are going to be, or how far we will go with Him, but because He knows we do not know these things. He tests our hearts along the way to let us know the limits of our commitment to Him, and whether or not we will choose to go with Him, the distance to which He has called us to go. If we are willing after being tested, and continue with Him and do not get discouraged and give up, He will further cleanse us and pour out more grace on us to further aid us to go the distance. The reality is, although we will say to the Lord Jesus that we will do anything He wants us to do, those are only words. Many have said yes to the Lord Jesus, only to flee and abandon what He had called them to do, once they are tested with the reality of the call.

When I use the term "our commitment," I am speaking about the commitment that our beloved Lord has called us to, whatever that may be, and we in turn commit to Him to go the distance that He has called us to go. We do this although we usually do not know the extent of those distances, or the difficulties we might face, or the things we will be called on to do along the way, or when we get to where He has called us to go. Yet we will be faithful in doing all that He has called us to do. This is what I call, "our commitment."

You see, we cannot of ourselves decide what we are going to do, and then make a commitment to the Lord Jesus based on that. No, that is not how it is done. God is the One who initiates the things we are to do in His Kingdom, for His purposes and glory. Then, in those things which He has initiated and called us to do, such as to go to some far off place, or to die to our carnal desires, or to give up some of what we have, or even everything that we have that is keeping us at bay from Him, in order for us to follow Him and draw closer to Him, we in turn make a commitment to Him to do the things He has called us to do, or to go through the difficulties the Lord Jesus has called us to go through, or to go where He has chosen to send us. We then choose to commit ourselves to be faithful to the calling He has placed on our lives. In the process, we also make a commitment to the Lord Jesus, to choose death to those areas where He has revealed lack of commitment, disobedience, fears, uncertainties, unfaithfulness, etc., and therefore lack of faith – sin. We must then deny our flesh in those areas, and do the things which the Lord Jesus requires us to do. This is what I call, "our commitment."

I once heard a pastor with a nation-wide radio program, say on the air that his limit would be, as far as his walk with the Lord is concerned, if some man were to hit his daughter. He said, if that were to happen, that would be the day he would walk away, and from the context, I assume He meant from the ministry and from the Lord Jesus. Here, he is blaming the Lord Jesus in advance, that if any such thing would happen, he would quit. This is not what I would call a commitment, for this seems to be in words only. Such commitments will not stand. At the moment that you are tested, you will then give up, for the decision has already been made in the heart that the day that things get too rough in ways that you do not like, you will just give up and abandon your commitment to the Lord Jesus.

> For we are God's workmanship, created in Christ Jesus to do good works, which God prepared in advance for us to do. Eph. 2:10

Our Lord tends to test us in these commitments, while giving us the grace to go through the test. The dimension of the test however, will depend on the importance and danger of the call to which He has called us. He gives us understanding of His will as to where He wants to send us, and the things He wants us to do or to go through or to suffer through. At the same time, He gives us the opportunity to make good our commitment to Him in that which He has willed for us to do, whether internally or externally. If we agree to go with Him the distance He has chosen for us to go, He then tests us along the way to reveal to us that which is real from that which is false in our commitment to Him. This could be to go through afflictions, beatings, imprisonments, sicknesses and sufferings of all kinds, even unto death like Paul, who nothing could stop, for his purpose and focus were not about himself. His commitment was to the Lord Jesus unto death.

In the process, as we choose to continue with the Lord Jesus, in spite of the difficulties that we might face or maybe because of them, our shortcomings, lack of commitment or unfaithfulness, etc., will be revealed. When this happens, if we acknowledge them in truth and sincerity before the Lord and repent of them, we are being cleansed as we go. This is so, because the difficulties we face along the way, reveal the true state of our hearts towards the Lord Jesus, and towards the things He has called us to do, as we face the lies, dishonesty, deceit, falsehood, pride, hypocrisy, selfish ambitions, greed, envy, jealousy, selfishness, wrong motives – and in general, the sins in which we may be walking, while being blind to them or not. But as we are being tested in this way, they are being revealed by His grace, to allow us to face them, repent of them and turn from them, and from then on, to deny our flesh in those areas of the sinful nature where sin seems to be reigning. Our Lord will then cleanse us of all these evils along the way, so that our mouth will no longer be saying, "Yes" to the Lord Jesus, while the heart is murmuring and accusing Him, saying "No." The purpose of the beloved Lord Jesus in all of this is to reveal hidden faults/sin, to get us to repent of them so that He can cleanse us of them, and bring us closer to Himself. This is sanctification.

If in faith we embrace the tests that the Lord Jesus sends our way, we will be cleansed of these things as we continue with Him. On the other hand, if we do not choose to embrace the tests that our beloved Lord Jesus sends our way, the result will be to accuse Him, rebel against Him, and withdraw from Him. However, He only sends tests our way to reveal the true state of our hearts, to bring us into agreement with Him through repentance and prayer. In this way, He is then able to cleanse us of evil/sin, in order that we may grow and mature, and so draw closer to Him. Without these tests, we will continue to believe great things about ourselves that are not true. Therefore, we will not come to know who we truly are, and so be able to surrender those areas of weakness to the Lord Jesus, to be able to develop and mature. These tests could simply be in the areas of truth and sincerity of heart, faith, submission, obedience and faithfulness to our Lord. There must be sincerity of heart in order for us to be able to walk with the Lord Jesus. Without truth and sincerity of heart, we cannot walk with the Lord Jesus, for He is the God of Truth.

However, the manner in which our beloved Lord chooses to send the tests into our lives does not matter. What matters is those tests are designed to reveal, not to God, but to us, whether we are sincere in our commitment to Him or not – what is real about us and what is false. In the process, He gives us the opportunity to face our weaknesses – the selfishness, the uncertainties, the self-will, the fears, the doubts, the falsehood, the pride, the lies, the exalted state in which we may be walking, the deceit, etc. Once we face these, we are then able to take whatever the problems are to the Lord Jesus, as He permits us to see them. We can now either run and hide them from Him, or we can choose to face them in repentance before Him, asking Him for the faith, the strength, or for whatever else He permits us to understand that we might need to go the distance in whatever He has called us to do.

If we are truthful and honest with the Lord Jesus about our problems, He will cleanse us of these sins, and supply in abundance all that we need to go on. However, if we are dishonest with Him, we will remain right where we are in dishonesty, pride, fear, doubt, falsehood and even confusion, until we have chosen to come clean and to be sincere in all that we believe, desire, think, choose or do before our Lord.

> Consider it pure joy, my brothers, whenever you face trials of many kinds, [3]because you know that the testing of your faith develops perseverance. [4]Perseverance must finish its work so that you may be mature and complete, not lacking anything. James 1:2-4

> Blessed is the man who perseveres under trial, because when he has stood the test, he will receive the crown of life that God has promised to those who love him. James 1:12

There were many times that I would fall when I went to the bathroom, because I was so weak in my body. However, each time that I became sick, the one who was responsible to help me was very reluctant to do so, and would get very angry.

Several times at nights during this period, the devil challenged me to get up from off the bed. At other times, he dared me to go to the bathroom, and by God's grace, each time I would take him up on his challenge, and do that which he said I could not do. All these attacks were meant to subject me to live under the fear and intimidation of the devil, to discourage me and cause me to give up, but my beloved Lord Jesus used them all to strengthen me in faith even more, and to enable me to grow in grace and in love for my Lord. He again turned that which was meant for evil into good, for those who love Him.

This is the same devil and his demons that would, in the future, by the power of the living Christ, be fleeing in droves from my presence, begging me for a chance. This is the same devil and his demons that would be screaming to get out of people in a hurry. Yes, the beloved Lord Jesus had permitted all these things to happen, to prepare me to confront demons and command them to loose people and flee from them, so that they would be free to go to their Lord and God and embrace Him.

> Therefore we do not lose heart. Though outwardly we are wasting away, yet inwardly we are being renewed day by day. [17]For our light and momentary troubles are achieving for us an eternal glory that far outweighs them all. [18]So we fix our eyes not on what is seen, but on what is unseen. For what is seen is temporary, but what is unseen is eternal.
> 2 Cor. 4:16-18

Although we may have been hurt, or experienced a small amount of suffering, and at those times it might even seem to us that we cannot trust our beloved Lord Jesus because we are being afflicted, nevertheless, the whole point is, will we continue to trust Him? Because that is exactly what the devil is trying to keep us from doing through all of the afflictions, torments and troubles. What is important therefore is that we must keep on trusting the Lord Jesus, and not yield to the tricks of the enemy.

The more the devil afflicts us, the more we need to trust our Lord Jesus – never giving up. Our God and Lord deserves such children, who will not shrink back, not even from death, and so dishonor their Lord, but rather will, in the face of death, take a stand in faith with their Lord to honor Him, regardless of the circumstances or the consequences.

> But my righteous one will live by faith. And if he shrinks back, I will not be pleased with him."
> [39]But we are not of those who shrink back and are destroyed, but of those who believe and are saved. Heb. 10:38-39

> They overcame him by the blood of the Lamb and by the word of their testimony; they did not love their lives so much as to shrink from death. Rev. 12:11

One day, while I was in the city, the devil afflicted me in ways that I now realize I am not permitted to share the details of, at this time. Yes, I was being tested. Was my commitment unto death? Here is the moment of testing. Now, am I going to be murmuring and accusing the Lord Jesus, or will I stay the course, trusting Him? Will I stay trusting, regardless of the fears and uncertainties concerning my overall health, without demanding anything of my beloved Lord Jesus, but rather walk faithfully with Him, with a pure heart attitude of, Thy will be done Oh Lord, trusting Him all the way?

> But we have this treasure in jars of clay to show that this all-surpassing power is from God and not from us. [8]We are hard pressed on every side, but

> not crushed; perplexed, but not in despair; [9]persecuted, but not abandoned; struck down, but not destroyed. [10]We always carry around in our body the death of Jesus, so that the life of Jesus may also be revealed in our body. [11]For we who are alive are always being given over to death for Jesus' sake, so that his life may be revealed in our mortal body.
> 2 Cor. 4:7-11

The truth is we do not always know for sure whether or not we are going to be delivered or healed. Only God knows for sure what His will in each situation is. Therefore, when we ask the Lord Jesus to heal us or deliver us, we are asking according to His will, and not ours. For only He, the beloved Lord Jesus, knows the true purpose of each test that He allows. However, one thing that we do know for sure, and that is everything our Lord permits in our lives is always for our highest good and never for anything less.

Yes, I trusted Him to heal me, if that was His will. And yes, His will was to heal me in some limited way, but not at that time, because the testing of my faith and the cleansing of my heart were much, much, more important than the healing of my body. Again, the testing was to purge and cleanse me, in order to prepare me for His eternal purposes, while the healing of my body was only for my temporal and physical benefits.

My commitment not only remained strong, but it deepened and broadened. The Lord gave me much grace to sustain me through these difficult times. So, I became more confident in facing my difficulties because of the grace He gave me through the process. My physical life began to lose its importance, and now it did not matter as much, whether I lived or died. The tests that the Lord sends into our lives do have such effects.

As time went by, because of my surrender/death with the Lord Jesus, self-denial became a natural part of my life. Therefore, physical death did not seem to have much meaning any longer, other than to launch me into the presence of my God, Lord and Father. Over the years, for these and other reasons, the Holy Spirit has been putting to death much of the old ways of my sinful nature.

Indeed, I have not gone to a doctor even once, neither have I taken a pill or any other medication in almost thirty-nine years, although before coming to the Lord Jesus I was frequently at the doctor, going at least six times per year. This was so because my body was in such a bad state, which in those days, required that I follow a strict diet. I was healed of this condition after coming to the Lord Jesus. Since then, I have simply trusted my life into His hands. This was a conviction that I had received from the Lord Jesus, and therefore going to doctors was not an option for me. Unless the

Lord Jesus has called you to this however, I do not recommend that anyone follow this example, because you will die.

I previously said that I have not visited a doctor in almost thirty-nine years. The reason why I used the term almost is because of the fact that after my first year in Mexico, I visited my former hometown in California, and a doctor friend of mine told me that because I am coming from Mexico, he needed to examine me. So, I allowed him to do so. At that time, I had a very bad cough for which he gave me a prescription, but I did not fill it. That was thirty-five years ago, and it was the first and last time that I have seen a doctor since coming to the Lord Jesus.

On another day I had to go to town, and while there I felt like every disease in the world was upon me. My body became so weak that I had problems standing, and had to be assisted by someone who was with me. In all of this, the beloved Lord Jesus, who we serve, and to whom we belong, is inestimably good. I would like to express my eternal gratitude to Him for who He is and for His inestimable goodness, but I can find no words that are adequate enough to tell of His marvelous greatness, kindness, love, generosity, faithfulness and inestimable goodness, which have no bounds. The Lord Jesus is just inestimably good, and words cannot express the wonders of His marvelous and great name.

In the year 2002, the Lord Jesus revealed what true goodness is, and led me to write about it in the chapter, "The Only Good One" which appears in the book, "The Promised Blessing to the Nations." However, the more He revealed and the more I wrote, was the more I realized that using the word "good" to describe our beloved God and Lord, was far from being appropriate as it relates to Him. This is because of the simple fact that in our language and vocabulary, there are so many things that are called good.

It is common to hear people say that they have a good dog, a good cat, etc. This is how common this word is. Therefore, how could we, with this knowledge, use the same word, which we have been doing for centuries, that is used for our dog and everything else, without qualifying or distinguishing it, as it is used in relation to our God and Lord? To me, this should not have been and must not continue. This therefore became a concern and a priority for me, which had to be the work of the blessed Holy Spirit in me.

With this concern in my heart, I began to ask my Lord Jesus for a word to set apart the word "good," as it relates to Him. It is now 2007, five years later, when He gave me this word – INESTIMABLE. This word means immeasurable, great, unfathomable, enormous, incalculable, infinite, tremendous, invaluable, not able to be measured, too great to be estimated and priceless. These meanings were taken from two different dictionaries. This word truly describes so much of who God is, so much so that when I saw its meaning, along with the way it came to me, I believed that this was the answer to my prayer. This is indeed the will of my Father and Lord. "Thank You Lord Jesus."

> You are forgiving and good, O Lord, abounding in love to all who call to you. Psa. 86: 5

> As it is written: "There is no one righteous, not even one; [11]there is no one who understands, no one who seeks God. [12]All have turned away, they have together become worthless; there is no one who does good, not even one." [13]"Their throats are open graves; their tongues practice deceit." "The poison of vipers is on their lips." Rom. 3:10-13

Therefore, this word – "INESTIMABLE" is to be used with the word "good," whenever it is used to refer to our God, Lord and His Spirit. Therefore, we are to say, for example, "The inestimable goodness of God," "The Lord is inestimably good," etc. I do pray that everyone who reads this will gladly adopt this word, INESTIMABLE to refer to our Lord, God and Father.

> "Why do you call me good?" Jesus answered. "No one is good—except God alone. Luke 18:19

Let us return to our study. In all that my beloved Lord and Father permits to touch this life, He is never far. He is always there watching, covering and protecting me through it all. I will always praise and thank Him for His watchful eyes upon me at all times. He will never leave us nor forsake us.

> He ransoms me unharmed from the battle waged against me, even though many oppose me. Psa. 55:18

> Cast your cares on the LORD and he will sustain you; he will never let the righteous fall. Psa. 55:22

I remember those first days without my legal status, how terrible it felt as a Christian to be in a country illegally. It felt as if I had no ground under my feet, and spiritually I felt like a hypocrite. I was embarrassed and I felt ashamed. These were the circumstances that my beloved Lord Jesus chose for me. Therefore, I must learn to live with them and choose to be contented in them. It was not easy for my mind to accept, but by the grace given me, I submitted myself to God's will in obedience to Him, and then I chose to be contented in all circumstances, while using it all to grow in faith. "Thy will be done, Oh Lord."

> I am not saying this because I am in need, for I have
> learned to be content whatever the circumstances.
> [12]I know what it is to be in need, and I know what it
> is to have plenty. I have learned the secret of being
> content in any and every situation, whether well
> fed or hungry, whether living in plenty or in want.
> [13]I can do everything through him who gives me
> strength. Phil. 4:11-13

To be contented was a daily, moment-by-moment choice that I had to make. But the Lord Jesus gave me the grace to do so – lots of grace. And oh, how the enemy would use the sound of those sirens, which seemed to be unending, and the fear that would grip me as I believed that the police were coming for me – how difficult those moments were in that place where I stood!

Without God's grace, which allowed me the privilege of choosing faith moment-by-moment, I would have been history, for it would have been over for me right then. But His grace did allow me to choose faith every step of the way, and to take my stand with Him while in prison, and unto death, even at those times when fear covered me. And oh, how He would use those situations to build faith in me, to trust this life into His hands without reservation, unto death.

Here I am, thirty-one years since my legal status was removed, and my beloved Lord Jesus still has not changed my status. I am still living there without any legal standing, but by the power and authority of the living Christ, He keeps me safe in the midst of all those who have chosen to be enemies of mine, and who know about my status in the country.

I believe that we all know how easy it is to say, "I trust the Lord Jesus." You hear it said every day from all quarters, yet when real difficulties, or in some cases even minor difficulties, hit home, many who had just said, "I trust" no longer trust. Now, the first words that pop out of their mouths are, "Why me?" or "Why Lord?" etc. From then on, they take their lives into their own hands, trusting themselves to do for themselves, while murmuring and accusing the Lord Jesus.

> During the days of Jesus' life on earth, he offered up prayers and petitions with loud cries and tears to the one who could save him from death, and he was heard because of his reverent submission. [8]Although he was a son, he learned obedience from what he suffered [9]and, once made perfect, he became the source of eternal salvation for all who obey him Heb. 5:7-9

Yes, our wonderful beloved Lord solidifies sincere faith in our hearts through what we suffer. I do not see myself as one who has suffered anything, for when I look at Calvary and see our Lord Jesus, I am fully convinced that He is the only One who truly suffered, while the rest of us only experience such things as sicknesses, pains, the loss of loved ones, disasters, some injustice, loss of property, and various other problems, difficulties, inconveniences, etc., here and there. My intention here is not to minimize people's difficulties, losses, suffering and sicknesses, because I know that people are suffering. What I am saying is, when I compare our difficulties and sufferings to that which the Lord Jesus went through, I see no comparison whatsoever.

The reason why some see themselves as suffering so much is because they are self-centered, and very important in their own eyes. They focus on self, and therefore give themselves too much attention. This is not good, because in that state, they believe that they deserve a better and an easier life. It will therefore be easy to see themselves suffering, while never considering the suffering of our Lord Jesus. But when I look at the suffering of the Lord Jesus, which I often do, it makes me feel as if I have never suffered anything.

I cannot remember ever contemplating on any of these things that have happened to me. In fact, I had forgotten about them all, and in reality, never discussed them. It is only as I write that my beloved Lord Jesus brings them back to my mind, one by one, and as He brings them I write them down. Yet, I cannot get in touch with any of them emotionally. It is as if they never happened. Apart from writing this account of them, they don't seem to exist, although I live with them every day.

## CHAPTER 5

# SATAN'S INTIMIDATION AND ATTACK

One morning at about 11:00 a.m., I had some difficulty getting up from the floor where I was because I was extremely weak. As I sat there, I saw satan, the master deceiver, in the far corner of the room opposite to where I was, and in a rage, he lunged at me with vengeance on his face. This time he did not come as he did at first, when he had appeared to me handsome and well dressed, offering me power, which by the Spirit of the Lord, I rejected. No. This time he came as a dirty, scar-faced, wicked criminal, intent on murder, and in this state, he launched at me.

I was covered in fear when I saw him. Because of the fear I was experiencing, my head felt swollen beyond measure, and my body felt equally enlarged, as if they were not a part of me. I was frozen in fear to the extent that my body felt numb, yet in my spirit, I was not afraid. In fact, I was as bold as a lion, because the Lord Jesus was with me.

In that moment, knowledge seemed to have been taken from me. However, there were two things that I was certain of: firstly, that God IS, and the name of the Lord Jesus was in my mouth, and secondly, I could see satan in the far corner of the room, and in that moment I was given full knowledge that it was him.

As satan launched at me, although I was in that extremely weak state, I remember saying in my heart, "I am not going to run from you." and, "I am going to face you down." I also said, "Lord Jesus, I am coming home," fully believing this was "it" for me, as I was so certain that my death was imminent. There was a tremendous fear over my whole body, yet I had great boldness in spirit – that is grace. That day, I could clearly understand and experience the separation between spirit and body, for although my body was covered in fear, yet in my spirit I had great liberty and boldness.

> But he said to me, "My grace is sufficient for you, for my power is made perfect in weakness." Therefore I will boast all the more gladly about my weaknesses, so that Christ's power may rest on me. [10]That is why, for Christ's sake, I delight in weaknesses, in insults, in hardships, in persecutions, in

difficulties. For when I am weak, then I am strong.
2 Cor. 12:9-10

As the devil came towards me, as weak as I was I went at him, moving my head and upper body forward towards him, showing him that I was not afraid of him, and neither was I going to back away or run from him. To my surprise, he passed right through me! Immediately as this happened, right in the other corner of the room, appeared – guess Who? He was there all the time! He gave us His sure Word, for He said in Hebrews Chapter 13:5, **". . .Never will I leave you; never will I forsake you. . ."** if you are truly His. You still cannot guess Who it was? I'll give you another clue. In John Chapter 14:3, He says, **"And if I go and prepare a place for you, I will come back and take you to be with me that you also may be where I am."** Yes, it was my beloved Lord Jesus!

When I saw Him, my heart leapt with joy. He had a sword on His right thigh, and His hand was poised on the handle, as if in readiness to draw. The casing and handle of the sword were covered with many different shapes and shades of gold. All fear was removed from me, and at that time, the beloved Lord Jesus strengthened me and gave me His sure peace. I was at rest and was so delighted and thrilled with the fact that my well Beloved was there, watching over me and helping me. He gave me the boldness and strength to face down satan. I realized that His heart was glad as He watched me, His little one, with His enabling, take on satan by the power of His Spirit, and did not shrink back from what I presumed was my physical death. I was so thankful and grateful to the Lord Jesus for giving me this boldness to confront satan. "Thank You Lord Jesus."

The real beauty of it all is that He was there. My sweet and beloved Lord Jesus was there all the time! For years, tears would come to my eyes whenever I spoke of His appearing at such a time.

That day, the Lord Jesus put an end to the heavy weakness I was experiencing in my body, by delivering me from what caused it. The enemy attacked me again in a similar way a few months later, but this time when it was over, I saw angels all around me. I was completely surrounded by them. "Thank You beloved Lord Jesus."

In these recent years, the Lord Jesus has given me health that I never had before, in different areas of my body. Apart from satan's attacks, which are now less than they used to be, there are tumors throughout my body, but the Lord Jesus has removed mostly all other weaknesses and most sicknesses from me.

Through all these afflictions and attacks of the enemy over these many years, my Lord has always given me the strength to run each morning. I do feel healthy and strong. I give much thanks to my wonderful Lord and Savior, for so blessing me. They that wait upon the Lord in faith, without murmuring or accusing Him, will be strengthened, filled and renewed. Glory to His holy name. If it is the Lord's will, He will deliver and cleanse me of these other afflictions. I do trust Him with them all. "Thy will be done dearly beloved. Thank You beloved Lord Jesus."

# CHAPTER 6

# SEPARATED · A STAR BECAME MY ONLY FRIEND

The years of testing mentioned were very lonely for me according to the flesh. There was no one I knew who could understand the call of our beloved Lord Jesus on my life. Neither could I explain it, because I myself did not understand a lot of the things that had happened and were happening, or many of the things that the Lord Jesus had called me to.

It was many years later before I had a vague understanding of some of these things, and even as I am writing, I am just now beginning to understand the true meaning and significance of them, and the way the Lord Jesus has been leading me. Also, at that time I did not know or understand the significance of the many visions I had been given, until I was made to write about them. Indeed, I was blind to what the Lord Jesus was saying to me through them over all those years, and still am to a great extent. It is only now as I am writing that the Lord is opening my eyes to understand them one by one, giving me the clarity of their meaning, which I confess, I had no idea of.

I was also cut off from all friendly faces, and I did not understand why. It felt like a sharp cut had been made around me. This separated me completely from any, and everyone in the flesh who would give me any kind of consideration, understanding or support, or with whom I could have even a brief conversation.

There was hostility towards me from all sides, and nothing made sense. Even those persons whom I had known very well had become hostile towards me, and when I would approach someone to ask a question, or to have a friendly conversation or for any other reason, I would be rebuffed, rejected, ignored, or simply given no attention. I just could not understand these things, and although I knew I was separated, for some reason, I could not connect the two – the separation with the rejection I was experiencing. Although it was obvious from what was happening that the rejection was the result of the separation, yet while these things were taking place, I did not understand them that way. Indeed, I did not understand them at all.

One day, I was taken to the home of the head of a large ministry, and although I had known this person before, there I was standing in his house in front of him, and he did not acknowledge my presence. Neither he nor his wife even offered me a seat as I stood there looking on, being totally humiliated. Meanwhile, the person who took me there was laughing and talking with them, as if nothing was happening. Yes, I was totally cut off from anyone who would understand what I was going through. Not even I understood what was happening.

On another occasion, I went along with someone to the office of a pastor who we both knew, and I sat quietly as they talked. When they paused, I said to the pastor, "You came to my city; why didn't you call me?" That was all that I said to him. He immediately jumped to his feet, pointed his finger at me, and told me to get out of his office. I was simply stunned. It did not make any sense to me, because I did not say or do anything wrong that could possibly offend anyone. Moreover, I had always liked him from when we first met. Yet, this was his reaction to me.

In another case, a friend went to see a "Christian businessman," whom he knew well. I did not know this person; neither did he know me, because I was not known to many people in that area. Yet, in their conversation, the businessman in anger, declared concerning me: "That man, someone needs to put a bullet in him."

Yes, strange things were happening that could not be explained, but in all that was happening, my dearly Beloved kept me safe and strong in faith in Him.

One day, someone who I knew, asked me, “What do you do?” I replied, “I am waiting on the Lord Jesus.” The person then said to me in a mocking way, “Did you know that Jesus already came, and you do not need to be waiting on Him any longer?” I simply responded with, “Thank you.” I have found this same attitude to be common among many Christians.

When I mention that I am waiting on the Lord Jesus, it is usually ridiculed, and I am looked upon as strange. With those to whom I have spoken, “waiting on the Lord Jesus” has no place in their beliefs and vocabulary; at least not the kind of waiting in which I am involved.

At first, I was saddened and affected by these things, and there was no one to share them with who would understand or empathize – no one in the flesh that I knew of. Nevertheless, the beloved Lord Jesus sustained me strong in faith in Him. There were several similar situations that occurred, and it is only now, as I am writing about some of them, that the Lord Jesus is opening my eyes and giving me understanding of what was really happening.

The Lord Jesus had cut me off from family, friends, country, language, church-family, etc., separating me for His purpose, and no one could understand what I was about, or what was happening to me. They just saw me as strange and rejected me. All this happened because I was being separated by the Lord Jesus.

The Lord Jesus is just now opening my eyes for me to see, that it was He who blocked all my attempts over all these years to get close to anyone to befriend them. He also blocked any and everyone from coming close, or making any kind of connection with me. At the same time, He put an end to all previous relationships, apart from the few students He has placed with me, who were also suspicious of me. If He had not, the devil would have tied me up in relationships, so that my Lord would not be able to prepare me for His day. So indeed, He had to cut me off to sanctify and prepare me, according to His will and purpose, and that was His way of accomplishing this, because it is usually easy for me to make friends.

My beloved Lord Jesus just brought back to my mind, one occasion when He sent me back to my old hometown of Santa Barbara, where one of my best friends for many years lived. We were very close, and we never had any difficulty in our relationship. We never got even slightly angry with each other, but on this trip, things were going to change. I went to visit him, and we greeted each other warmly. He and his wife invited my wife and I out for dinner the following evening. We went, and we had a lovely time together, as we always did.

When we had finished eating, I simply said to him, "You're always paying, let me pay the bill this time." That was all that I said, when, for no reason at all, he turned red and exploded with a tremendous amount of anger and wrath against me. In all the fifteen years of our being friends, I had never seen him or known him to be like this, and I was stunned. Whatever he said, I do not recall. I just kept quiet and said nothing. That was the last time I saw him. We were separated. I was also cut off from my second best friend in a similar fashion.

At about that same time, since I was in the area, I decided to stop at my brother-in-law's workplace to say hello to him. When I saw him, I had hardly said hello before he burst into a rage, and in the presence of quite a few persons who were in the lobby at that time, he came at me as if he wanted to hit me. He then pointed his finger in my face and told me to get out. I said nothing, and I simply turned around to leave. As I did, he pushed me, and while I walked to the door, he pushed me again. This was someone who I had not seen for a long time, and as far as I knew, there was no problem between us then, or prior to this. Yet, this happened. To this day, I have not told my sister.

The Holy Spirit is now just making clear to me the details of what took place, for it had gone from my mind all of this time. He is also showing me what really happened that day. The devil was pushing me to retaliate so that I would start a fight right there, and so discredit God's working in and through me. But by God's grace, He did not permit me to retaliate. I simply walked out in shame, and that was that.

Following this, I went to visit another friend. Although I was told that he was there, he went and hid, and sent to tell me he was not at home. That was the end of that relationship. There was another friend who I called and told that I was in town and would like to visit with him. He said he would call me back, but he never did. Again, this was the end of that relationship.

There was also another friend, who all of a sudden one day, became hostile towards me, and although I tried to understand why this had happened and to resolve the problem, I just could not. I was instantly cut off from him also. There was yet another friend who I had helped to establish his own business. He simply refused to respond to my letters or phone calls. There was also another, who I had helped to buy a home, and all of a sudden, he too turned against me.

Even now, as I look back on these things, they seem so strange and so unreal, as if things like these could not have happened, but they did.

I remember this wonderful family with whom I was very close. We had a beautiful relationship, until one morning I happened to stop by to spend a few moments with them. When I did, the wife, out of nowhere, began to curse me and accuse me of all kinds of things, which I could not relate to or understand, yet she kept going on. I found myself in a state of shock, and I could not respond. I remember standing there listening to things that I knew nothing about, things that I could not relate to and was totally unaware of; things that I had never heard of, or thought of before, yet I was being accused of them. The lady was very emotional and very loud. Eventually, her husband joined us. He did not say very much, but in a quiet way, he communicated to me his agreement with her in what she was saying.

For years, I tried to understand what that was all about, but never could. Yet, a beautiful relationship was destroyed over something which I knew nothing about. I am just now realizing that all of this had to do with my separation. "Thank You Lord Jesus."

My Lord just brought to my mind another family, who seemed to have loved me very much, and respected me as a man of God. We had a very loving and friendly relationship. Then one day, all of a sudden, everything changed. Where they had loved me, now they hated me, and where they had respected me, now they seemed to be mocking me and laughing at me. That was the end of that relationship too. The Lord was making His cut all around me, and it was total.

I was also cut-off from my pastor, along with all the friends I had made in church. Ever since I fell at the pulpit as shared in Volume 1 of this book, they all became very suspicious, cold and indifferent to me. There were also two assistant pastors at the church, who also became suspicious and indifferent towards me, although previously they were very friendly.

The knife of my Beloved was making its rounds as it cut around me, and these cuts were deep and clean, and they would last. Whenever I would try to develop a relationship, or even a conversation with anyone, before they even got started, complications would enter and put an end to them, and this has been consistent to this very day.

One day, while on another visit to Santa Barbara, my sister drove my wife to visit one of her brothers. While my wife went in to visit with him, my sister remained in the car in front of their home. Even though I had visited with him in his home before, he was convinced that it was I who was sitting in the car outside his gate that day. According to him, I believed that I was better than him, and that is why I did not come in. He thought I had belittled him, and so on, and so forth. From that day to this, I have been separated from him. I was also separated from her three sisters and her other brothers, with whom I previously had a very close relationship, and from the rest of her family, as I was from mine. There were also other separations, including some that took place in Jamaica and in Mexico, but I think I have gotten the point across with the few that I have mentioned.

I remember when my father died and my sister called me to give me the news. She told me that the family would be meeting in Miami so that we could all travel to the Caribbean together. She said, "So we expect to see you there," at the time she had set. While she was speaking, I was asking the Lord Jesus what was I to do: would He permit me to go immediately? However, there was no answer, although He gave me His deep peace, so much so, that I was not concerned about anything. Along with this peace, came an assurance that all was well with my father, as in his latter years, he had given his life to the Lord Jesus.

While all of this was happening, I was waiting for an answer from the Lord as to what to do. Would He permit me to go or not? As I waited for an answer, I remained quiet and did not respond to my sister. So finally, with an impatient voice, she asked, "Why aren't you answering me?" By then, I realized that I had to say something. However, having not heard from the Lord, I said to her, "Call me back later in the day, and I will let you know if I can go or not." Her response was what one should expect under such circumstances. She said, "What? Do you mean to tell me that you might not go?" By this time, she was understandably ruffled by my responses.

Meanwhile, my Lord kept me in a state of profound peace throughout that whole day. Later on in the day, the understanding became clearer and clearer that I was not to go. My sister called back later that day, and when I told her that I could not go, you can imagine her response. We will just say that she got a little emotional, and so did the rest of the family. My Lord did permit me to visit there a year or so later, and then I realized how ugly and detestable I had become in the eyes of some of the family, and others who knew me.

Some years had now passed, when my sister called and told me that my other sister was planning a family reunion, and they wanted me to be there. I responded, "If the Lord permits." She then said, "Do you think that the Lord separates people and keeps them from seeing their family? God does not do that!"

I would definitely agree with her that God does not usually separate people from their family, or keep them from seeing their family, because He is the author and creator of the family, and His will is for families to have a close and loving relationship. However, for a higher good, He does at times bring separations, although very rarely and only to accomplish His divine purpose to save lives.

Throughout history God has, through different means, separated individuals from their families, friends, and at times, even from their country, customs and language. As I was writing this, my beloved Lord Jesus just now made me aware of a few, and I will list them: Noah, Abraham, Jacob, Joseph, Samuel, Moses, Elisha, John the Baptist, Paul and Luke, along with several of the prophets, apostles, disciples, etc.

> Another disciple said to him, "Lord, first let me go and bury my father." 22But Jesus told him, "Follow me, and let the dead bury their own dead."
> Matt. 8:21-22

These types of separations always seem ugly and ungodly to the natural mind, simply because we do not understand God's purpose for them. Every separation that God brings about is always for the good of the many. He always separates to save others through that one who He has separated. Yet, at times it will be rejected by people as not being of God, especially in the days in which we are now living.

There is no one in this world to whom I could explain my separation who would accept it as of the Lord Jesus, apart from the few that He has placed with me, whose separations are no different. People see them as fools, deceived to believe that they could be so separated to be waiting on the Lord Jesus. According to some, "Don't be a fool, Jesus has already come; so what could you possibly be waiting for?"

Strange things continued to happen all around me that could not be explained. I just could not understand what was happening, and although I had clear knowledge that I was separated, I did not connect these strange happenings to it. It is just now as I am writing that the beloved Lord Jesus is permitting me to understand them, some twenty-five years later.

The hostility towards me was very great, and it was from all sides. I was cut off from my brothers and sisters in very unusual ways. Strange things had developed in our relationships to bring about these separations, which has caused them to last over all these years. I was also separated by similar circumstances from other family members with whom I still had a good relationship. There are many more strange things that occurred to separate me, but they are too numerous to write about. For example, I have not mentioned the several strange separations that took place in Jamaica, or in Mexico, because they are simply too numerous for me to list.

At the same time all these things were taking place, I was being accused of being a loner who was isolating himself from the body of Christ, and I was therefore branded a cultic leader by some. However, the Lord Jesus put in me not to answer these charges. I therefore could not explain, and I knew if I tried, I would only make matters worse. This is how I have lived all these years. Nevertheless, my Lord has kept me strong, secure and immovable in faith in Him.

I know within my spirit that my Heavenly Father has chosen this path for me to walk, and although it does not feel good, I must walk it, giving Him thanks every step of the way. This might be speaking to my future as well, when I might be standing alone, although I pray not. Yet, it is my Father's will that I want, and not my own. However, I have had some preview of what that future could be like. I have often said to my Father and Lord that I am a coward, so please do not let things get too rough for me.

By this time I was isolated, and no one in Mexico, apart from the few students that were left was talking to me, and even they resented me. To mention my name was like mentioning the plague. To add to all this, students who were expelled had to justify to their family and friends why they had left, so they told all kinds of negative stories which automatically put me in a worse light. Many lies were told about me, even that they had left because they found out that I was leading a cult.

> . . .If the head of the house has been called Beelzebub, how much more the members of his household! Matt. 10:25b

The devil was piling it on. He wanted to destroy me, but the beloved Lord turned it all into good for me. He used it all to cement me more and more in Him, and to make me into a man of faith. The Lord Jesus used this, along with the sirens and all the other difficulties I was facing, to teach me to stand with Him alone, looking only to Him, trusting only in Him, knowing that my security is in Him alone, and this brought me into a deeper rest in Him.

## A STAR BECAME MY ONLY FRIEND

One night as I was driving along the highway on my way home, feeling quite lonely, I happened to look up at the sky through the windshield, and I saw a star that stood out among all the other stars. I also noticed that this star was on the move. It was travelling ahead of me going in the same direction I was, as if it was leading me and guiding my path. After looking at the star for an hour or so, I had a sense that this star was given to me to keep my company. It remained in front of me until I got home. Then it stopped when I stopped; right over the "House of Life" where I lived in the compound where the ministry is located. It remained there for approximately three to four months. It was the lowest and largest star in the sky. This made it easy for me to identify it.

I remember in those days, I would go into the backyard at nights and look up at the sky. I felt that I was given a connection to this star. I felt that this star was special, as if there was something personal about it. As strange as it may seem, I felt that the beloved Lord Jesus had sent this star to be my friend. I actually felt a connection to this star. Each night I would go outside, and there it was, my friend, the star. This lasted for three to four months.

Then one night, I went out and looked up, and it was no longer there. The star, which had become my only friend, was no more. I searched for it in the skies, but it could not be found. It was gone, and although there were many stars in the sky, there was none to replace that one. I finally hung my head in sorrow and went back inside.

In those days, I had no words even to utter a prayer to my Lord, because all utterance in prayer had been removed from me. The only prayer I now had was the prayer in the spirit – deep within my spirit. In all those years since I left the school that the Lord used to discipline me, my Lord Jesus remained as if very distant, and even when He would appear, He rarely permitted me to sense His presence.

> You have taken my companions and loved ones from me; the darkness is my closest friend. Psa. 88:18

It would be reasonable in the natural, to think that after all the afflictions that satan has hit this body with, by now he would give up. But no! In the years 2010 and 11, satan raised the bar of affliction. At times he hit my scalp with tenderness, itching, and a sharp pain when certain areas are touched. When he is not hitting the scalp, he would hit my throat with itching and pain, my gums with swelling and pain, and a burning sensation in my tongue. There would also be pain in my neck, shoulder and in my right ankle, and the bone of my upper left arm and in the shoulder joint. Then he would hit my stomach with terrible gas pains and this would cause further pain in my prostate tumor. This along with repeated vomiting; emptying my stomach several times over a period of months, to the point where only bile would be coming out, and nothing is able to enter the stomach, not even water. When I took a sip of water, it came right back up. Once, for two days nothing would enter the stomach although it was empty. Then late on that day, the Lord intervened and I was able to drink water and some oat porridge. This affliction comes with an extreme weakness and sleepiness in the whole body; still I was not able to sleep at all. All that I could do each time was to lay there on the bathroom floor for five or six hours, until the Lord Jesus intervened and stopped the vomiting and eased the pain and the extreme weakness and sleepiness over my mind and body.

When satan is not tormenting me in this way, he is hitting me with pain in my left kidney, and in the joint of my right hip, or in both of my knees, or in the back or side of my legs or in the very large tumor in my prostate, and in my back. Some of these afflictions would go on for months, others for years. Then there would be for a time, extreme itching over my whole body, from my head to my feet, and also extreme heat and burning in my feet and this is more extreme in my toes. Then he hit my index finger, the finger I use to write, with stiffness, pain and swelling, to make it difficult for me to write. He also hits my eyes with itching, burning and tears.

The last thing he hit me with was a large blood-red rash (for lack of words to describe it) on my leg, which measured 6 inches by 5 inches. This affliction is most unusual – I have never before seen anything like it, and it scares those who see it. It is rough and scaly, and seemed as if ready any moment to breakout and consume my leg. He hit me with the same rash on my back, only it was much smaller in size. I imagine this was to scare me to cause me to disobey the Lord Jesus and go to the doctor, and to divert and drive fear in me to get me to give up, but he will not succeed, for the Lord Jesus is my mainstay.

In all of this, the grace of the Lord Jesus continues to be sufficient in all areas of this life. I believe that all of this has to do with preparing me for what the Lord Jesus has planned in the future for this life. I must therefore learn to trust Him now through all these seemingly scary things which, by the grace given me to go through them, have failed to scare me. Thank You Lord Jesus.

I give thanks to the beloved Lord Jesus for sustaining me through it all, while strengthening me in the inner man, because I can actually feel His strength within me, even while I lay there on the bathroom floor. Each time, in the flesh, it seems as if I am given over to death, yet within me, the life of the Lord Jesus is pouring in. This has been a very strange experience each time. My body seems to be dying, while life is expanding and strengthening within. This was repeated several times; once I only had a three day break before it started all over again.

Therefore we do not lose heart. Though outwardly we are wasting away, yet inwardly we are being renewed day by day. 2 Cor 4:16

CHAPTER 7

# SEPARATIONS BY GOD

Separation from family, friends and in some cases, country and language, in the eyes of most is an ugly and despicable thing, and it is if it is done by men for selfish, carnal reasons. But when God does it, He does it always for the highest good of the many. When God separates a man or a woman from their family, He has a set plan and purpose for such separations, as in the cases of Noah, Abraham, Jacob, Joseph, Moses, Samuel, Ruth, Daniel, Elisha, John The Baptist, Luke, Anna in Luke Chapter 2, Paul, and many of the prophets, apostles, disciples, etc. I mention these few who the Lord Jesus has again brought to my mind, but of course there are many others.

It is important here for me to note, that in every case that God separates one from family, friends, country, etc., His intent is to do great things on this earth that will affect the lives of everyone living here. Those who will accept the one He has separated will be affected positively by that separation, but those who reject that one, will be affected negatively by it.

Let us take Noah for instance. Although the Scripture does not say specifically that he was separated, yet God has revealed that yes, Noah was separated for a long time, longer than any of the others in Scripture. After this revelation came, I went back to the Scripture, and there it was. The Lord permitted me to see that long before that day when God told Noah to enter the ark with his wife, their three sons and their three wives, Noah had been cut off from family and friends, so much so, that there was no family member around. Neither was there any mention by God, nor by Noah, of any of his family or his wife's family or the families of his three sons' wives. None of them were around; neither was any of them mentioned. Noah also did not seem preoccupied with family, although between them they must have had thousands of family members, since in those days people lived for such a long time. What could have happened?

Principally, Noah was a righteous man, and hate for righteousness was all around him. All this hate and rejection of God was manifested against Noah, the preacher of righteousness. At a point, no one wanted to hear him preach anymore, as his preaching of righteousness was contrary to their lifestyle, and therefore offensive to them. They hated him for opposing their way of living, and for putting God and the way of righteousness before them. Not only was Noah hated by them for this, but he was cut off from family members and from everyone else, for their hearts were totally turned against God. Consequently, they hated being around Noah, who continually kept God before them.

> The LORD saw how great man's wickedness on
> the earth had become, and that every inclination
> of the thoughts of his heart was only evil all the
> time. [6]The LORD was grieved that he had made
> man on the earth, and his heart was filled with pain.
> [7]So the LORD said, "I will wipe mankind, whom I
> have created, from the face of the earth – men and
> animals, and creatures that move along the ground,
> and birds of the air – for I am grieved that I have
> made them." [8]But Noah found favor in the eyes of
> the LORD. [9]This is the account of Noah. Noah was
> a righteous man, blameless among the people of
> his time, and he walked with God. [10]Noah had three
> sons: Shem, Ham and Japheth. [11]Now the earth was
> corrupt in God's sight and was full of violence.
> [12]God saw how corrupt the earth had become, for
> all the people on earth had corrupted their ways.
> [13]So God said to Noah, "I am going to put an end

> to all people, for the earth is filled with violence because of them. I am surely going to destroy both them and the earth. Gen. 6:5-13

Noah's family, his wife's family, the families of his three sons' wives, along with all the other people, hated God with a vengeance, and because Noah was seen as a righteous man of God, representing God, they vented their hate for God towards him. So they rejected him, seeing him as a fool, and worse, as an agent of a God that they did not care for. Therefore, his building the ark without any possibility of getting something that big to water, justified them in their beliefs that the man Noah was just as they had thought – the man had gone mad! To them, he was the fool they had thought him to be all along for believing God and holding to Him.

In these beliefs, they totally justified themselves so that they could go on ignoring and rejecting any and everything he had ever said to them. In this way, they closed their ears and their hearts to God's Word through Noah, and darkness continued to multiply upon the earth. The result of this was disaster for all who lived on the earth, because God had to put an end to the wickedness which was before Him.

Yes, God did use an ugly situation, which was their rejection of Noah, to separate Noah, through whom He saved the whole human race. God only separates to save and to bring about good to mankind. In this case, He separated Noah to rescue and save the whole human family from self-destruction, because by their wickedness, that was where they were all headed. Through Noah, God saved mankind physically, to later save them spiritually through Abraham's Seed – the Lord Jesus Christ.

> The LORD had said to Abram, "Leave your country, your people and your father's household and go to the land I will show you. [2]"I will make you into a great nation and I will bless you; I will make your name great, and you will be a blessing. [3]I will bless those who bless you, and whoever curses you I will curse; and all peoples on earth will be blessed through you." [4]So Abram left, as the LORD had told him; and Lot went with him. Abram was seventy-five years old when he set out from Haran. [5]He took his wife Sarai, his nephew Lot, all the possessions they had accumulated and the people they had acquired in Haran, and they set out for the land of Canaan, and they arrived there. Gen. 12:1-5

As God separated and used Noah to save the natural and physical man, so He will now separate and use Abraham to save man spiritually, through his Seed, according to the flesh, our beloved Lord Jesus Christ.

> The promises were spoken to Abraham and to his seed. The Scripture does not say "and to seeds," meaning many people, but "and to your seed," meaning one person, who is Christ. Gal. 3:16

I am sure that Abraham's separation was not easy, for no separation is ever easy. This is so because, no matter who you are, or where you live, people will not understand or accept that it is God who is separating you from your family, friends, country, etc., for their own good, and for the good of many others. By God's grace, Abraham believed God and obeyed Him, regardless of the criticisms and the accusations he might have received from family, friends and others.

> Consider Abraham: "He believed God, and it was credited to him as righteousness." [7]Understand, then, that those who believe are children of Abraham. [8]The Scripture foresaw that God would justify the Gentiles by faith, and announced the gospel in advance to Abraham: "All nations will be blessed through you." [9]So those who have faith

> are blessed along with Abraham, the man of faith.
> Gal. 3:6-9

Remember, Abraham did not have much knowledge of God, yet he believed and obeyed the few words which God had spoken to him. Oh, how I pray that I could say as much about us, the church, today. Although we have been gifted with so much more knowledge of God than he was, yet none of us come close to believing God as Abraham, the man of faith, did. He had very little knowledge of God, yet when God spoke, he believed and obeyed Him. This was counted as righteousness. For these reasons, he possessed the land, but because of the Israelites disobedience and rebellion, they could not.

> Then the word of the LORD came to me: [24]"Son of man, the people living in those ruins in the land of Israel are saying, 'Abraham was only one man, yet he possessed the land. But we are many; surely the land has been given to us as our possession.'
> Ezek. 33:23-24

Here, by faith, Abraham possessed the land as one man, yet they were many, and they could only possess the ruins of the land, although they had so much more knowledge of God than he did; for by now they had the law of God, and he did not. Does this sound like the church today; having much knowledge of God's Word, yet very little faith?

I have often heard it preached that Abraham disobeyed God when Lot went with him. Don't be foolish! This was God's doing, in order that Abraham would feel secure along the way, because Abraham did not yet know God in this way – that God would protect him from the harm of men. This lack of knowledge was also manifested when he went into Egypt and into Gerar. In both places, he asked Sarah to say that she was his sister, which she was, rather than his wife, which she also was.

This was not because Abraham did not have faith in God, for the Scripture clearly says that he did. Rather, this was simply a case of his ignorance of God, in that and other areas of his life. He simply did not know God to be the God who protects. He did not know at that time that he could believe God for such things as protection from man's wickedness to man, but he will come to know this later on.

In those early years, Abraham did not know that he was under God's protection, and so he feared men, believing that they would kill him and take his wife, because she was so beautiful. And he was proven right, for this was what took place in many parts of that area of the world, as was revealed both in Egypt and in Gerar.

Pharaoh, king of Egypt, and Abimelech, king of Gerar, did take Sarah, just as Abraham had believed and feared that they would, and they would have killed him to have her, just as he had said, if they knew that she was his wife. But God was protecting both him and Sarah, only he did not know this.

God had to intervene so that neither of those kings would touch Sarah, while at the same time, He protected Abraham from them. God used these situations to reveal to Abraham that He does protect those who are His. Many times God permits strange things to happen in our lives to teach us of His protecting arm around us. Through such happenings, Abraham did indeed come to know of God's protecting arm, and learnt to trust Him in all these areas.

God already knew of Abraham's fears. The reason therefore why God permitted Abraham to take Lot along with him, was so that he would not be afraid to go, for Abraham knew the danger that was lurking along the way. You see, God's plan is perfect and cannot be thwarted by anyone. In the same way that God separated Abraham from his father and other family members, He had His plan to also separate him from Lot at the appropriate time. And as Scripture has revealed, He did so, no sooner or no later than He had planned.

As in almost all separations, an ugly situation had developed – in this case, between Abraham's men and Lot's men. It was now very clear that they had to separate, for the union and friendship among their people had been broken. This, along with the fact that the land could no longer support both of their herds, made it necessary for them to separate. This was God's time and doing.

God's time of final separation had come, and so, even if they tried to stay together, they would not be able to do so. The conflict between their people would only get worse, and would therefore consume them if they had tried to stay together. God's time for Abraham to be isolated from his last family member and all that was had come, and no one could change that.

In reality, without some ugly situation developing between people to force a separation, most separations would not happen. God found His man in Abraham – a man who would believe and obey Him. I pray that I could say the same for us – the church. Here again, God's separation of a man was instrumental in bringing Salvation to the entire world.

> Christ redeemed us from the curse of the law by becoming a curse for us, for it is written: "Cursed is everyone who is hung on a tree." 14He redeemed us in order that the blessing given to Abraham might come to the Gentiles through Christ Jesus, so that

> by faith we might receive the promise of the Spirit.
> Gal. 3:13-14

Abraham is our spiritual father according to the Scriptures, yet so many preachers seem to spend a lot of their time discrediting him. I do not remember ever hearing a positive message about Abraham. Why is that so? How often have I heard it preached that we are to honor our father and mother? Doesn't this apply to our spiritual father as well, and maybe should even be more so? When Abraham is preached about in such negative ways, as has been the custom, isn't it really God who they are riling up against by saying to Him, "Why did You give us such a bad example of a spiritual father, as Abraham?" Why are we ridiculing him? Obviously because we are so righteous and perfect – aren't we?

On several occasions, I have heard Abraham being called an adulterer, which is a lie, for God has never charged Abraham with any such sin. Why? Because it never happened. In addition to this, the law had not yet been given, and according to the Scripture, without law, sin is not counted against anyone.

> because law brings wrath. And where there is no law there is no transgression. Rom. 4:15

> for before the law was given, sin was in the world. But sin is not taken into account when there is no law. Rom. 5:13

Apart from this knowledge and understanding in the Scriptures, the fact is, in the whole area of Mesopotamia where Abraham came from, their laws and customs were that a childless wife had an obligation to give her maidservant to her husband, through whom they may have children, and this is exactly what Sarah did. Abraham went along with it, simply because it was their law and custom – a way of life for them.

At this point, God still had not yet revealed Himself to Abraham in a way that would say to him his old customs had ended, as He has done to us, so that Abraham would know to abandon and deny them. Therefore, because this had not yet happened, Abraham simply did what their custom demanded. For these reasons, God has never charged Abraham with sin for this act, or the others for which he has been, and continues to be accused of, by his offspring, the church.

Which of you being childless, and at the same time not knowing God's will in this area (for God had never told him not to), if based on that, you were given the opportunity to have children both in a legal way, and in keeping with your customs and traditions, would tell me that you would reject such an opportunity to do so? Would you not do it, especially if you were at Abraham's and Sarah's age, unless of course, you were so righteous? Then, this would prove how self-righteous you are.

> Now Sarai, Abram's wife, had borne him no children. But she had an Egyptian maidservant named Hagar; [2]so she said to Abram, "The LORD has kept me from having children. Go, sleep with my maidservant; perhaps I can build a family through her." Abram agreed to what Sarai said. [3]So after Abram had been living in Canaan ten years, Sarai his wife took her Egyptian maidservant Hagar and gave her to her husband to be his wife. [4]He slept with Hagar, and she conceived. When she knew she was pregnant, she began to despise her mistress. Gen. 16:1-4

As this Scripture states this is precisely what happened. This is not adultery. Abraham was not sneaking around trying to have sexual relations with Sarah's maid. No! The purpose for this type of arrangement was not for sexual gratification. Rather, it was to build a family for themselves, in keeping with the custom of their region, seeing that Abraham and Sarah were already old and well advanced in years, and Sarah was past childbearing age according to the natural. Again, this is simply Abraham's ignorance of God, for at that time, he did not understand God's plan for their lives in the way we do today. Yet, many preachers take advantage of his ignorance, to brand him negatively in every possible way. Shame on you who do such a thing!

Every time I hear such preaching it sickens me, but I realize that this is because of the darkness that is over the church. Instead of honoring our God, by honoring His elect, through whom He has chosen to bless us in such a mighty way, they choose instead to dishonor Him, through their outright belittling of God's elect – our spiritual father Abraham. In addition, he has been put down and ridiculed over and over again concerning his taking Lot with him, along with all the other false accusations that they have leveled against him, including his being an adulterer and a deceiver. If this would only help us to look at ourselves, to see the dimension of darkness that we are in, then that would at least be a step in the right direction, to turn us from these evil practices.

In my case, I knew that I was separated thirty-nine years ago – yet it took me over twenty-nine of those years to begin to understand the separation and its implications, as revealed through the writing of these books. Until today, I cannot say that I have fully understood it. Yet, we expect Abraham to instantly understand and embrace his separation in its totality, although he had so much less knowledge of God than we have today. Abraham died without understanding the implication or significance of his call and separation.

I pray that we will all understand that it is God's will to vindicate His friend, Abraham. I fear God, so I have chosen to respect and honor His elect servant and friend, my spiritual father, Abraham, through whom the whole world is blessed. I have not seen or said anything negative about him, simply because I know of none. Apart from that, the Holy Spirit has given me understanding about his life, and a fear to be looking for anything for which to accuse him of, and by so doing, to justify myself.

Ever since I came to the Lord Jesus, He has planted this truth in me concerning His elect servant and friend, Abraham. I have never spoken a negative word about him to date, because I see no reason to do so, and by the grace of my God, I pray that I never will, in honor of my God, Lord and Father.

My Lord has given me love and respect for my spiritual father Abraham, and I love and honor him. I am very offended when I hear those who say that they are men of God, yet speak ill of him. Please stop and begin to honor your spiritual father, who happened to be a friend of God. I would think that anyone who fears God would avoid speaking ill of His anointed servant and friend, Abraham – the father of the church.

In the case of Joseph, his brothers hated him with a vengeance. They envied him because he was his father's favorite child, and so, out of this envy, they decided to kill him. But look how God is going to use this evil act of his brothers to deliver him from them, and separate him from his entire family and country and language. Although this separation caused much pain and suffering, yet it had to be done to fulfill God's purpose for the higher good of the many. This does not mean that God intended for Joseph's separation to have happened the way it did. Yet it did happen in this way, because of the evil of envy and jealousy of his brothers towards him.

Separation is often very ugly and difficult for all those who are separated, myself included. If it was up to us we would not be separated, simply because none of us human beings want to be cut off from our families and loved ones, for it is too difficult and lonely while it is happening. I remember how ugly the final separation from my youngest sister was. If it were not so, we probably would never be separated, because we love each other, and we were always very close. So yes, separation may have to be ugly for it to take place and last, but only God knows why for sure.

Joseph's brothers saw him coming at a distance, and they said,

> "Here comes that dreamer!" they said to each other. [20]"Come now, let's kill him and throw him into one of these cisterns and say that a ferocious animal devoured him. Then we'll see what comes of his dreams." [21]When Reuben heard this, he tried to rescue him from their hands. "Let's not take his life," he said. [22]"Don't shed any blood. Throw him into this cistern here in the desert, but don't lay a hand on him." Reuben said this to rescue him from them and take him back to his father. [23]So when Joseph came to his brothers, they stripped him of his robe – the richly ornamented robe he was wearing – [24]and they took him and threw him into the cistern. Now the cistern was empty; there was no water in it. Gen. 37:19-24

Now, to have had his own brothers do this to him must have been a terrible blow for Joseph. Can separation get any uglier than this? How awful it must have been for him, to first of all face the despicable plan of his brothers to kill him, and then to later change their plan. Instead, they now put him in a pit to, as far as he knows, slowly pine away, suffering every moment of every day, until death comes. This must have been agonizing, for it was such a traumatic blow for him. Imagine the disappointment, the fears, the anxieties and the torment to his mind that he must have experienced to have had his own brothers do this to him. What betrayal! What a letdown!

I can remember when my own sister was used by the enemy to lie so viciously against me, to make me out to be a thief and a robber; when in front of so many people, my brother-in-law, for no reason at all, insulted me and pushed me, telling me to get out of the lobby of his workplace. How belittling and humiliating those things were, and yet they were nothing in comparison to what Joseph had to face. But God was there with him taking him through it all, otherwise he could not have gone through such things.

> Judah said to his brothers, "What will we gain if we
> kill our brother and cover up his blood? 27Come,
> let's sell him to the Ishmaelites and not lay our
> hands on him; after all, he is our brother, our own
> flesh and blood." His brothers agreed. 28So when
> the Midianite merchants came by, his brothers
> pulled Joseph up out of the cistern and sold him
> for twenty shekels of silver to the Ishmaelites, who
> took him to Egypt. Gen. 37:26-28

This is yet another big blow for Joseph – being sold just like one would sell an animal, where it would be dragged off to the marketplace, tied to a post, and sold to the highest bidder. Would

Joseph rather be dead than to be sold into an uncertain future, not knowing what would become of him? This must have been very traumatic for him and tormenting to his mind, especially when facing such a long journey to Egypt.

The journey must have taken a few weeks, and as he went along, he was no doubt being tormented by the enemy. With such an uncertain future before him, there would have been a tremendous state of worry, anxiety and fear. Knowing who the devil is, he would have made sure that Joseph had no peace of mind, and no rest from the agony he was experiencing. But because Joseph put his trust in his God, the Lord was there with him all along the way.

> You will keep in perfect peace him whose mind is steadfast, because he trusts in you. [4]Trust in the LORD forever, for the LORD, the LORD, is the Rock eternal. Isa. 26:3-4

> Meanwhile, the Midianites sold Joseph in Egypt to Potiphar, one of Pharaoh's officials, the captain of the guard. Gen. 37:36

Here is another terrible blow for Joseph, being sold a second time as a slave; from the favorite son to a slave, and there is nothing he can do about it. Yet, our loving Lord and Father was with him, and

He is going to turn it all around for good for Joseph, although it is going to take a very long time – over thirteen years.

Joseph is now sold in Egypt to Potiphar.

> Now Joseph had been taken down to Egypt. Potiphar, an Egyptian who was one of Pharaoh's officials, the captain of the guard, bought him from the Ishmaelites who had taken him there. [2]The LORD was with Joseph and he prospered, and he lived in the house of his Egyptian master. [3]When his master saw that the LORD was with him and that the LORD gave him success in everything he did, [4]Joseph found favor in his eyes and became his attendant. Potiphar put him in charge of his household, and he entrusted to his care everything he owned. [5]From the time he put him in charge of his household and of all that he owned, the LORD blessed the household of the Egyptian because of Joseph. The blessing of the LORD was on everything Potiphar had, both in the house and in the field. [6]So he left in Joseph's care everything he had; with Joseph in charge, he did not concern himself with anything except the food he ate. Now Joseph was well-built and handsome, [7]and after a

while his master's wife took notice of Joseph and said, "Come to bed with me!" 8But he refused. "With me in charge," he told her, "my master does not concern himself with anything in the house; everything he owns he has entrusted to my care. 9No one is greater in this house than I am. My master has withheld nothing from me except you, because you are his wife. How then could I do such a wicked thing and sin against God?" 10And though she spoke to Joseph day after day, he refused to go to bed with her or even be with her. 11One day he went into the house to attend to his duties, and none of the household servants was inside. 12She caught him by his cloak and said, "Come to bed with me!" But he left his cloak in her hand and ran out of the house. 13When she saw that he had left his cloak in her hand and had run out of the house, 14she called her household servants. "Look," she said to them, "this Hebrew has been brought to us to make sport of us! He came in here to sleep with me, but I screamed. 15When he heard me scream for help, he left his cloak beside me and ran out of the house." 16She kept his cloak beside her until his master came home. 17Then she told him this story: "That Hebrew slave you brought us came to me to

> make sport of me. [18]But as soon as I screamed for help, he left his cloak beside me and ran out of the house." Gen. 39:1-18

After all that Joseph has gone through, some would think that by now he would be bitter towards God – but no. What this passage of Scripture reveals is that Joseph was a young man who was totally committed and faithful to his God. He would not satisfy his flesh at the cost of sinning against his God. Yet, he is lied on and wrongly accused; a great injustice has befallen him. These are heavy blows for anyone, much less one who has already been through so much. Oh, how I desire Joseph's heart attitude, and his faithfulness towards God.

I wonder could we receive such blows and not curse God? How many of us could take such unjust blows without being bitter and so accuse God of wronging us? Yet, Joseph showed no sign of bitterness or even the slightest resentment against his God; neither was there any accusation in his heart against Him. This is precisely how we should walk with our God, trusting Him every step of the way, regardless of our circumstances or what we are going through. God is faithful, and He is going to reward Joseph mightily for his faithfulness to Him. He is going to use all these evil acts that have been done against Joseph, and work them all for good for Joseph, and for the saving of many lives. He is also going to use them to train him to be the leader that He had called him to be – the leader of Egypt and young Israel.

> When his master heard the story his wife told him, saying, "This is how your slave treated me," he burned with anger. [20]Joseph's master took him and put him in prison, the place where the king's prisoners were confined. . . Gen. 39:19-20a

Imagine, Joseph being faithful in honoring both his God and his employer, Potiphar, and for doing so, he was lied on by Potiphar's wife and thrown in jail, and even then, he did not defend himself. This must have been an awful and terrible situation for him, yet in it all, he remained faithful to his God, and God sustained him through it all, and kept him faithful to Him to the end.

> . . .But while Joseph was there in the prison, [21]the LORD was with him; he showed him kindness and granted him favor in the eyes of the prison warden. [22]So the warden put Joseph in charge of all those held in the prison, and he was made responsible for all that was done there. [23]The warden paid no attention to anything under Joseph's care, because the LORD was with Joseph and gave him success in whatever he did. Gen. 39:20b-23

This is again another horrible blow for Joseph. He is thrown into prison, but his God and Lord is there with him, giving him favor. He was there with him all the time – through all the fears, difficulties and suffering; He was in it all with him. Joseph was therefore never alone. This is the God to whom we belong.

> Keep your lives free from the love of money and be content with what you have, because God has said, "Never will I leave you; never will I forsake you." [6]So we say with confidence, "The Lord is my helper; I will not be afraid. What can man do to me?" Heb. 13:5-6

Those who believe their God and Lord, holding firmly to Him through His Word and not letting go, will always find that after coming through the fire, their beloved Lord Jesus was there all the time, and that He never abandons us, although at times it might seem that way.

Joseph found favor and kindness because he held to his God, believing Him, and through all his difficulties, he never doubted or accused Him for a moment. This is pure and sincere faith in the living God and Lord. This is a testimony of God's faithfulness and His inestimable goodness to those who will believe in Him, to those who will hold fast to His Holy Word, never letting it go.

If this is who you are, you will find that God will always be there with you in all your struggles and through all your difficulties, and in the end, He Himself will lift you up and reward you.

> Humble yourselves, therefore, under God's mighty
> hand, that he may lift you up in due time. [7]Cast
> all your anxiety on him because he cares for you.
> [8]Be self-controlled and alert. Your enemy the
> devil prowls around like a roaring lion looking
> for someone to devour. [9]Resist him, standing firm
> in the faith, because you know that your brothers
> throughout the world are undergoing the same kind
> of sufferings. [10]And the God of all grace, who called
> you to his eternal glory in Christ, after you have
> suffered a little while, will himself restore you and
> make you strong, firm and steadfast. [11]To him be
> the power for ever and ever. Amen. 1 Peter 5:6-11

This is God's promise to the faithful, to those who put their trust in Him, and wait upon Him.

After God had lifted Joseph up out of the dungeon, and had him stand before Pharaoh, we then see Joseph acknowledging and revealing the great God of Heaven to Pharaoh. Isn't this precious? How beautiful is faithfulness unto our God and Lord!

> So Pharaoh sent for Joseph, and he was quickly brought from the dungeon. When he had shaved and changed his clothes, he came before Pharaoh. [15]Pharaoh said to Joseph, "I had a dream, and no one can interpret it. But I have heard it said of you that when you hear a dream you can interpret it." [16]"I cannot do it," Joseph replied to Pharaoh, "but God will give Pharaoh the answer he desires." Gen. 41:14-16

Through Joseph, God gave Pharaoh the interpretation of his dream. God also gave Joseph favor with Pharaoh, which He used to exalt Joseph from a prisoner, to be the head of the Government over all of Egypt. Only Pharaoh, because he was the king, was higher in position, authority and honor than Joseph. Glory to the name of our Lord and God. Is there anything impossible for God to do? No! There is nothing. From this honored position, Joseph will now be able to rescue Israel from the famine to come.

> Then Pharaoh said to Joseph, "Since God has made all this known to you, there is no one so discerning and wise as you. [40]You shall be in charge of my palace, and all my people are to submit to your orders. Only with respect to the throne will I be greater than you." [41]So Pharaoh said to Joseph,

"I hereby put you in charge of the whole land of Egypt." [42]Then Pharaoh took his signet ring from his finger and put it on Joseph's finger. He dressed him in robes of fine linen and put a gold chain around his neck. [43]He had him ride in a chariot as his second-in-command, and men shouted before him, "Make way!" Thus he put him in charge of the whole land of Egypt. [44]Then Pharaoh said to Joseph, "I am Pharaoh, but without your word no one will lift hand or foot in all Egypt." [45]Pharaoh gave Joseph the name Zaphenath-Paneah and gave him Asenath daughter of Potiphera, priest of On, to be his wife. And Joseph went throughout the land of Egypt. Gen. 41:39-45

(See also Gen. 41:25-38)

Here, God exalted Joseph from the low place of a slave, the lowest place that any human being could ever be placed in, and vindicated him from the wrongful charge of being a rapist, for which he was imprisoned. From this low place, God reached down and lifted him up, making him the head of government over Egypt and his family/his brothers. Is there anything impossible for God to do?

Joseph suffered blow after blow and was in a constant state of humiliation for thirteen long years, yet he never let go of his faith, but rather remained faithful to His God, never judging or accusing Him. And look how God used all of that suffering to prepare him for this high place of honor, which He had willed for him to hold. Look at the honor poured out on Joseph. They that wait upon the Lord will be renewed.

Now it is time for Joseph to reveal himself to his brothers.

> Then Joseph said to his brothers, "Come close to me." When they had done so, he said, "I am your brother Joseph, the one you sold into Egypt!" Gen. 45:4

I pray that everyone will understand that I am not writing a story about Joseph, because if I were, it would go on for a long time. What I am writing about is the process of separation: the hate and hostility which awaits one along that path; the rejection of you, the doubting by others of who you are and what you are about; the shame, the humiliation, the suspicion, the gossiping, the ridicule, the mocking, the persecution, the suffering, the setting of traps for you so that you will fall into sin, the looking in your face and laughing at you, the looking down on you, the seeing you as a deceiver, as of the devil, as nothing, etc.

There are also the accusations, the outright lying to you, and deceiving you, the criticisms, the insinuations, the rejections, the afflictions, and the judgments that you are not of God. Then there are the isolation and the separation from all family and friends, with no one wanting to understand that this is of God, who is at work in you to accomplish His purposes, and in the end through such a separation, to rescue the blind and the lost. And it really comes down to this question: "Does anyone care?" From the responses all around you, the answer is a clear "No," but I think it is best that way. In fact, it is necessary, for God uses all of this to build you into a man or woman of God. However, in the end, God restores, and as we can see, the day of restoration is great. Joseph was restored to his family. In my case, I believe that my restoration will take place in heaven.

Here, we now see Joseph comforting his brothers from their guilt of selling him into Egypt.

> And now, do not be distressed and do not be angry with yourselves for selling me here, because it was to save lives that God sent me ahead of you. [6]For two years now there has been famine in the land, and for the next five years there will not be plowing and reaping. [7]But God sent me ahead of you to preserve for you a remnant on earth and to save

> your lives by a great deliverance. [8]"So then, it was not you who sent me here, but God. He made me father to Pharaoh, lord of his entire household and ruler of all Egypt. [9]Now hurry back to my father and say to him, 'This is what your son Joseph says: God has made me lord of all Egypt. Come down to me; don't delay. [10]You shall live in the region of Goshen and be near me – you, your children and grandchildren, your flocks and herds, and all you have. [11]I will provide for you there, because five years of famine are still to come. Otherwise you and your household and all who belong to you will become destitute.' Gen. 45:5-11

Here Joseph is telling his brothers not to feel guilty about what they had done to him, for it was God's will to send him ahead of them to Egypt. Therefore, he received all that had been done against him as from God, and not from them. And indeed, if you are truly the Lord's, that is the only way to look at it, since all that you are is the Lord's. This will also help you to avoid resentment, hate, bitterness and vindictiveness towards those who do those things to you.

It is God who uses the selfish acts of those around us to put us through the fire, in order to purge us of everything that contaminates;

everything that He sees will hinder us from accomplishing His divine purpose. The Lord Jesus has to therefore take us on a path for the purpose of working death in all those areas of our lives, where there are so many weaknesses/sins. The Lord Jesus has to cleanse us of them, but He first reveals them, at times through some tough circumstances. May we trust Him to lead us along that path, as difficult as it may seem. If we hold firmly to Him and His precious Word, the Holy Spirit will be sanctifying us along that path, and it will not seem so difficult. In the end, we will look back at it all and say, "Oh, it wasn't difficult after all."

Joseph has now come through that rough road, that difficult path, and yes, he suffered a lot, and he must have pained tremendously. He was humiliated, belittled, and seen as a nobody, a poor thing, a slave and a rapist. Oh, how lonely he must have been at times. How he must have missed his father and longed to know his younger brother, Benjamin. But through all of this, God was leading him through the valley of the shadow of death, for him to grow up and mature, so that at the young age of thirty, he would be prepared to assume the great position and responsibility as ruler of all Egypt. Yes, suffering does bring forth greater faith, development and maturity, and closeness with God.

If we could now ask Joseph if he would have chosen a different path, if that was possible, he would definitely tell us, no. He would say, "The path that God has led me on was quite satisfactory, thank you! I would not have had it any other way." Seeing the maturity in his life, and how God had used all the injustices that were perpetrated against him for his highest good, for his own development at such a young age, so that he would be mature enough to take on that great responsibility, he must have thanked God every day, for so leading him on that rough road. "Thank You, dearest, beloved Lord Jesus."

Joseph's preparation however, took a long time. It took thirteen years for God to prepare Joseph to save that entire section of the world from the famine that was to come, and to keep the light that had been lit through Abraham from going out. This was the real reason why Joseph was separated – to be prepared to save lives, even our lives, through our Lord and Savior Jesus Christ, by saving Israel, along with the rest of the people in that vast region of the world, from the devastating famine which was to come.

So yes, separation always seems hard and even cruel to some. But look at the results, and you will see how wonderful it is for those of us who are the beneficiaries of such separations. I believe that what we are seeing here is, without exception, separations for godly purposes are usually not very beautiful, but in the end the results are always so wonderful for the one separated, and for those who are blessed by it.

Moses is now about to be separated for the purpose of leading Israel out of Egypt. God saw the suffering of His people in Egypt, and for this reason, he needed to separate a man from his family, friends and country, to prepare him for the purpose of delivering His people.

As Joseph was separated, so now, Moses is going to be separated by God. Why? Again, to prepare him to save lives – our lives, as well as Israel's.

> During that long period, the king of Egypt died. The Israelites groaned in their slavery and cried out, and their cry for help because of their slavery went up to God. [24]God heard their groaning and he remembered his covenant with Abraham, with Isaac and with Jacob. [25]So God looked on the Israelites and was concerned about them. Exodus 2:23-25

This preparation for such a massive undertaking was absolutely necessary, in part because of Moses' immaturity, as revealed in his choice and action to run ahead of God, which resulted in his killing the Egyptian. Yet, through this very act, God was able to separate Moses and to get him out of Egypt and into his desert. Here, God could then work in Moses' life, to humble him and cleanse him from all the ways of Egypt, and so prepare him for this important mission. God did this over a period of forty years, during which time He was able to bring him to maturity, and put to an end the ways and influences of Egypt in his life, thereby equipping him for the purpose of delivering God's people, Israel, and giving them the Law.

As we can see, all four of these men were types of saviors in the hand of God – Noah, Abraham, Joseph and Moses. When I read the accounts of these men's lives, what I see are footsteps coming across the desert; those beautiful footsteps of our dearest and beloved Lord and Savior, the Lord Jesus Christ. And with each of these lives, another step was being taken on the way to Calvary's Cross, to save wretches like you and me.

These men's lives represent hope, hope for you and for me. With each of these lives we were one step closer to being redeemed, and one step closer to going home to our Father and Lord, who loves us dearly. Their lives represent the footsteps of our Lord Jesus, marching through that arid desert, marching to Calvary's Cross.

The Lord was on a mission to save lives, and when I read the Old Testament, what I see throughout are the footsteps of our beloved Lord Jesus, coming to Calvary's Cross to die, and to pay the price which we could not pay – the price for our sins, and to buy us out from under the degradation of sin. "Thank You dearest Lord Jesus."

We tend to see these men, and their separation and suffering, rather than seeing the true reason for it all. And because our eyes are fixed on them, we fail to see the One who really suffered as He marched through their lives. He too was separated. The Lord Jesus was cut off from His Father, from His place of abode – the beauty and splendor and comfort of heaven, and from those who attended and worshiped Him, to the point where, on the Cross, because of our sins, He cried out, **". . .My God, my God, why have you forsaken me?"** (Matt. 27:46)

This separation stands out above all separations. The Lord Jesus felt that separation more than any of us could ever understand or experience. That is because He is so bound up in His Father; the oneness in life and purpose which they share, and the profound bond of love that they have in each other, set His separation apart and above all other separations. Our beloved Lord Jesus set all this aside and was separated, to rescue and save wretches like you and me.

Nothing could stop our beloved Lord Jesus. He kept coming, and although He knew the pain and suffering awaiting Him, and the fact that He was going to lay down His life in such a cruel and awful way to save ours, this did not deter Him or slow Him down. He just kept coming through judges, prophets, servants and kings. He kept coming, with full knowledge that He would be rejected, beaten, stripped, mocked, insulted, laughed at, spat upon, His beard ripped off His face and His inestimable good towards us called demonic.

Man's cruelty and demonic vindictiveness were poured out on the Lord Jesus in an ugly and wicked way. He knew all this was waiting for Him, yet He kept coming. Yes, regardless of the suffering, the pain, the rejections, the insults, the beatings, the mocking and being spat upon, which were all awaiting Him, He kept coming. None of these diverted Him from His purpose to rescue us, whom He so loves. He just kept coming, with a determination to lay down His life to buy us out from under the power of the devil, and from the slavery to sin in which we were held prisoners.

Look with me across the landscape as you read the blessed Scriptures, and see if you too do not see the beloved Lord Jesus coming, coming to suffer and to lay down His precious life unto death to pay the price for the sins of wretches like you and me. "Thank You beloved Lord Jesus."

Yes, Moses was separated from family, friends and country for forty years, one year of separation for each year he had spent in

Egypt. God was cleansing him of all the ways and customs of Pharaoh's palace and of Egypt, and preparing him, so that through him, He could take another giant step through that desert, to save lives. And yes, He did come and lay down His precious life for wretches like us, to buy us out from under the control of the devil and from under the power of sin.

So the reason all these men were separated, was because Jesus our Lord was on a mission to save lives, and He is still separating people today, through whom He is going to save even more lives. Why? Because He has seen the suffering and misery of His body, the church. In my case and in the cases of those few He has called to be with me, He has separated us for His purpose – His church.

> The LORD said, "I have indeed seen the misery of my people in Egypt. I have heard them crying out because of their slave drivers, and I am concerned about their suffering. [8]So I have come down to rescue them from the hand of the Egyptians and to bring them up out of that land into a good and spacious land, a land flowing with milk and honey. . .
> Exodus 3:7-8a

CHAPTER 8

# DEEP BREATHING

In January 1991, the Spirit of the Lord came into me in a way I had not known of before, and remained. I then became very weak, and deep breathing overtook me. The state of weakness that came upon me was extreme, so much so, that at times I would find it difficult to lift my arms. I cannot explain this, nor do I understand it. Until this day, my Lord has not permitted me to understand exactly what had happened. Indeed, I had not known, understood or heard of this happening to anyone before in this way.

> But he said to me, "My grace is sufficient for you, for my power is made perfect in weakness." Therefore I will boast all the more gladly about my weaknesses, so that Christ's power may rest on me.
> 10That is why, for Christ's sake, I delight in weaknesses, in insults, in hardships, in persecutions, in

> difficulties. For when I am weak, then I am strong.
> 2 Cor. 12:9-10

I would inhale and exhale for long periods, and at times, it would seem to me that there would be no end to the span of breathing. Sometimes it sounds somewhat like a very deep sigh, only it is much, much deeper. From the day that I first experienced this, and for the next three years, I spent every day, with very few exceptions, on my belly on the floor before the Lord, breathing deeply, and yielding up the life to the Lord Jesus at deeper levels which I did not know existed, as He brought these areas to me.

During the three years of deep breathing while laying on the floor, my body became even weaker, indeed, extremely weaker than it had been in previous years, and when the breathing began, it would weaken me even more. At the end of the three years, this extreme state of weakness diminished to a point. This diminished state continued for several years.

After that three year period had ended, the breathing would begin when I least expected it, with only a very short advance notice. At times, it happened when there was a need for deliverance, repentance, cleansing, etc. I have seen it result in conviction of sin, deliverance, transformation of lives, etc. People have testified of experiencing a tenderness for the Lord Jesus; great care, love and admiration for Him; a desire for Him, His Word and His ways; deep rest, hope and security in their relationship with their Lord Jesus; gratitude, thanksgiving and appreciation to the Lord Jesus; a reverent fear, respect, honor and exaltation of Him; a deep cleansing within, etc.

In the process of deep breathing, one person was even transformed from what seemed to be mental and physical retardation, to normalcy before my very eyes, and the eyes of their parents and those who were present. These are only some of the results that have been testified to, which have occurred throughout, and after deep breathing has taken place. The following are a few illustrations from the Scriptures, which speak on the Breath of God. These are the Scriptures that I found, which come close to explaining the heavy blasts of breath through my nostrils, and at other times, through my mouth.

> And then the lawless one will be revealed, whom the Lord Jesus will overthrow with the breath of his mouth and destroy by the splendor of his coming. 2 Thess. 2:8

> After he took him aside, away from the crowd, Jesus put his fingers into the man's ears. Then he spit and touched the man's tongue. [34]He looked up to heaven

and with a deep sigh said to him, “Ephphatha!” (which means, “Be opened!”). [35]At this, the man’s ears were opened, his tongue was loosened and he began to speak plainly. Mark 7:33-35

Again Jesus said, “Peace be with you! As the Father has sent me, I am sending you.” [22]And with that he breathed on them and said, “Receive the Holy Spirit. John 20:21-22

The valleys of the sea were exposed and the foundations of the earth laid bare at the rebuke of the LORD, at the blast of breath from his nostrils. 2 Sam. 22:16

From the west, men will fear the name of the LORD, and from the rising of the sun, they will revere his glory. For he will come like a pent-up flood that the breath of the LORD drives along. Isa. 59:19

but with righteousness he will judge the needy, with justice he will give decisions for the poor of the earth. He will strike the earth with the rod of his mouth; with the breath of his lips he will slay the wicked. Isa. 11:4

The grass withers and the flowers fall, because the breath of the LORD blows on them. Surely the people are grass. Isa. 40:7

Then he said to me, "Prophesy to these bones and say to them, 'Dry bones, hear the word of the LORD! [5]This is what the Sovereign LORD says to these bones: I will make breath enter you, and you will come to life. [6]I will attach tendons to you and make flesh come upon you and cover you with skin; I will put breath in you, and you will come to life. Then you will know that I am the LORD.' " [7]So I prophesied as I was commanded. And as I was prophesying, there was a noise, a rattling sound, and the bones came together, bone to bone. [8]I looked, and tendons and flesh appeared on them and skin covered them, but there was no breath in them. [9]Then he said to me, "Prophesy to the breath; prophesy, son of man, and say to it, 'This is what the Sovereign LORD says: Come from the four winds, O breath, and breathe into these slain, that they may live.' " [10]So I prophesied as he commanded

> me, and breath entered them; they came to life and stood up on their feet – a vast army. Ezek. 37:4-10

> But you blew with your breath, and the sea covered them. They sank like lead in the mighty waters. Exodus 15:10

> See also: Isa. 30:28 & 33, Job 15:30, Job 4:9, Job 37:10, Job 33:4

Since then, deep breathing has evolved, and at times has manifested itself in tremendous blasts of breath through my nostrils, and at other times through my mouth. I do not control the breathing; it comes from within me when the beloved Lord Jesus has a purpose for its use. Knowledge that it is about to begin is given to me only minutes before it starts. However, the beloved Lord Jesus is in full control of it, and He uses it to accomplish His purposes when He chooses. I am surrendered to His will, for Him to do in and through me whatever He so wills, and I am at all times in full agreement with whatever He chooses to do. "Thank You beloved Lord Jesus."

# CHAPTER 9

# THE ANOINTING

On the night of Tuesday, March 26, 1996, sometime between the hours of 8:00 and 9:00 p.m., I went upstairs to my apartment to retire for the night, and as is customary, I began reading my Bible. Part of my Bible reading for that day happened to be 1 Samuel Chapter 3, which records the call of Samuel. As I sat on the couch and began to read, the tender presence of the Lord Jesus began to engulf me, and tears began to flow. As I read through the call of Samuel by the Lord, the presence of the glorious, beloved Lord Jesus grew stronger, and the tears increased.

It was not long before I became totally enveloped with the precious presence of the beloved Lord Jesus, and tears were now calmly flooding out. When I reached verse 11, it seemed as if I was no longer reading, but rather, the words of this verse which said: **". . .See, I am about to do something in Israel that will make**

**the ears of everyone who hears of it tingle."** leapt off the page and spoke to me, as if the Lord had spoken these words afresh to me. At this point, I was tenderly broken and overwhelmed by His gentle presence, and I could no longer read.

As the tears continued to flow, I sat there a while longer, enjoying the sweet presence of the Lord Jesus, which I had not felt in this way for twenty-two or so years. Then the Lord Jesus spoke to me, instructing me to enter a large room that is next to the chapel, and remain there for seven days. This room, measuring twenty-three feet by forty feet, had been prepared on the instructions of the Lord Jesus seventeen years earlier, when in 1979, He guided me in every detail as to its furnishings and exactly how it was to be decorated, which I followed until it was finished.

When the decoration of this room was completed, the instructions of the Lord Jesus were for it to be sealed, meaning, tightly locked up. He however gave us liberty to enter this room once each year, for the purpose of cleaning it. This liberty lasted for approximately six years, after which it was removed. The room then remained completely sealed for the next eleven years, during which time He did not permit any further access to it.

I knew that this room was set apart for the purposes of the Lord Jesus, who I believe will make His presence known there one day. Therefore, after I regained my composure, in awe, reverent fear and with a touch of hesitancy, I got up and shared with the brethren that the beloved Lord Jesus had instructed me to enter the room and remain there for seven days. We then washed ourselves and put on clean clothes and new socks. Then shoe-less, in fear and trembling, not knowing what I would find there, we unsealed the door, and at approximately 12:00 midnight, I entered the room.

I was still in much awe and reverent fear, and without any clear understanding as to what was going to happen, although for many years, I had been waiting to be anointed at any time, as my Lord had always kept me in a low state of consciousness and anticipation that this would happen one day.

From the day my Lord saved me, He planted this knowledge within me that I would be anointed one day. A day did not go by that I was not conscious of this fact. So this was something that I was always looking forward to, expecting it to happen any day. I therefore suspected that this was it, but with the Lord Jesus, one never knows for sure when He will move in our lives, and how He will move.

For the first three days after I entered the room, I spent the time laying before the Lord Jesus. During this time, demonic thoughts came to my mind, such as: nothing was going to happen; how foolish I was to be there; what was I waiting for; my being there was not of the Lord, etc. This went on for hours. However, by the grace of God, I ignored them; I put my trust in the Lord Jesus and continued to wait upon Him.

These thoughts persisted, along with many others, and at times they were even accompanied by heavy, negative feelings. I therefore had to hold on to what the Lord Jesus had said to me to be able to remain there. If I had focused on all that was being said through these thoughts, along with all the negative feelings that were hitting me, I would not have been able to remain there.

These three days seemed to have been days of testing, as at times, the feelings were so strong that one could easily have gotten up and walked out of the room. However, the Lord Jesus gave me the grace to resist them, and by faith, to hold on to the words that He had spoken to me. After these three days had passed, the negative thoughts and feelings left me.

On Sunday morning, March 31, 1996, my fourth day in the room, at approximately 11:15 a.m., I heard what sounded like sharp "clicks," echoing throughout the whole room, as if many persons had jumped into the room. This sound was similar to that which would be made by several sharp spikes, all hitting the floor at the same time. Immediately following this, I was conscious that angels had entered the room.

I looked and saw images of angels, with what appeared to be arms in hand, positioned along the walls of the room. It seemed to me that they were shoulder to shoulder, so as not to allow any space between each of them. In so doing, they completely covered the walls. I could not see these angels clearly, as their images were somewhat obscured or blurred. This could have resulted from the fact that the room was very dark. However, I had full knowledge of their presence and of their keeping guard for the coming of someone very important. I had only a very small light in one corner of the room where I was, leaving the rest of the room very dark, and so I could not see clearly around it. Yet, I was able to see the forms of the angels along the walls.

On the morning of Monday, April 1, 1996, my fifth day in the room, two huge objects from heaven entered the room, one after the other. The only way I could describe them, is they looked as if they were miniature islands. They were incredibly beautiful, with one of them having a very young lamb laying on it, in a very restful posture, along with other things that I cannot describe. After this, two demonic counterfeits entered the room. They appeared to be almost identical to the previous two, but there was a slight difference in the way the lamb looked. However, the Lord Jesus gave me instant knowledge that the two that followed were satanic counterfeits.

Following this, I saw a huge valley filled with angels on both sides of it, with hands lifted up worshiping God. After this, I saw several distorted demonic figures in a rage, pointing their fingers at me in a threatening way, as if to harm me and to afflict me with fear. However, the beloved Lord Jesus did not permit them to harm me, nor was I afraid. Devils even have access to such sanctified and solemn occasions.

This surprised me very much, and then I remembered Job as he was tried, and Judas who was right there in the presence of the Lord Jesus every day for three years.

> On another day the angels came to present themselves before the LORD, and Satan also came with them to present himself before him. Job 2:1

> Then Jesus replied, "Have I not chosen you, the Twelve? Yet one of you is a devil!" John 6:70

Then there was Joshua, the high priest.

> Then he showed me Joshua the high priest standing before the angel of the LORD, and Satan standing at his right side to accuse him. [2]The LORD said to Satan, "The LORD rebuke you, Satan! The LORD, who has chosen Jerusalem, rebuke you! Is not this man a burning stick snatched from the fire?" Zech. 3:1-2

On Tuesday, April 2, 1996, my sixth day in the room, I again saw many twisted, ugly, demonic figures, with all kinds of scars, and what looked like melted lumps of flesh hanging off different parts of their bodies and faces. They surrounded me, and in a rage, they did everything possible to drive fear in me. Along with this rage, there was what looked like bolts of electricity or fire coming through their fingers as they pointed them towards me.

I was amazed at how the Lord Jesus sustained me and kept me from being afraid, because under any such circumstances, without the Lord Jesus being there with me, I would have fled in fear, if it were possible to flee, or rather, collapse under the fear, because these figures were so terrifying to look at. Thanks to the Lord Jesus, He kept me safe, feeling absolutely no fear at all. Yet it was difficult to look at those horrific distorted figures.

On Wednesday, April 3, 1996, my seventh day in the room, at 12:20 a.m., I was awakened by the most beautiful song, the beauty of which simply cannot be expressed. Along with this song came the following words: "Wake up Lee Lee, your time has come – your time of anointing is here."

For the last twenty-three years, I have had clear knowledge that one day, I would be anointed by the Lord Jesus to be His servant, which He has called me to be. This knowledge was planted in me by the Lord, and I have lived with it over all these years. So, for all those years I had been expecting this to happen any day, and suddenly that day had arrived. Yet, I was not overwhelmed by it, because it was a spiritual experience. My experience was in my spirit, and not in my flesh. Therefore, there were no emotional highs or lows or any other feelings in my flesh.

Yet, the part that moved me, was the simple touch of my Father, who called me through the angel by my childhood name, "Lee Lee," as He did when He visited me as a child. He still saw me as His little boy, and that was a tender touch which moved me deeply, from my Father and Lord, the God of the universe, the maker of heaven and earth and all that exists, and who is sovereign over all. All this took place in my spirit.

After this, I went to the bathroom. The whole experience was so calm and natural, that it did not seem to be supernatural; neither did it seem abnormal for me to get up in the middle of all that was happening to go to the bathroom. I had knowledge that what was happening was indeed supernatural, yet it did not seem that way to me. In other words, there were no feelings in my flesh that would allow me to relate to this experience as one would under normal circumstances.

Although I had the liberty to get up and go to the bathroom, which I did, when I returned to the room and sat down, there was a sense of reverent fear, so much so, that even though I was cold, I did not take the liberty to put on my over-shirt. Therefore, when I was told by the angel to put on my over-shirt, I was touched by the concern, and the loving, tender care of the Lord Jesus for me. This I did, and reverently laid face down again before my Lord.

Then the angel said to me: "Turn to God!" My immediate response out of surprise was: "I turn to God – I turn to God with all my heart, soul, mind, spirit and body." I also said; "I turn from self, the world, the devil and the ways of the flesh." I was taken aback at this instruction, since I had thought that all that I am had been turned over to the Lord Jesus, and that is why my response was in such surprise, as if being caught off guard. This is how blind I am, no different from the rest of the church, believing that we are in the light, when indeed, darkness is all that we know.

Immediately after this, I experienced a wonderful sensation, like a gentle, cool breeze in a circular, clockwise motion (like a drill), coming into my forehead. It was a very small, (about the size of a pencil), uniformed, pressurized, intense, and concentrated flow, of what seemed to me to be some kind of air, coming into the center of my forehead. This continued consistently for some minutes, and my spirit was moved into worship and praise to God my Father, to the Lord Jesus Christ, and to the Holy Spirit.

After some minutes, this praise ceased, and deep breathing overtook me, which continued for the remainder of the time. Then, that beautiful song began again, and these words were spoken: "Bye, bye, Lee Lee. You are no longer your own; you now belong to the living God; you are anointed to be the servant of the living God." The song then continued, but I cannot remember the words or the tune. It was all removed from me. You have never before heard singing, until you hear the song I heard that night. I actually listened to a song from heaven. I heard this beautiful heavenly voice, singing a precious and most beautiful heavenly song that thrilled my soul. That night, I actually heard an angel from heaven singing.

As the song faded away with a long echoing sound, the following words, **". . .Feed my sheep."** John 21:17b, were repeated to me three times, and imprinted in my spirit in such a way, that I felt the impact of them.

The entire experience of the anointing on Wednesday, April 3, 1996, lasted approximately twenty or thirty minutes.

When this was over, I continued to lie before the Lord Jesus in a solemn state, giving thanks to Him. Suddenly, my mind-set changed and everything was back to normal. Then thoughts and concerns about the students and my other responsibilities returned to my mind. I then began to ask the Lord Jesus questions regarding these concerns, such as: "What if. . .?" – "What is to be done. . .?" – "What do You require to be done in this person's situation?" – "What am I to do about this particular case?" As I asked these questions, what I found unusual and surprising was the instant, clear-cut and to-the-point answers which were given to each of them. Up to this point, I had asked about four questions. I then asked another question, "Should this other person go and carry out a particular task?"

All the questions that I had previously asked were through thoughts in my mind, and to each of them came an instant, clear-cut response from whom I thought was the Lord Jesus, but they were not from

Him. However, my last question was not asked in that way. Rather, it was made through a very quiet impression in my spirit, to which I received no response. I asked the question again in the same way, and there still was no answer. At that moment, the Lord quickened me to the fact that I was being deceived by the enemy to think that it was He, the Lord Jesus, who had answered my previous questions, when in fact, it was the devil who had answered them.

Believe me when I tell you that the devil's counterfeit was almost as if perfect. This was so to the point where, if the beloved Lord Jesus was not there to intervene, I would not have known that it was not He who was answering my questions.

In hindsight, the only clue to the fact that I was being deceived, would have been the rapid, clear-cut responses I received to each of my questions. Yes, I was suspicious and somewhat concerned about this, nevertheless in my mind it was justified because of the solemn occasion and the circumstances; therefore I thought it was the Lord Jesus who was responding to my questions. For this reason, I did not give much attention to the suspicion I had, and so I continued to ask those questions.

Of course, I was surprised at this turn of events, yet at the same time glad, because my Lord was there with me to take me through this experience, and to teach me what really goes on in these areas of our lives. In this way, He was not only teaching me, but His whole body, the church, regarding our ignorance of the workings of satan in our lives. By this revelation, our Lord has chosen to bless us, His church, with this knowledge, so as to put an end to the deceits that the enemy brings to our minds about so many things, in so many different ways. This ignorance is also part of the reason for the darkness that is so prevalent over the church.

The devil also deceives us so that he can continue leading us in the realm of the flesh, through thoughts, feelings and impressions. We have all heard over and over again from those who listen to voices in their minds, and then proclaim that God has said thus to them, without realizing that they are being deceived. God does not speak through our minds – the devil does. When God speaks, He speaks through our spirits, and mostly through a very gentle and quiet impression, deep within our spirit, with clear knowledge of what He is saying, which remains with you.

Through this experience, the Lord Jesus also taught me that the devil indeed speaks through our thoughts and understands them. The only thing he does not understand is the very quiet impressions in our spirit, by which the Holy Spirit communicates with us through our spirit, and likewise we, through a quiet impression in our spirit, are able to communicate with Him. Therefore, in this case, the devil did not know what the last question was that I had asked the Lord Jesus through the quiet impression in my spirit, and that is why there was no response to it from him.

The devil and his demons understand all the thought processes, which are formulated in the mind. However, they have no understanding of the Spirit to spirit communication that takes place between the Holy Spirit and our spirit; only the Holy Spirit and the person do.

In some instances, depending on its importance, the master of demons will himself handle the case, whatever it might be. However, in most cases, demons are given the job of dealing with individuals, and they pass the information on to a higher authority, as it is required or necessary, according to their system.

After all this had ended, I was given knowledge that the room was to be left dressed the way it was, and sealed again, to be opened sometime in the future, when the Lord Jesus Himself will appear there – I assume to empower this work for it to begin. I believe that this will happen, and I am looking forward to that day. Everything else is in place, and the writings that the Lord Jesus is sending to His body, the church, which will follow this one, are still being written.

I entered the room on Tuesday night, March 26, 1996 at 12.00 midnight and came out early on Wednesday morning, April 3, 1996 – a total of seven days, during which time I ate no food.

Several years after this experience, I heard on the morning of May 31st, 2012, a pastor that I respect very much, preach that angels do not sing, but rather they say. (I think he means they say things.) He also quoted from a book written by another pastor that confirmed this to him. I had no idea that in the body of Christ, there were beliefs that angels do not sing.

When I heard this message the second time, the Lord brought back to my mind that when He anointed me to be the servant of the Living God, He began the anointing with an angel singing, coming from a distance, and it stopped when it reached me. The voice of the angel and the song were so delightful, beautiful and sweet, they were beyond words to describe. They were so beautiful; the only thing that comes to mind to describe them is they were a heavenly voice and song.

I used to think that the Lord chose to bless me with that song, which He immediately removed from my mind at the end of the anointing so I was never able to recall it, but after hearing this pastor, I then realized that there was a greater purpose for the angel singing than just to bless me. The reason why the Lord sent a singing angel at the anointing was to reveal to His body, the church, that yes, angels do sing, and to debunk the beliefs held by some that angels do not sing. I am a witness of God to this fact – angels do sing – whether you believe it or not!

> Then I looked and heard the voice of many angels, numbering thousands upon thousands, and ten thousand times ten thousand. They encircled the throne and the living creatures and the elders. [12] In a loud voice they sang: "Worthy is the Lamb, who was slain, to receive power and wealth and wisdom and strength and honor and glory and praise!" [13] Then I heard every creature in heaven and on earth and under the earth and on the sea, and all that is in them, singing: "To him who sits on the throne and to the Lamb be praise and honor and glory and power, for ever and ever!" Rev.5:11-13

I had previously written in Volume 1 of this book, about an experience I had while returning from Mexico City, over eighteen years prior to the anointing. This was in regards to an accusation against the Lord Jesus that came from deep within me, without any understanding of how such a thing could ever happen. It is now twelve years since the anointing, when while in bed one Sunday morning, the beloved Lord Jesus woke me with the connection I had been waiting for over all these years. He revealed that the understanding He had given me at the end of the anointing, concerning the works of satan in our lives, is the connection I have been waiting for. This means that it was the enemy, through my very thoughts, who had made the accusation back then, which said that it was God's fault why the students were not doing better than they were.

I remember how certain I was that I did not make that accusation, yet it came from deep within me, through my thoughts. But I knew it was not I who had made it. I had struggled to understand what had happened, and how such a thing could be, because at that time, my beliefs were firm that satan could not interfere with our thought life in any way, or have any such access from within a Christian. For this reason, over the years, I was concerned about what had happened, but the Lord did not give me any understanding of it then.

However, clear understanding of the connection has now come as I am writing, some twenty-six years later from the time that it took place, as the Lord used this deceit of satan to open my eyes to what had happened back then. Obviously, the intention of the Lord Jesus, through these experiences, was to begin to open up the dark world of satan's work in the lives of His people, through our sinful nature. It is through that nature that satan has such access in us. However, this access will continue to diminish in our souls, area by area, through the sanctifying work of the blessed Holy Spirit, as He cleanses us and brings death to those areas of the sinful nature in our souls where darkness/sin has yet to be cleansed.

As I wrote this, the Lord Jesus brought before me the vision He had given me back in 1978, of the whole earth covered with a solid black covering. At the time, I had thought that it was either the whole earth or the whole church, but now I am understanding that it is both which are covered with this solid blackness. Although this blackness should not have been applied to the church, yet it has. This revealed the influence the world has on the church. We see this in the way the people of the church and the people of the world behave, Mondays through Fridays. For most, the only difference in behavior is going to church on Saturdays and Sundays. Then after church, everything reverts back to the way it was. We see it in the way they do their hair, in their make-up, in the way they talk, and in the way they dress, etc. For instance, observe the jeans that the ladies of the world wear, and the jeans that the ladies in the church wear. You will see that they are equally skin tight; each drawing attention to themselves by revealing all the contours and crevices of their bodies.

I remember at the time, the Lord had opened the black covering of the heavens for me to see a double-headed serpent looking down on us. I am now understanding from the Lord, that what He was showing me then, is the very dark world of satan and his demons that He has been opening up and revealing to me over all these years, which He is now confirming for the purpose of His body, the church. These revelations of the work of satan against the church will continue until it is all exposed, so that God's children will no longer have to live under this black covering of satan's deceit, in the same way the world does. This subject is dealt with in depth in the book, "The Two Natures" that will follow. "Thank You Lord Jesus."

Following is a recall of what I had previously written in Chapter 28 of Volume 1 of this book, entitled "The Accusation." I have brought this forward to refresh our memories of what took place then.

## The Accusation

Midway on my journey back home from Mexico City, a very sweet and tender presence of the beloved Lord Jesus enveloped me. I had not felt His sweet, adorable presence in this way from before I left school and would not experience it again until 1996, eighteen years later, when I would be called to be anointed. I just could not stop weeping. I was melting away inside. All this was happening while I was driving, and my heart was filled with worship, praise, adoration and gratitude, just loving my Lord and giving thanks to Him for being who He is. He filled me with much love and tenderness towards Him.

In the midst of it all, I heard coming from deep within me, an accusation against my beloved Lord and God. This was the first experience I have ever had of such evil against my God and Lord, so naturally, I was surprised and stunned. I immediately pulled over and stopped the car. This was way out there in the open countryside, with nothing but bushes and tall trees in sight, and there was no one else around, except an adult and a small child who were in the car with me.

I quickly got out of the car and ran over to an empty field that was next to the road. There were lots of large holes there in the ground, and although I did not know what kind of holes they were, apart from the fact that some kind of large animal lived in them, I did not care. The greater fear won out again. I knelt down, surrounded by those holes, and I cried out as loud as I could, "Lord Jesus, please forgive me for the accusation that came through me, for it is wickedness, it is sin against You, and I do not want such evil in me." Then I said, "Lord that was not me. I did not say that, and I know that I did not say it, yet there it was. It came through my own thoughts, yet it was not me." I thought – how could that be?

Still, I was very sorry, I literally felt the agony and the pain of it all in my whole being, for accusations should never be made against such an inestimably good, loving, kind, gracious and wonderful God and Lord. It just should not be. It is not right; it is wickedness, it is evil, and I will not stand for it.

The accusation said that it was God's fault why the students were not performing better than they were. I was hurting that such a thing came out of me against such a wonderful God and Lord who is so inestimably good and loving and who loves us so much, and who I love with my whole heart, soul, mind, and strength. I wanted to get to the bottom of this, but it was not given at that time; it would be twenty years later that the Lord Jesus would connect it and give me the understanding as to what it was, at the anointing. And some years after this, came the revelation of the black covering of the entire earth and the church that you will read about in Volume 2 of this book. The Lord Jesus is affirming and confirming to us the tremendous darkness that is over the church. Thanks again to our beloved Lord.

Remember, **". . .they that wait upon the LORD shall renew their strength; they shall mount up with wings as eagles; they shall run, and not be weary; and they shall walk, and not faint."** Isa. 40:31 (KJV) "I will wait upon You, dear Lord."

CHAPTER 10

# ABRAHAM AND THE ROOTS · GOD SPEAKS

This is an experience that could easily cause anyone who hears or reads of it, to ridicule it, but I know that the Lord Jesus is in charge of the things which are written in this book. Therefore, I am at rest and at peace with it all, for I only write the truth concerning the things that took place as the Lord Jesus leads me to write. This is because I am able to write only the things that He brings to my mind to remind me of them, since I am not able to remember them. If He does not bring them, then I have nothing to write, neither would I be capable of writing anything.

One night, I had this extremely unusual experience of being taken back in time. I had clear knowledge that I was going back in time to meet Abraham, and that I was traveling at a rate of speed which definitely was not of this earth. Indeed, the only thing that I could assume it to be would be the speed of light. I actually felt the thrust from the speed in my body, although it was extremely subdued. I believe the Lord Jesus made it happen this way, because if it was any other way, my body could not have withstood the journey.

While it was happening, the journey back in time seemed to me to have taken a long time, although in reality it did not. I thought this way because of the knowledge I had of the speed at which I was traveling, along with the thrust I felt in my body from this speed. I therefore anticipated that I would have been there instantly, and because I was not, I thought it was taking too long. Foolish me!

Immediately as those thoughts ended, I suddenly arrived at a large tent, and as I entered, I saw Abraham sitting at a large round table in an area of what seemed to be the section of the tent where they reclined and dined. (The tent seemed to have three sections to it and it was very large.) In front of him there was some type of lighted lamp, which seemed to have been made out of animal skin. He was a broad and stocky man. Neither one of us spoke. In his hands was a root that had many fine strands/rootlets, which were light golden brown in color, as if they were taken from the earth and washed clean. The stalk at the top of the root was cut very, very low, so the root was the dominant part of what I saw. This root was also very clean, as if it had never been in the earth. Yet, its color was as if it was washed clean from being in the earth. The root was large enough that both his hands were filled with it with space between them, with its hundreds of strands/rootlets hanging down, so that as he held it out to me, I could see that both his hands could not come together so as to touch each other. In fact, as he held the root out to me, the distance apart between the fingers of both of his hands, was approximately 4 inches.

As I approached the table where he sat, we looked at each other, and he immediately reached out his hands across the table with both of them overfilled with the root. It was as if he was sitting there waiting for me to arrive. Similarly and simultaneously, I stretched out both my hands across the table to receive the root. Our hands met in the middle of the table, where I received the root from his hands. He continued sitting as he handed it to me, while I remained standing. As I took hold of the root from his hands, I was suddenly taken away, and that was the end of the experience. (I really do not know what else to call it.)

As I am writing this account and thinking about how I was suddenly taken away, the Lord impressed upon my spirit this Scripture from Acts Chapter 8.

> When they came up out of the water, the Spirit of the Lord suddenly took Philip away, and the

> eunuch did not see him again, but went on his way rejoicing. Acts 8:39

The clear impression that I had from the Holy Spirit, was that a torch had been passed from Abraham to me. This was the only understanding that I was given. However, I left it at that, as the whole thing seemed too high for me to contemplate or to comprehend. So over the years, whenever it would come to my mind, I really never gave much thought to it, apart from having a good laugh at the whole thing, because it seemed so way-out to me. Until today, I do not have any understanding of this matter beyond what I have written here, but I do know that one day, He, my glorious and beloved Lord Jesus, will connect it when His time has come to do so, and His time has not yet come. But they that wait upon the Lord will renew their strength.

I had another experience of traveling across the earth at a rapid rate of speed. I could see the earth beneath me going at a very fast rate of speed in the opposite direction. I was not in a vehicle of any kind. The only understanding I have been given of this, are the words – for the future.

As previously mentioned, these experiences which have been given to me by the Lord Jesus, were real-to-life experiences. I could actually feel that I was living them out as I went through them. Indeed, I was fully involved in what was happening, to the point where all my faculties, senses, emotions and feelings were interacting with what was taking place, and my decision-making process was also fully involved. These were therefore experiences that I lived out, as one would live out any experience in their daily lives.

The only things my mind retains are those things which come from the beloved Lord Jesus. The images of all these experiences and visions that I have shared in these writings, are as sharp and vivid as if I had just experienced them a moment ago. I can still see the Lord Jesus in His many appearances, as well as Abraham and all the other visions, and they are very clear and very fresh. Even those appearances that the Lord Jesus made to me when I was a child remain crystal clear, as if they occurred only moments ago. I have instant recall of all these appearances at all times.

## "I AM GOING TO BLESS YOU"

During those three years when I was on the floor experiencing the deep breathing, one morning at about eleven a.m., I got up and went to the bathroom. As I was washing my hands, I looked in the mirror, and immediately my beloved Lord and Father began to speak. I felt His reverent presence, and I quickly went down on my knees right where I was, and remained silent while He spoke. He spoke for some minutes; I do not know for sure how long. The last thing that He said was, "I am going to bless you, and every nation, every people, every language, every tribe, and every tongue will hear your voice." Then He stopped speaking. That was over twenty-eight years ago, and I am also waiting for its fulfillment.

> But they that wait upon the Lord shall renew their strength; they shall mount up with wings as eagles; they shall run, and not be weary; and they shall walk, and not faint. Isa. 40:31 (KJV)

## CHAPTER 11

# VISION OF GOD'S HOLINESS - ABRAHAM AND THE ROOTS

One day, the beloved Lord Jesus permitted me to see in a vision, the impact of His holiness as it fell on the earth. As far as I could see around me, even far off into the distance and beyond – there it was. I saw people falling to their knees under conviction of their sins, as they cried out in remorse to God, acknowledging their sins and repenting. Some were walking along the sidewalks; some were entering the gates to their homes, while others were going up the steps to their verandahs. They all fell right where they were, some on their faces, and others on their knees. All were in great awe and reverence of the Almighty God and His Son, the Lord Jesus Christ.

I had knowledge that at the same time, people were under conviction in their homes, in hospitals, and all over the city, or possibly the world – I do not know for sure. Indeed, it could have been the whole church or the whole world, but I do not know. I could also see inside the supermarkets, although I was far away from them. There, I could see people on their knees, all over the floors, weeping in repentance over their sins. This was all that He showed me, and I do not know what it means.

## REVELATION OF ABRAHAM AND THE ROOTS

I had previously written of the experience regarding my going back in time to receive the roots from Abraham. At the time I wrote about it, I did not understand its meaning up to that time, for it had not been given. But now, three days later as I was writing, the revelation came from the Lord Jesus, with clear knowledge and understanding of its meaning. The interpretation of this extraordinary experience that the beloved Lord Jesus gave me is: the root Abraham held in his hands and handed to me, represent Abraham – the root of the church. This root symbolizes Abraham, the root of the church, whereas the stalk that was cut very low, which barely appeared at the top of the root, represents me, the end of the church. This is the end of the revelation.

I had lived with the knowledge of this experience for all these years, yet never understanding its meaning or significance until today, when this revelation came. It clearly reveals that the root, with its hundreds of strands/rootlets hanging down, represent Abraham as the beginning of the church, and the stalk that was cut very low and protruded from the root, represents me, the end of the church.

> Consider Abraham: "He believed God, and it was credited to him as righteousness." [7]Understand, then, that those who believe are children of Abraham. [8]The Scripture foresaw that God would justify the Gentiles by faith, and announced the gospel in advance to Abraham: "All nations will be blessed through you." [9]So those who have faith are blessed along with Abraham, the man of faith. Gal. 3:6-9

## REVELATION OF THE PROMISE

Thirty-nine years ago, a promise was given to me by the beloved Lord Jesus, when He spoke to me in the church in Santa Barbara, California. (Please see Volume 1 of this book.) He said to me, "Look around at all the people." As I looked, He said to me, "None of the people you are looking at are living the abundant life that I brought," meaning, that He the Lord Jesus brought – speaking of the church as a whole. And here is the promise He gave me that day. He said, "But you are going to live the abundant life, here on this earth, in the flesh."

That is the promise, and although in the beginning I never saw or understood it as a promise given to anyone beyond myself, I nevertheless had a vague sense that it was also given to the church. But now the revelation and understanding have come from the beloved Lord Jesus, that this was a promise given to me, and through me, to the church.

# CHAPTER 12

# MIRACLES

My Lord has blessed me, giving me grace to be able to get up and run in the mornings, and I do this five days per week – Mondays through Fridays. One morning, I got up as usual and rode my bicycle to the park where I ran. After completing my run, I got on my bicycle again and started my journey back home.

On the way, while riding down a long boulevard, I noticed that there was hardly any traffic. At a point however, I happened to look back, and I saw a car coming behind me. For some reason or another, although I became suspicious of this car, I ignored it and continued on my way. The next thing I knew, after coming to my senses, was that I was flat on my back on the concrete sidewalk. I looked around to see what had happened, but saw nothing. I then noticed that the skin on the top of my left shoulder, next to my neck, was completely gone. However, there was no bleeding, and I felt no pain. I only felt some weakness and a little dizziness.

By this time, the car had gone. It did not stop. I wondered what had happened. Until today, I do not know for sure, for I heard nothing, and I felt nothing. Yet, there I was on my back, on the sidewalk, approximately five feet from where I had been riding, with the bicycle at my side, and the skin at the very top of my shoulder completely gone. Obviously, that is where I had taken the fall, because there was no other part of my body that showed any sign of a bruise. I then realized that if that was where I took the fall, my neck and head would have had to be out of the way, or else my neck would have been broken.

The place where I had landed clearly signaled that for me to have landed there, I would have had to be knocked across the grassy strip that was between the street and the concrete sidewalk, which at times runners use as a track. Yet, as mentioned before, I heard nothing, and I felt nothing. From that day until this, there has been no after-effect. "Thank You beloved Lord Jesus."

My Lord has not permitted me to understand this mystery, as He has done in so many other cases. Yet I know that He was there protecting me as usual. "Thank You beloved Lord Jesus, for being You."

On another occasion, as I was riding to the park to get in my morning run, a car with two men in it, pulled up next to me. The driver said to me, "Do you know where I can buy some drugs?" I responded, "No, I do not know." With that said, he became angry with me and tried to run me over. It was still dark, and so there was no one else around, except for one person who was with me. He therefore could have easily accomplished his goal, and no one else in the flesh would have seen, apart from the person with me, who yelled out to alert me that the car was coming at me. However, my Lord was there protecting me, as usual. If He were not, the man would have accomplished his purpose, because he came very close to doing so. Again, my beloved Lord Jesus rescued me. "Thank You Lord Jesus."

On another morning, while running in the same park, a pickup truck suddenly appeared before me. As far as I could see, this truck was coming at me head-on, and the more I tried to escape it by running to the left, to somehow get onto the sidewalk, it just kept following me. I just could not escape it. As I tried to turn to the right, there it was in front of me, ready to run me over. Finally, just as it was about to do so, it stopped abruptly.

The driver of the pickup came out, full of remorse, begging me to forgive him. He was sweating from anxiety and fear. He explained that he could not control the vehicle as it followed me, neither could he stop it, until that moment when it was about to run me over. He said that only then was his leg free to slam on the brakes, and the vehicle stopped suddenly. Thanks to my Lord, it was not going very fast.

Through all of this, I could clearly see that the Lord Jesus is with me wherever I go, protecting me from the clutches of the enemy. Here, once again, the enemy was clearly trying to put an end to my life, but my Lord did not permit him to. The Lord Jesus was there all the time. "Thank You Lord Jesus."

On yet another morning, as I was running, an SUV suddenly appeared behind me. Immediately as I heard the sound of the motor, I looked around and saw that it was about to run me over. Thanks to my Lord that I was next to the sidewalk, and so I was able to quickly jump onto it to get out of the way. As I did, the SUV sped up and went right by, exactly in the same path where I had been running. With the help of the Lord Jesus, I barely made it out of its way. The SUV then made the circle and made another attempt to run me over, but I was on guard and saw it coming, and was therefore able to get out of its way. The devil was determined to slay me, but my Lord was more than determined to protect me.

On another morning, I saw the driver of the SUV in the park. As I passed by, I heard him telling the man he was with, how he had tried to run me over. I said nothing. I simply went on my way, putting my trust in my Lord. He never attempted to do so again. This had to be the enemy himself, because I did not know this man, yet he tried to kill me.

One morning, while on my way back from running, I rode along a one-way street, which had two lanes. I then entered a wide intersection, and as I reached the middle of it, and was proceeding across it, suddenly, a car came from behind and made a right turn directly in front of me. It knocked me off the bicycle, and I lost consciousness. When I regained consciousness, it took me a little while to get up from where I had fallen. As I sat there in the middle of the street in that weak state, I saw someone looking at me and laughing mockingly at me.

Once again, my Lord was there protecting me, while the devil was having his fun, mocking and laughing at me. Apart from a few bruises, my Lord did not permit me to suffer any further harm. "Thank You beloved Lord Jesus."

## MIRACLE IN SMOKEY VALE

Early one morning, two of my students and I were returning from our usual morning run. While running backwards, very fast, down a long and extremely steep road on the side of a mountain (I had been doing this for some time as part of my exercise, and it felt very good, until that morning), before I knew what had happened, I fell over backwards, landing on my bottom. As I did, my upper body flipped backwards at a rapid rate, and with such force that I hit the back of my head very hard on the asphalt pavement. This resulted in my sustaining a deep wound to the back of my head. As that happened, there was an instant, automatic response (or reflex) to get up, but I could not.

All that happened was I flipped forward to a sitting position, and instantly I again flipped backwards, hitting my head very hard a second time, obviously widening the opening in the back of my head even more. I could clearly hear each time that I went backwards, the loud noise as my head hit the pavement. After the second hit, I could no longer move from where I lay in the road. One of the students who was with me, instantly ran to my aid. He immediately lifted my head from off the asphalt and rested his hand under it. Shortly thereafter, someone brought something to rest my head on.

While all this was going on, my faith was firmly fixed in my beloved Lord Jesus. My desires and thoughts were towards Him, and so there was no fear or thoughts of what might be. He gave me these blessings. After laying there a few minutes, I tried to get up a few times, but I realized that I could not, so I gave that to the Lord Jesus as well.

By then, others had gathered around to help in whatever way they could. Some fanned me, while others stroked my arms and face. They all did their best to comfort and encourage me, but in the process, I realized that some of those present thought that I was going to die. For a time, I myself thought that I was going home to be with my Lord, because for the first half an hour after I fell, I was steadily drifting away. The thought of dying however, did not bother me, and neither did it last for long.

Those who were with me, along with those who came by, thought that I should immediately be taken to the hospital, but I steadfastly refused, because I knew that is not the will of my God and Lord for me. Rather, His will for me is that I must trust Him in all things, at all times, and in all situations and circumstances. So, there was no way that I could have gone to the doctor, or to a hospital. After laying there for about half an hour, my Lord began to revive me.

In about forty-five minutes, one of my students who had gone to get his motor vehicle came back for me, visibly shaken and in tears. By then, my Lord who was reviving me, had given me enough strength to get up. The students then helped me to my feet and held me until I could move, and then walked me to the vehicle. What was left of the dizziness and weakness that I had felt, began to dissipate.

A short while after they got me home, I seemed to be okay. At this point, I felt very good, although they told me that the back of my head was open, and my hair was full of blood. However, the beloved Lord Jesus had put an end to the bleeding and the pain immediately after it had started. And so, throughout the whole process, I felt no pain whatsoever, and there was hardly any bleeding. The only blood we saw was in my hair around the opening. "Thank You beloved Lord."

However, all those who were with me at home believed that I needed to go to the doctor to get my head stitched to close the opening there, and so they kept insisting that I do so. But I simply said no, because my Lord had given me the faith to put my trust in Him, and in Him alone; and so I did.

I eventually went and took a bath and got dressed. By then I felt fine, as if nothing had happened. I finally had breakfast, by which time I had forgotten about the seriousness of the wound that was in my head. This happened because I felt no pain at all. My beloved Lord Jesus had taken all the pain away.

Meanwhile, a lady happened to pass by that day. After seeing my head, she stated that she once knew a man who had a similar accident. She shared that this man had sustained injuries to the back of his head in the same way as I did, and the next day he died.

The devil obviously sent this lady to "encourage" me, but my Lord did not permit this to affect me in any way.

I had classes scheduled for all that day, and so I got busy teaching. This I did throughout the entire day, until seven o'clock that evening. Apart from feeling a little tired, I felt alright; as normal as one could be. After classes I had dinner, and because I felt normal, and there was no pain all day, I thought that the wound I had received in my head that morning was closed. It was no longer visible, as I had not washed the blood away from around it that morning, for fear that water might have entered the wound, and somehow got into my head. So I had left it the way it was, believing that sometime during the day the opening would have been closed by my Lord, and I would then have been able to wash away the blood in the evening.

With that belief in place, after dinner, at approximately 8.30 p.m., some fourteen hours later, a few of the students and some members of their family, proceeded to examine the area where my head was opened. They attempted to do so with much difficulty, because by now the blood which had saturated my hair surrounding and covering the wound, had dried and hardened, making it difficult for the hair to be parted.

However, from what little they were able to see, it was enough for them to recommend that they cut away the hair from around the wound, to be better able to examine it. I consented to this, and after cutting away some of the hair, I heard various reactions and sounds around me, which clearly said that something was very wrong, for they were all very frightened by what they saw.

There were six persons present in all. One of them backed away out of fear of what she saw. Finally, they told me that I needed to go to the hospital urgently to get my head stitched, for it was open and looked very bad. One of them said that the opening was at least one-quarter of an inch wide. Upon hearing this, I too became afraid, because I had thought that by then, all was well.

Nevertheless, I asked them to continue cutting away the rest of the hair, and the more they cut, the more afraid they became. However, I continued to hold to my Lord, trusting Him with the situation. I realized that this thing was very serious, yet my trust and hope must remain in my Lord alone. Someone said, "My friend's father is a doctor, please let me call him; he will come." But I said, "No." Another person came to look, and after seeing the opening in my head, she quickly disappeared, saying that she could not cope with what she saw.

I could hear whispering around me, as if they thought that I was going to die. Everyone around me was in fear. I could actually feel in the atmosphere, the tension of fear all around me which they were in, and the devil used that to hit me with further fear. So by this time, being in the midst of such fear, I myself was now covered in fear, which I did not submit to. One of them again spoke up, giving a clear description of the condition of the wound in my head.

When I heard this, the fear that I felt over my body grew even more, and in the middle of the fear, he asked me directly, "Do you want me to take you to the hospital? The wound in your head is very bad and needs to be stitched to close it." In faith in the Lord Jesus, I simply said to him, "No, for I am trusting the Lord." As I said those words, the wound closed up – right in front of their eyes!

That step of faith obviously was necessary for me to take in the middle of the fear that I felt, for the Lord to do His work, and this is His Word.

> Then Jesus said, "Did I not tell you that if you believed, you would see the glory of God?" John 11:40

However, their minds just could not cope with or accept what their eyes saw. At first, there was silence, as if everyone was in shock. Finally, I heard someone say, "I saw nothing." Another exclaimed, "What!" Still another said, "Maybe I did not see very clearly before," etc. They were all in a state of unbelief. Their minds would not accept what their eyes had seen. It took them some time to come to terms with what they saw, but days later, they eventually did. Glory to the name of the beloved Lord and God.

After the Lord Jesus closed the wound in my head and the excitement had died down, I went and showered, and I washed my hair. I was surprised as I scrubbed around and over the area of my head where the opening had been, because there was no pain, and I felt only a slight tenderness there. It was as if nothing had happened. Thanks to our dearest and beloved Lord Jesus.

Looking back at this experience, I realize how much the enemy uses fear to keep us from trusting the Lord unconditionally. So, we are forever kept from moving forward in faith to deeper and deeper levels of trust in our Lord Jesus, whereby we are able to embrace our God and Lord unconditionally with the confidence that is of faith, in which we should be walking.

## MIRACLE – THE ECLIPSE

One morning, at about 8:30 a.m., I left home to go to the city. I was driving on a main street where I had the right-of-way, when on reaching an intersection six blocks away from home, there suddenly came from my left an ambulance traveling without its sirens on. It ran the stop sign and we collided in the middle of the intersection. The knowledge that came to me from my Lord Jesus was that the ambulance came right over the car I was driving, which was very small.

There was a collision, yet there was no evidence of one, because the moment it happened, the Lord intervened, and in a flash, I found myself across the intersection, continuing in the direction I was traveling, while at the same time, believing that I was dead. Nevertheless, I happened to look back to see what had taken place, and I saw the ambulance crossing on its side of the street, at about the same distance from the intersection as I was. Neither the people nor the vehicles manifested or suffered any effects from the accident. There was simply no damage to either vehicle, or harm to anyone.

I thought – how could this be? In that moment, I had knowledge from the Lord Jesus that there was divine intervention at the moment of the collision, and in that I was given a reprieve, and a new lease on life. This clearly reinforced to me the fact that this life is not mine, but the Lord's, for Him to do with it as He sees fit.

I did not intend to write about this experience, simply because I was not given permission to do so before, along with not wanting to be laughed at, because this story sounds too bizarre, as with Abraham, for the mind to embrace. But recently, the Lord Jesus also brought this and kept it before me as something He required to be included in this book. However, I did not know how to describe such an occurrence.

That night while I was in bed, I asked the Lord Jesus how to describe it. The following morning, I was awakened with the word "Eclipse," to describe what had taken place, because that was what occurred. The ambulance went over the car I was in. (For example, an eclipse of the sun is when the moon is positioned between the earth and the sun, shielding it from the earth.) This was indeed a great miracle of the Lord Jesus. "Thank You beloved Lord."

I will now try to explain how I felt as both vehicles were about to collide, and in the moments that followed. As I approached the intersection and saw the ambulance to my left, I knew then that an accident could not be avoided, because we were too close to each other, and at the speed we both were traveling, there was simply no possibility of stopping in time. That was as far as I got in my thoughts, when there came a moment of what I call nothingness, or a void, along with total silence. When I came out on the other side of the intersection, I had this eerie feeling; a very strange feeling that I had died, and I left there with the clear knowledge that in fact, I had died. In what had taken place, I heard nothing; there was just this strange silence that lasted a while. "Thank You dearly beloved Lord Jesus."

If this life was not already the Lord Jesus' before that day, you can be assured that from that day on it certainly must be, because on that day, this life ended as I knew it. That which the natural man would call "mine" was already not mine, but on that day, this reality was affirmed and confirmed.

As mentioned before, I really did not want to share this story because, as you can see, it is really bizarre, and I did not want to be laughed at and be ridiculed as a nut or a basket case. But the Lord Jesus wanted it told, and in obedience to Him, I have written it down here. "Thank You Lord Jesus."

# CHAPTER 13

# OVEN OF PURIFICATION

After three years, I finally graduated thirty-three of the students with a beautiful ceremony, and sent them on their way. With this, the school as we knew it came to its end, but the congregation continued for a few more years. Now, I was to focus on those few students that the Lord Jesus had chosen to remain, along with my own life.

There were fourteen live-in students who remained, who had committed their lives to full-time service to the Lord Jesus in this ministry. I continued to work with these few students, teaching them. The Lord Jesus began to open their hearts more and more to show them, along with myself, the reality of the darkness that He is seeing in their lives and in His church. He began to move mightily, revealing their state of deceit.

For instance, they were doing their Bible reading, repentance and prayer, and seeing these as works, doing them as substitutes for giving over their lives to the Lord Jesus. In their minds, these were good works they saw themselves doing, and therefore they expected the Lord Jesus to reward them for doing these works. At the same time, they were using these self-efforts to justify the way they were living. In so doing, they could continue having their own way, while accusing the Lord Jesus for not rewarding them for their good works.

In other words, spending a lot of time in Bible reading, prayer, and what they call repentance, was their way of justifying themselves to remain aloof from their Lord. In this type of work attitude and self-efforts, they believed that they could prove to themselves and to others that they were really committed and dedicated Christians, rather than simply being one. They would rather do this than to surrender their lives, trusting them to the Lord Jesus, for His will to be done in them.

The students believed that these self-efforts gave them favor with men and rights before God. They believed they had rights, because they saw their many hours of Bible reading, prayer and repentance, as making great sacrifices for God. When you believe that you have made such great efforts, it will then be easy to believe that the Lord Jesus owes you and that you are deserving. So to them, having rights before the Lord Jesus is a given. Therefore, demands and rebellion will automatically follow when you believe that you are not getting that which you have earned and deserve through your efforts.

So, the students used these self-efforts to believe that the Lord Jesus was obligated to do for them, and give them what they deemed to be their rights, because they had earned them. And because they did not get their way with Him, which, thanks to the Lord Jesus, no one can – they demanded of Him and accused Him even more, saying, "We have read the Bible, we have prayed, and we have repented, and He has done nothing for us. Yet, He has given to others. That is because He does not love us," etc.

With such beliefs in their hearts, their resentment and bitterness toward the beloved Lord Jesus would grow and fester, driving a greater wedge between Him and them. It is only by His great mercy and grace, that such obstacles can be overcome. Believing the devil, rather than God's Word, pushes people into these dark holes, where darkness and blindness overwhelm them. The Lord Jesus is using all this to teach me of these realities in the church, which I did not know existed.

The beloved Lord Jesus continued to plant themes in me such as: "Love"; "Faith"; "Hope"; "Submission"; "Obedience";

"Faithfulness"; "Perseverance"; "Suffering"; "Deny yourself to follow Him"; "Salvation"; "The lies in which we live"; "The rejection of God in His church"; "Rejection of His Word"; "Hypocrisy"; "Self-will, Self-reign, Self-goodness, Self-righteousness and Self-efforts"; "Selfish ambitions"; "Lovers of the world instead of lovers of God"; "Self-exaltation"; "Competition"; "Hate for truth", and a host of others. In the end, He also revealed, "Defiance"; "Hate and Hostility towards God in the church."

But you say, "No, hate for God in the church cannot be!" Yes, not only can it be, but rather is the reality for many who call themselves Christians. If you listen closely to their conversation, you will hear subtle accusations against the Lord Jesus, which they see as nothing, for this is their heart and custom. Indeed, many such souls do not even know that this is their heart attitude towards the Lord Jesus. And, if you were to bring this truth to their attention, they will resent you and hate you for doing so, for they believe that they love the Lord Jesus.

Many Christians live in a state of demand before the Lord Jesus, where they accept Him based only on what they perceive He can do for them carnally, on a daily basis. They further expect Him to give them, at their own command, the things that they desire, and when they desire them. This is coming out of a belief that says, "I have earned it through my own efforts, and therefore I have rights before the Lord." This means that they can demand of the Lord Jesus whenever they want. This is an evil work attitude in the hearts of many, and a tremendous state of arrogance before our God and Lord.

When I, by God's mercy and grace, began to tell the students that they were hostile towards the Lord Jesus, they frowned on it. And when I told them that they did not love the Lord Jesus, they were angry with me, for they swore that they loved Him with their whole heart. But our great and awesome God prevailed, for He is the God of truth, and shortly thereafter, He began to open their eyes for them to see these realities. As He revealed their hostility towards Him, they would hide from it, cover it, and would not face it for a long time thereafter.

Why was this so? The students had come to the Lord Jesus with hearts filled with carnal, worldly expectations for all their carnal desires and demands to be met, believing that to be spiritual is to be successful in this world. When He did not deliver the success that they had expected, this only added to their disappointment and frustration with the Lord Jesus, which they had already been carrying since their youth. They therefore rejected the Lord Jesus and became hostile towards Him, accusing Him and withdrawing from Him in their hearts even further than they already had. Yet, in that state, they continued to be in the church, covering this state of hostility, as if this was not the reality of their hearts. This is the way they were living, yet not wanting to believe that this is what they were doing all along.

I have learnt that many souls, although having knowledge of God's Word, and are able to correctly verbalize it, yet, they will not bring it home and believe it in their hearts, and therefore apply it to their lives, or respond to it in anyway. Rather, they continue to believe what they feel, and therefore act accordingly, although it is contrary to all the knowledge that they have of God's Word. This is due to the dishonest state in which they choose to live. This is the way of the sinful nature.

In reality, much of this state in which they walked has been covered. It was so covered that they themselves did not know their true state, and in fact, did not want to know what they have been believing, and how they have been living. This was so, because their whole lives had been spent making excuses to justify themselves, while accusing God for all their problems. So, the consequences of such choices were now upon them, and they were not willing to take responsibility for their choices/sin. They therefore continued to blame the Lord Jesus for all their circumstances and problems to escape taking responsibility for their choices.

It was also revealed, that much of this hostility had been in their hearts since their youth. They had held to the belief from then that because of their circumstances, which they blamed God for, He therefore owes them a lot. And so they believe that they deserve much but got nothing, and nothing can fill such demands, which only breed more mistrust, more dissatisfaction and hostility against God. These hostilities were deeply buried, because throughout their youth, adolescence and adulthood, they held issues in their hearts against God.

Some of these issues had to do with how they see themselves – their ways, their desires and their thoughts, and they blame God for making them this way. Additionally, they believe they deserve better, more attractive parents, and according to them, God short-changed them by giving them the parents they have. Furthermore, they believe that they deserved to be treated better than their parents treated them, etc. They also believed that the Lord Jesus did not give them or allow them to have the positions and possessions, which according to them, they should have had.

In addition, they held issues in their hearts because of the different kinds of problems and sicknesses that they believed they have suffered through, believing that this should not have happened to them, and for which they also blamed God. Because they refused to face the truth about these things, they continued to hold the

Lord Jesus responsible for all their misfortunes, their errors, their irresponsibility, their laziness, their sins and for all their problems. All these lies that they held to in their hearts, made it difficult for them to let go and trust their lives to the Lord Jesus, and indeed they could not while holding such evil beliefs in their hearts against Him. Yet, they insisted that they wanted the Lord Jesus, and that they loved Him.

This is all deceit, to cover the reality of the hate, hostility, bitterness, resentment, and therefore the rejection of God held to in their hearts. This rejection is the true reason for the self-efforts/work attitude of offering their works to God, which are to cover, hide and deny those evil beliefs held in their hearts against God. At the same time, these beliefs give them the reason they need, so that they will never have to submit their lives to the Lord Jesus. Doing works to deceive themselves and others to believe the lie that they love the Lord Jesus, is part of the dishonest life in which they live. It justifies them to continue escaping the Lord Jesus, while pretending before people that they are seeking Him.

Some of the students believed that in coming to the Lord Jesus, they had given up too much and got nothing in return, and that is how it had been all their lives. According to them, they were always giving and never receiving what they deserve. These lies serve to add to and confirm their hate for God, which kept them in a state of rebellion against the Lord Jesus. This is so because, for most souls, God is responsible for all that has ever happened to them. They blame Him for their circumstances and for all the disappointments, difficulties, sickness, rejections, belittlement and problems that they have faced in their lives since their childhood, and they are not about to let Him off the hook. So, in coming to the Lord Jesus, they expected Him to make up to them for all that they believed they should have had and did not get. They therefore blame the Lord Jesus for every bad and negative thing that has ever happened to them over all their lives.

Others believed that their friends and families had success, and the Lord Jesus did not give them success in the same way they believed they deserved. They saw themselves deserving of great ministries, and if not that, then worldly positions, where they would become famous amongst men. This would then have given them the stature they believed that they deserved and should have had, which would have made them even more successful than their family and friends. So, because they did not have these desires of their hearts fulfilled, they became more hostile to the Lord Jesus. Others said that they believed that God should have given them success – period, and it seems to me that this could be in any form, meaning, spiritual or worldly. They thought they deserved this, even more so now since according to them, they have given their lives to the Lord Jesus, but they got nothing. This is how meaningless and without value Calvary really is for so many in the church. Salvation seems to be so cheap to them. Because of their demands of the Lord Jesus, it is seen as without value, it is cheap, and can be trampled on. When you hold wrong beliefs in your heart about God, you will always see yourself as innocent, and therefore never see anything wrong with sinning against Him. "Thank You beloved Lord Jesus for having mercy on us."

These students just would not let go of such desires and beliefs, and therefore would not trust their lives and their dreams to the beloved Lord Jesus. These were some of the problems that they would not face, and so the complaints and accusations were only used to cover this fact. These are only some of the things that are keeping them separated from the Lord Jesus, but they are buried so deeply, that in order to bring them to a place for them to face these truths, it is a struggle – it is really like pulling teeth, or much worse. This is God revealing the darkness over the church, and I was not understanding.

This is just what the Lord Jesus showed me in the vision of the jungle. There I was, chopping and pulling on the branches of those tall trees for what seemed to be a lifetime, yet darkness continued. This is the chopping that the Lord Jesus was revealing; therefore, I must continue to chop (whatever that means) until the Holy Spirit sends His light into the hearts of His children across the church. This heart attitude covers a great part of the church.

There was no end to these types of complaints and accusations against our Lord Jesus that had been covered up and hidden under the lie of, "I love You Jesus." There were many other reasons for this state of hostility against the beloved Lord and God, but I am not permitted to go into them now.

Even those who had come to their Lord without these same expectations, ended up being disappointed with Him. So, this type of rejection of the beloved Lord Jesus is across the board, although covered up and deeply buried ever since their youth, while their mouths have been saying, "I love You Jesus."

The Lord Jesus was revealing hearts. He was revealing those things which were deeply covered, which some call secret sins. These are also the attitudes of everyone who comes to the Lord Jesus with the belief that they are important, good and have something to offer God, and who see themselves as persons of value.

These beliefs make such persons see themselves as special, and therefore having rights before God. They therefore believe that they can come before the Lord Jesus, with hearts full of expectations, like the Pharisee did, as recorded in Luke Chapter 18. He came with rights and demands, because in his beliefs, he had met all of God's requirements out of his own perceived goodness. He therefore believed that he had earned a place in heaven.

Instead, they should have come before the Lord Jesus with hearts as wretched sinners coming to a merciful and gracious Lord to ask for mercy, like the tax collector in the same chapter did – he came as a sinner seeking mercy. In this way, they would not have come to the Lord Jesus with hearts full of expectations and demands, for they would have known that they were sinners, needing to be saved by God's grace.

At about this time, the beloved Lord Jesus ordered that the church be closed. This was for the purpose of purifying the hearts of the students who had dedicated themselves to Him in full-time service, along with myself. When I announced this to the congregation, many persons were angry, and some even became bitter and hostile, saying that only the devil would close down a church, meaning that I was a devil.

Although I explained in the best way that I could, I had now become a devil to them, and so most of them got together and decided to throw me out of the country and take over the work. Their words were, "Let's get rid of him by sending him back to his own country." But glory be to our gracious God and Lord, He sustained me in a mighty way – indeed, His grace is sufficient. He gave me His peace, and although they met to decide how to get rid of me, they could not agree on how to do it. By God's grace, it all came to nothing.

At the same time, I received a letter from the Immigration Department in Mexico City, informing me that they had rejected my petition for permanent residency, because I had filed under the wrong code. This was after seven years of waiting. It is possible that I did, but if this was so, why then did they accept my application and give me temporary residency status for seven years prior to this? However, even before I touched the letter, the beloved Lord Jesus told me that He had done this, meaning, that it was He who had closed the door, so that I would not receive permanent residency in Mexico. With that, I knew I did not even have to open the letter. Nevertheless, after a short while I did, and this was confirmed. They wanted me to refile, but I could not since this was not the will of God for me.

I also knew that my legal status in Mexico was removed by my Lord. I had obtained legal temporary residency in Mexico seven years prior to this, for which I paid an annual fee, while I was awaiting approval of my permanent residency. This I was supposed to be qualified for, and should have received after being in the country for five years, but it never came.

Then I remembered, that on the Sunday morning when I had announced the closing of the church, I was sitting at the back of the chapel, and while the congregation sang, I opened my Bible and it opened to Zechariah Chapter 13, and the Lord Jesus spoke to me through the following Scripture verse:

> "This third I will bring into the fire; I will refine them like silver and test them like gold. They will call on my name and I will answer them; I will say, 'They are my people,' and they will say, 'The LORD is our God.'" Zech. 13:9

I knew from that moment that things were going to be different, but only I did not know how different. When the Lord Jesus spoke to me through the Scripture that He would **"refine them like silver and test them like gold,"** I realized then, that I too was going to be refined, tested, tried and purified, and I was a little scared. This turned out to be much beyond what I had thought. He had chosen to sanctify/purify each of us who He had selected in Mexico and in Jamaica. The Lord Jesus therefore ordered the church to be closed, in order for Him to immediately begin His refining and purifying work in those very few whom He had chosen to remain. This is an example of the purifying work that He will be doing in His church in the future.

From that day on, His "oven of purification" became very hot. He kept turning up the temperature, and the more He did, the deeper the revelation of the hearts became, and this has continued over all of these years. However, the students had never sincerely embraced His purifying work, and so they struggle and resist their Lord, to this very day. At the same time He was sifting the students, so that only those few who would agree with Him of their need to be refined/purified, would remain. We give our beloved Lord Jesus thanks for His blessed work of refining and purifying us all, for we so desperately need it. However, whoever thought that this purifying work of the Lord Jesus in our souls would have lasted for so long over all these years, and still continues to this day.

> May God himself, the God of peace, sanctify you through and through. May your whole spirit, soul and body be kept blameless at the coming of our Lord Jesus Christ. [24]The one who calls you is faithful and he will do it. 1 Thess. 5:23-24

All of this time, throughout all those years, the Lord Jesus was revealing to me the heart of the church, but I was not understanding, and so the struggle continued. Although I could see satan's work in and through the lives of the students, and although I spoke to them about this, I continue to struggle with them because the work of satan is so subtle. In my state of ignorance, it was hard to deal with it, since I too was under continual attack, as he afflicted me in every area of my body, every day, seven days per week. Even till today he has not let up. Notwithstanding, the Lord Jesus has used all that has happened to now begin to open my eyes, as He uncovers and reveals the working of satan and his demons against the church. This is now ongoing. "Thank You beloved Lord Jesus."

# CHAPTER 14

# MEANINGLESS OFFERINGS

One day, the Lord Jesus moved me to stop all singing and all praise in our meetings and classes, for He was displeased with the attitude of heart in which we worship. This happened within three years after He had revealed His displeasure with our worship and praise, through the vision He gave me in Mexico City of Himself enjoying the fragrance of those beautiful beds of flowers, which represent the worship and praise He desires from the pure hearts of His children. This I previously wrote about in Volume 1 of this book. Therefore, I was ordered to stop all praise and the singing of songs, until He, the Lord Jesus, has purified the hearts of His people, the church. Then the praises which will be offered, will be from pure hearts that are pleasing to Him.

> "The multitude of your sacrifices – what are they to me?" says the LORD. "I have more than enough

of burnt offerings, of rams and the fat of fattened animals; I have no pleasure in the blood of bulls and lambs and goats. [12]When you come to appear before me, who has asked this of you, this trampling of my courts? [13]Stop bringing meaningless offerings! Your incense is detestable to me. New Moons, Sabbaths and convocations – I cannot bear your evil assemblies. [14]Your New Moon festivals and your appointed feasts my soul hates. They have become a burden to me; I am weary of bearing them. [15]When you spread out your hands in prayer, I will hide my eyes from you; even if you offer many prayers, I will not listen. Your hands are full of blood; [16]wash and make yourselves clean. Take your evil deeds out of my sight! Stop doing wrong, [17]learn to do right! Seek justice, encourage the oppressed. Defend the cause of the fatherless, plead the case of the widow. [18]"Come now, let us reason together," says the LORD. "Though your sins are like scarlet, they shall be as white as snow; though they are red as crimson, they shall be like wool. [19]If you are willing and obedient, you will eat the best from the land; [20]but if you resist and rebel, you will be devoured by the sword." For the mouth of the LORD has spoken. Isa. 1:11-20

The beloved Lord is tired of the bankrupt and corrupt praise that we the church have been offering Him. I know that the students and I will not be offering praise or songs in worship to the Lord Jesus or to our Father in heaven, until He has come and purified our hearts, thereby enabling us to do so from pure hearts. I have therefore avoided doing so for all these years, and only on rare occasions has the Lord Jesus put words of praise in my mouth. He had prepared me for this from Mexico City, when He showed me in that vision, the beds of beautiful flowers and His enjoyment of their fragrance, and how delighted He was with their aroma.

That vision was all about His enjoyment of the aroma of praise and worship that flows from the pure hearts of His children. Those beautiful flowers represent the pure hearts of His children. His desire is to enjoy the fragrance that flows from sincere and pure motives that guide us into worshiping Him from a pure heart.

I thank the Lord Jesus for stopping us from singing songs and "praising" Him with impure motives, from impure hearts. I look forward to the day when praises will ring out anew from the pure hearts of His children, that our God, Lord and Father will fully enjoy, as He showed in the vision, His pleasure and enjoyment of the fragrance of those beautiful flowers. Glory to His holy name!

After I had stopped the singing and praises, and after we had again begun classes with the few live-in students that remained, the themes that were given to me by the Lord became more and more piercing, for the truth was dividing spirit and soul.

> For the word of God is living and active. Sharper than any double-edged sword, it penetrates even to dividing soul and spirit, joints and marrow; it judges the thoughts and attitudes of the heart. [13]Nothing in all creation is hidden from God's sight. Everything is uncovered and laid bare before the eyes of him to whom we must give account. Heb. 4:12-13

The students were uncomfortable, and you could see that they wanted to hide, but there was no place to hide, for the light of the Almighty Lord was shining ever so brightly. The lies and deceit in which they lived could no longer be covered with praise and songs. No! He had put an end to their pretense, and their justifying and covering their sins with tears while praising and singing. He did this, by exposing their evil beliefs, motives and practices, so that He could now put them on the road to acknowledgement and repentance, in order that He could cleanse them. The Lord Jesus also revealed that they did not love Him, which they swore they did.

Indeed, we are either being corrupted or being purified, for I could again hear them using terms to justify their sins, such as: "I have repented"; "I have prayed"; "I have read the Bible"; and these insincere acts would now be their substitutes for resisting and opposing sin, and would further become another "cover" for their true state of rebellion and rejection of God. Through these acts and sacrifices, they deceived themselves to believe that they were sincerely committed to the Lord Jesus, although never choosing to obey Him, and therefore submit their lives to Him, by turning from and resisting sin. Now however, they could no longer use "praising" and singing and "worshiping," as part of this deceit to make-believe that they truly love the Lord Jesus.

When one is "praying" deceivingly, using it to cover one's own sins, what then is prayer? When you do not want truth, you definitely do not want to hear from the Lord Jesus. Such "prayers" are therefore a farce. Yet, they are praying: "Lord, we want to hear from You; we want Your truth." However, when the truth comes, they rebel against it and reject it, while continuing their works of sacrifice using Bible reading, "repentance" and "prayer," along with other types of self-efforts. This is all deceit, for it is designed for others to see them doing these things. This is also out of a work attitude, to cover the fact that they are escaping submitting to the Lord Jesus.

> "Come to me, all you who are weary and burdened, and I will give you rest. [29]Take my yoke upon you and learn from me, for I am gentle and humble in heart, and you will find rest for your souls. [30]For my yoke is easy and my burden is light." Matt. 11:28-30

Our beloved Lord Jesus wanted to cleanse the students of all the filth that they were holding to. But He first wanted them to face the true state in which they were walking, which they refused to do. I remember one of them asking me in class; "If I give up everything to the Lord Jesus (meaning, surrendering the life to Him totally), what then will I have left?" I said, "You would definitely not have that corrupted life to look forward to and the misery it brings, but rather, you would have purity of life, because all that you will be giving up is sin." I asked them if they all felt the same way as he did, and they all said yes. Then I began to understand when Paul said: **"I have no one else like him, who takes a genuine interest in your welfare. [21]For everyone looks out for his own interests, not those of Jesus Christ."** Phil. 2:20-21

> In the same way, any of you who does not give up everything he has cannot be my disciple. Luke 14:33

Those who belong to Christ Jesus have crucified the sinful nature with its passions and desires. Gal. 5:24

May I never boast except in the cross of our Lord Jesus Christ, through which the world has been crucified to me, and I to the world. [15]Neither circumcision nor uncircumcision means anything; what counts is a new creation. Gal. 6:14-15

because anyone who has died has been freed from sin. [8]Now if we died with Christ, we believe that we will also live with him. Rom. 6:7-8

For Christ's love compels us, because we are convinced that one died for all, and therefore all died. [15]And he died for all, that those who live should no longer live for themselves but for him who died for them and was raised again. 2 Cor. 5:14-15

I have been crucified with Christ and I no longer live, but Christ lives in me. The life I live in the body, I live by faith in the Son of God, who loved me and gave himself for me. Gal. 2:20

> Here is a trustworthy saying: If we died with him, we will also live with him; [12]if we endure, we will also reign with him. If we disown him, he will also disown us; 2 Tim. 2:11-12

What we are learning here, is if we are not willing to give up and renounce the ways of this world, and the ways and demands of this flesh, which allows us to continue having our own way, we will not have victory over sin. The problem the students all had as they spoke was, if they gave up everything they would not have the liberty to do as they wanted and when they wanted. And in the process, they might jeopardize their images, as well as the position and possessions which they desired. For these and other reasons, they were not willing to risk giving over their lives to the Lord Jesus. This further revealed that they were just not finished with sin, and this is what I find wherever I go, although it is very covered under the guise of, "Jesus, I love You."

> Remind the people to be subject to rulers and authorities, to be obedient, to be ready to do whatever is good, [2]to slander no one, to be peaceable and considerate, and to show true humility toward all men. [3]At one time we too were foolish, disobedient, deceived and enslaved by all kinds of passions and pleasures. We lived in malice and envy,

> being hated and hating one another. [4]But when the
> kindness and love of God our Savior appeared,
> [5]he saved us, not because of righteous things we
> had done, but because of his mercy. He saved us
> through the washing of rebirth and renewal by the
> Holy Spirit, [6]whom he poured out on us generously
> through Jesus Christ our Savior, [7]so that, having
> been justified by his grace, we might become
> heirs having the hope of eternal life. [8]This is a
> trustworthy saying. And I want you to stress these
> things, so that those who have trusted in God may
> be careful to devote themselves to doing what is
> good. These things are excellent and profitable for
> everyone. Titus 3:1-8.

But if you belong to the Lord Jesus Christ, why would you want to hold onto your old life and the sins thereof, and at the same time, expect to be guided by the Lord Jesus? One would think that now that you are His, you would want to do away with sin to be able to do everything with Him. You would want to be led by Him, and would no longer want to hide from Him to carry out any of your devious plans, which are all of the old carnal sinful nature. This condition simply manifests a lack of truth and sincerity of heart, and therefore an unwillingness to trust the Lord Jesus.

> This is the verdict: Light has come into the world, but men loved darkness instead of light because their deeds were evil. [20]Everyone who does evil hates the light, and will not come into the light for fear that his deeds will be exposed. [21]But whoever lives by the truth comes into the light, so that it may be seen plainly that what he has done has been done through God." John 3:19-21

The students were not willing to come into the light, because there was still unfinished business with darkness. Therefore, they would not give up the life, as the Lord Jesus requires us to do. They still had plans to one day be somebody great according to the flesh, by having a great ministry, or if not, then through something other that would bring them fame so that they could show-off to family and friends how successful they have been. And that is what is wrong with these desires. Each believed that if their plans were trusted to the Lord Jesus, they would risk not having their hearts' desires met, and so they would not trust Him and surrender their lives to Him. So why then do they remain in this kind of training?

Additionally, they wanted to have a big house, a nice car, an attractive family, etc., for they believed that they deserved these things. And nothing is wrong with having these things, if it is God's will and timing for you. They believed that if they gave up their desires and plans, and trusted them to the Lord Jesus, He would not give them these desires of their hearts, or at least not in the way they want to have them.

Many such persons came into the church to use the Lord Jesus to gain carnal success, which they believed they would not be able to gain otherwise. Some came to find a wife or a husband, because they believed that a Christian would make a better spouse. And so, they remain in the church, believing themselves to be Christian, without ever sincerely making a genuine commitment to Christ.

For these and other reasons, they would not trust the Lord Jesus with their lives. But above all this, they wanted the liberty to be their own men and women, and to make their own decisions and carry them out, independent of the Lord Jesus. Many souls would rather have their own way in these things than to submit them to the Lord Jesus and risk not getting what they want. In such cases, these souls are not willing to turn from the ways of the flesh. Therefore, trusting the Lord Jesus with their whole life, is to them, simply too risky.

If we are understanding what is happening here, for many, coming to the Lord Jesus is a means of achieving their "somebodyhood," and when they do not achieve it, along with their hearts' desire in these matters, this allows them to distance themselves from

Him even further. They also use this to justify their continual withdrawal from their Lord internally, and to doubt Him, and also to continue being justified in holding to their beliefs and pursuing them. They do all this while continuing in the church.

> Remain in me, and I will remain in you. No branch can bear fruit by itself; it must remain in the vine. Neither can you bear fruit unless you remain in me. [5]"I am the vine; you are the branches. If a man remains in me and I in him, he will bear much fruit; apart from me you can do nothing. John 15:4-5

If the Lord Jesus said that apart from Him we can do nothing, why do so many souls seek to hide their plans from Him? Could it be because they have refused to die to their old sinful way of life? If they had chosen to do so, they could have put their trust in the Lord Jesus, and deny their flesh. Then, they would have been able to take their place on the narrow way, and trust their plans to their Lord, with the willingness to be satisfied with that which He provides.

> Those who belong to Christ Jesus have crucified the sinful nature with its passions and desires. [25]Since we live by the Spirit, let us keep in step with the

> Spirit. [26]Let us not become conceited, provoking and envying each other. Gal. 5:24-26

In these writings, you are looking at the work of the enemy against the church that is going unnoticed, therefore satan has a free hand to slash and burn. The enemy is robbing the church right and left, and getting away with it, for we are all ignorant of his devices. But thanks be to the Lord our God, He has been over all these years, preparing to put an end to this work of satan that is against His church, and now this work is very close to beginning. Pray for this work of God to begin.

> in order that Satan might not outwit us. For we are not unaware of his schemes. 2 Cor. 2:11

CHAPTER 15

# THE HEART OF THE CHURCH BEING REVEALED · THE LORD APPEARS

Although many believe that they can testify to their faith, their devotion to God's Word, to prayer, to their love for the Lord Jesus, their loyalty, their service, their giving, their trustworthiness, their dependability, their acknowledgement of the Word, their holding to the Word, their obedience, their encouragement of others, their winning of souls, their involvement in different ministries in the church and elsewhere, and their submission to their pastor, assisting him in every possible way. Yes, as devoted to serving as some are, yet, without exception, darkness is over everyone in the church. This is the clear knowledge that the beloved Lord Jesus has imparted to me, and through me to the church.

Indeed, we need to look no further than our lack of faith to see that our all is not fully trusted into the hands of the Lord Jesus. This should help us to realize how much darkness we are in. Look how slow we are in every area of our lives to first put our trust in the Lord Jesus, and to wait upon Him because we truly believe His Word. This lack results in our picking up the life and carrying it, suffering under its burden, while at the same time worrying about it day and night. This is because we have not totally trusted the Lord Jesus with the life, and for some, it is the whole life they are carrying, and not trusting the Lord Jesus with any part of it.

Therefore, when the Lord Jesus said to me that no one is living the abundant life that Jesus brought, these are all signs of that truth. A further sign is the church is not believing the working of satan that is against it, and so he has free course in working havoc in the lives of God's children throughout the church. Another reason for the darkness over the church is, truth is not taken seriously and therefore embraced in the hearts of Christians to be their everyday reality. Therefore the whole church suffers as a result, for dishonesty and insincerity are rampant throughout. A further reason for the darkness is the way sin is so readily embraced – it is not taken seriously across the church. Sin, in many cases, is seen as a natural part of life. For most Christians, lack of faith, self-efforts and works of all kinds, are not seen as sin, and so they are accepted and lived out from A to Z as a normal part of the daily lives of many souls. This is so rampant across the church that everyone is seen as doing it. So, the deceitful belief is, if everybody is doing it and nothing has happened to them, why shouldn't I? What we are understanding here, is that darkness is over the church, and it is real.

Some will say that they "trust" the Lord Jesus, but this is only when they feel like it, if that could, in any way be called trust. There are those who will say that they trust the Lord Jesus, while having no understanding of what it means to trust Him. Some will only "trust" Him when the problem they face is too big for them to handle, and so they will demand of the Lord to fix their problem, and call this trust. This type of trust allows them to manage their problem every step of the way. Still, the "trust" of others will be like the turning on and off of a light bulb. These types of trust are only empty words uttered by such souls. We need to know that this kind of lifestyle is sin against the Lord Jesus, and our Father in heaven.

As terrible as these situations are, yet, I have seen over and over again, how God, in His great mercy, would reach out and extend His grace to such souls. And when He does, their response would only be for a short period, and then they would be right back to their old ways again.

How often have souls turned from faith to put their trust in their own understanding, abilities and know-how, without even giving a thought to the fact that they have turned from the beloved Lord Jesus and have gone their own way, carrying out their own will, making their own plans, fulfilling their carnal, selfish ambitions, etc.? This is a daily occurrence in the lives of many Christians. Yet it goes unnoticed, as if it never happens. But when the consequences of these choices come upon them, many accuse the Lord Jesus asking, "Why is this happening to me?" This is darkness over the church.

> A man's own folly ruins his life, yet his heart rages against the LORD. Prov. 19:3

There are those pastors who are faithful and diligent (as much as we understand faithfulness and diligence) in their service to the Lord Jesus and to His Word. These pastors are hard-working in serving the flock, and in many cases, they along with the many who assist them in serving their Lord, are making great personal sacrifices in doing so, as much as we understand these things, in the darkness that we are in. Yet, no one escapes this darkness, because most of the time we are not even aware of the deceit of our own hearts: the self-will, selfish ambitions, pride, the big ego, envy, greed, jealousy, striving, competition, the unfaithfulness, lack of trust in the Lord, disobedience, lack of submission, etc., that are behind the motivations that drive so many. In many of these cases, are we truly servants of the Lord Jesus, serving Him with all our hearts, or is it that we are fulfilling our own ambitions and interests, serving ourselves?

> I have no one else like him, who takes a genuine interest in your welfare. [21]For everyone looks out for his own interests, not those of Jesus Christ. Phil. 2:20-21

Yes, darkness is over the entire church and we do not recognize it. But the world knows, for they see us as hypocrites, and have been telling us this for a long time. However, we laugh it off, without ever giving it a serious thought. The question is, are they right in calling us hypocrites? Based on what the Lord Jesus is revealing, I think they are right. I believe I need to be the first to acknowledge that I am a hypocrite, because darkness is over us all.

Although I have barely touched on different aspects of the church, I give the Lord Jesus thanks for those faithful ones, whom He has sustained and used to hold things together. As I look at my own so-called service and faithfulness, all that I see is filthy rags, because as far as I can see, my best is filthy rags. These are not just words I am writing. This is the reality for me; this is how I see my service – as filthy rags. Sometimes I have to wonder aloud saying,

"Lord, how do You accept this service of mine, which is nothing but filthy rags?"

Although I speak of service, I only do so for the purpose of communication, because to this day, I personally have never seen myself as one who is serving the Lord Jesus in any capacity.

These things that I have touched on are just a small part of what the Lord Jesus has revealed, and continues to reveal to me concerning the church. He is showing me that the entire church is in darkness, and no part of it is living the abundant life that He, the beloved Lord Jesus, brought and gave to us. None of us have embraced this abundant life, because I do not think that we know what it is, and furthermore, we are so satisfied with the status quo that we embraced it without question. And although there are many in the church today, who are totally dissatisfied with that which they call a Christian life, and are therefore in misery, yet, in deceit, it is all covered under the guise of, "I love Jesus."

> Now while he was in Jerusalem at the Passover Feast, many people saw the miraculous signs he was doing and believed in his name. [24]But Jesus would not entrust himself to them, for he knew all men. John 2:23-24

But I think these questions should be asked: "Where is the abundant life that the Lord Jesus brought? Who is living it?" If you believe you are, do not tell me, show me; and even then, if that were possible, I would still tell you that you are deceived. Why? Because the Lord Jesus says that no one is living it, at least not the abundant life, which He, the Lord Jesus, brought. Therefore, if any of us believe that we are living it, then I would have to say, we are not believing that there is an abundant life. Why? Because, if we should call the Christian life that we are living, abundant, then indeed, there is no abundant life as far as we are concerned. One thing I can say for sure, and that is, I am not living it, at least not yet, but I will. I do believe that, because the Lord Jesus told me that I would live it here on this earth, in the flesh.

You might be living in abundance economically and materially, but that is not the abundance the Lord Jesus is talking about. He is speaking of spiritual abundance, a rich life of faith in our Lord and Father, which allows the new life in Christ to be our daily, moment-by-moment reality; where our all is rested in Him, trusting Him with it all; resulting in true peace, rest, contentment and a living hope to be home with our God, Lord and Father in heaven, not some of the time, but all of the time, regardless of how we feel or what our circumstances may be. The following Scriptures will reveal what a life in Christ really is all about.

> This is what the Sovereign LORD, the Holy One of Israel, says: "In repentance and rest is your salvation, in quietness and trust is your strength, but you would have none of it. Isa. 30:15

> "Come to me, all you who are weary and burdened, and I will give you rest. [29]Take my yoke upon you and learn from me, for I am gentle and humble in heart, and you will find rest for your souls. [30]For my yoke is easy and my burden is light." Matt. 11:28-30

> "Do not let your hearts be troubled. Trust in God; trust also in me. John 14:1

It could be that we do not believe there is an abundant life, one that is free from the worries, cares, the concerns and anxieties of life, where there are no more weights or burdens to carry. For the weight of life will be finally surrendered to the Lord Jesus to whom it belongs, and to Him alone. He is the only One who can carry it. It is only then that we will be free to clothe ourselves with, and to enjoy our dearest and beloved Lord, God and Father, looking to Him and receiving from Him all that we need to live this life. We are now able to walk in the abundant life of faith and love which He brought, and enjoy it because the focus will no longer be on self. This abundant life of faith and love gives true liberty and joy in the Lord Jesus to enjoy the life, which He, the beloved Lord Jesus bought and paid for with His own shed blood on Calvary's Cross.

When the Lord Jesus cleanses our hearts to live and to enjoy the abundant life that He brought, He will not only be joyfully embraced to be our life, but along with that, He, the Lord Jesus, will be the center of our attention. Our focus, our interest, and our hearts' desires will now be Him and Him alone. Our hearts will be filled with love, desire and admiration for our blessed and beloved Lord Jesus. Here, there will be no room for us to continue being or wanting to be the center of attention or interest, for we have died with the Lord Jesus to it all.

Our pursuit therefore, will no longer be for selfish, personal gain, and our selfish ambitions for positions, possessions and pleasures, will no longer be before us. We will no longer be protecting these things as if they are our most valuable treasures. Self-interest and having my way, being number one, the first and the greatest, will no longer be our desire or pursuit. To show-off and compete with others will no longer be attractive to us, in that our life, our love, our joy and hope will be singular – they will be unto our Lord and God, where we will be loving Him, desiring Him and admiring Him. Then and only then, will our eyes be opened to understand truly, what the abundant life really is, and what it is all about.

We should be interested to look beyond, to understand that there is a vibrant life of faith, which draws us and keeps us continually in the presence of our beloved Lord Jesus, where He becomes very real to us. The church needs this faith to remain true to its Lord, and it is by such a faith that we will fully lay down the life and come into total agreement with the Lord Jesus in His Word, so that we will come to know, and to live, the abundant life that He, the beloved Lord Jesus brought.

As stated in His Word, God has proclaimed all under sin, so that He could extend mercy to all. (Romans 11:32) Similarly today, God, by His great mercy and grace, has proclaimed all to be under darkness, simply because we are, so that He can shine His light into the hearts of all His children. Again, I call on the whole church, in the name of our beloved Lord Jesus, to acknowledge our state of darkness as individuals and as a body, and therefore repent of embracing this state of darkness and walking in it, as if all is well, when by God's Word, we should know that all is not well. This is what we have been doing all along, although some might not be aware of their true state.

We should understand from the continual battle that so many go through – the lack of understanding, the frustration, the giving up, the hiding and escaping the Lord, that all these things are caused by the lack of faith, resulting from their rejection of God. Just think of the struggles that so many have with uncertainty and doubt from time to time, and this state keeps them from moving continually towards the Lord Jesus. These are a result of their continual rejection of God, which is deep within their hearts. This state is much of what goes on in the church. Still, this is not the reality of the life that the Lord Jesus bought and paid for on Calvary's Cross.

I have heard it said over and over again, that every Christian battles with these problems of doubt, yet I never did. Nevertheless, I see no reason to pretend that I am not in darkness as the rest of us are, because I do read the Bible – God's Word, on a daily basis, and I am convicted by it continually of my own darkness. (If when you read God's Word you do not see that you have fallen short of its requirements, then I would say that you are a perfect man.) Why is this so? Simply because God's Word is perfect, and I am in darkness – imperfect, and when God's Word shines its light into my darkness, I cannot escape it, neither do I want to. I do desire to face the darkness that is revealed in my life, and in repentance face it before the Lord Jesus and lay it down. This I do on a daily basis, so that the light of God's Word will enter more and more, and continue to shine into my darkness; freeing me more each day by the cleansing power of the blessed Holy Spirit, to be able, by His precious grace, to walk uprightly before Him. This is called sanctification.

At this very moment, the Lord Jesus has brought before me the prayer in Daniel 9:3-19, as an example of what He requires of us today.

Daniel stood before God as one man, but a righteous man standing in that gap interceding for his entire nation, and taking responsibility before God by acknowledging his own sins, and the sins of all his people. In the same way today, men and women who believe that God is speaking, must likewise take a stand. This stand should be no different from that which Daniel took.

We should be interceding for ourselves and our brethren around the world, meaning the church; praying that we will be willing and ready to open our hearts to embrace the light which the Lord Jesus is about to send to His body, the church, and that we will hold fast to our Lord, and to His Word, so that His purifying work will be welcomed in the church, and therefore by each and every one of us.

The students were saying that they were not willing to give up everything, but if the Lord Jesus calls us to give up everything to be His disciples, and we rationalize it away to justify not giving up anything, what then will be the result? He also tells us that we must remain in Him, and without Him, we can do nothing. If we deny these truths, what will be the consequences? Obviously, we will continue in darkness.

Our beloved Lord Jesus further tells us that we must deny ourselves and die to our carnal nature. This means we are not to possess anything of this world in our hearts, because anything we possess in our hearts, will possess us, and that in turn will determine our choices and our actions. These will then determine our destiny. Again, if we ignore this truth, what then will be the result? Obviously, disaster – and our Lord knows this. That is why He tells us to die to this old carnal life – the sinful nature, so that we will be possessed by nothing apart from the Lord Jesus through His Spirit; being occupied with taking on His nature through His Word. For that which possesses us controls us, and that which controls us, determines what our choices will be and what we will do. What if we ignore the Lord Jesus and deny Him that place of complete reign over our lives? Doesn't that mean that darkness will reign, and the enemy who reigns in darkness will have great input into our lives, whether we believe it or not?

> In the same way, any of you who does not give up everything he has cannot be my disciple. Luke 14:33

> May I never boast except in the cross of our Lord Jesus Christ, through which the world has been crucified to me, and I to the world. Gal. 6:14

Shouldn't we indeed consider the fact that many souls are in the church, believing that they are children of God, yet their minds are always on earthly and carnal things? They desire these things and pursue them without any fear of being carried off by the enemy through them, not realizing that such a lifestyle is of the world, and the world is in darkness under the reign of the devil. Therefore, when we choose to fill our hearts and minds with that which is of the world, we have chosen to come under the control of him who reigns in darkness – the prince of this world, the prince of darkness. Yet, we blame the Lord and accuse Him for our condition and our problems.

> . . .the whole world is under the control of the evil one. 1 John 5:19

> Finally, be strong in the Lord and in his mighty power. [11]Put on the full armor of God so that you can take your stand against the devil's schemes. [12]For our struggle is not against flesh and blood, but against the rulers, against the authorities, against the powers of this dark world and against

> the spiritual forces of evil in the heavenly realms.
> Eph. 6:10-12

This is one of the reasons why so many Christians are confused about their Christian lives. They have their hearts filled with uncertainties, doubt and fear, and live under the intimidation of the devil, uncertain of who they are, or to whom they belong and where they are going. They are therefore empty and lonely, and are frustrated with life, so they deny their Lord at every turn, while carrying out the will of the devil. All of this is going on in the church unabated, and that is why so many are discouraged and are giving up. Yet, they are there in the church, going through the motions, discouraged and discontented as they are, believing that no one cares, not even the Lord Jesus.

> Then he said to them all: "If anyone would come
> after me, he must deny himself and take up his
> cross daily and follow me. [24]For whoever wants to
> save his life will lose it, but whoever loses his life
> for me will save it. [25]What good is it for a man to
> gain the whole world, and yet lose or forfeit his
> very self? Luke 9:23-25

Back to Mexico. The Lord Jesus was teaching me that wherever He would send me, from Santa Barbara, to San Francisco, to

Jamaica, to Texas, to Oklahoma, to New Mexico, to Mexico or to the ends of the earth, I would find the same darkness over the church. This is not a joke.

This darkness is real, it is universal, and part of this darkness exists because people are being told to come to the Lord Jesus for He will resolve all their problems, meet all their physical and financial needs, etc. And for many, these were their true motives for coming to the Lord Jesus, for they were told that the Lord Jesus will give you success; He will heal you, fix your marriage, give you a house and a better job, along with a whole list of earthly things.

Our Lord does do these things and much more for us, but these are not the reasons why anyone should come to the Lord Jesus. The reason for coming to Him should be a spiritual one, principally to have a spiritual life, and life eternal in the Lord Jesus Christ; laying down our old lives to Him, not for carnal reasons or for things. Some came because they saw the loaves and fish, and had their fill.

> Jesus answered, "I tell you the truth, you are looking for me, not because you saw miraculous signs but because you ate the loaves and had your fill. John 6:26

Now this is a terrible indictment against anyone, but can you imagine such an indictment against the church of the Lord Jesus Christ? Yet, this is the reality of much of it. We should not come to the Lord Jesus for carnal reasons, but rather we should come to Him to surrender this old carnal sinful life, so that we can receive a new life in the spirit from Him.

As I worked with the students, I realized that none of them wanted to surrender the old life to be able to enjoy the new life. What they wanted was an "add on." They wanted the beloved Lord Jesus to add His new life to their old life, and leave them to live the way they wanted, according to their own will and ways. Then, they would pretend to be His. But since the Lord Jesus has called us to first give up the old way of life, to be able to live according to the new, their responses were a silent withdrawal within, and a refusal to be open to Him, which definitely kept them in a state of quiet, yet open and ongoing rebellion against the Lord Jesus. The church was being placed right before my face, but I was not understanding the reality of what I was being shown.

The words of the Lord Jesus which said that no one was living the abundant life that He brought now rang louder and much clearer, as I was being awakened to what was being revealed. To have that victorious life, we must first die to the old. This indictment was for the whole church, which He has been keeping before me.

If we have been united with him like this in his death, we will certainly also be united with him in his resurrection. [6]For we know that our old self was crucified with him so that the body of sin might be done away with, that we should no longer be slaves to sin– Rom. 6:5-6

For Christ's love compels us, because we are convinced that one died for all, and therefore all died. [15]And he died for all, that those who live should no longer live for themselves but for him who died for them and was raised again. 2 Cor. 5:14-15

May I never boast except in the cross of our Lord Jesus Christ, through which the world has been crucified to me, and I to the world. [15]Neither circumcision nor uncircumcision means anything; what counts is a new creation. Gal. 6:14-15

Since, then, you have been raised with Christ, set your hearts on things above, where Christ is seated at the right hand of God. [2]Set your minds on things above, not on earthly things. [3]For you died, and your life is now hidden with Christ in God. [4]When Christ, who is your life, appears, then you also will appear with him in glory. [5]Put to death, therefore, whatever belongs to your earthly nature: sexual immorality, impurity, lust, evil desires and greed, which is idolatry. [6]Because of these, the wrath of God is coming. [7]You used to walk in these ways, in the life you once lived. [8]But now you must rid yourselves of all such things as these: anger, rage, malice, slander, and filthy language from your lips. [9]Do not lie to each other, since you have taken off your old self with its practices [10]and have put on the new self, which is being renewed in knowledge in the image of its Creator. Col. 3:1-10

Those who belong to Christ Jesus have crucified the sinful nature with its passions and desires. Gal. 5:24

When the devil saw that I was discovering some of his tricks, enemies began to spring up from all sides, and whereas I was loved before, now I was hated. Nevertheless, by the grace of the Lord Jesus, I pressed on.

When the students asked me what would they have left if they gave up the whole life to the Lord Jesus, they were talking about all the selfish ambitions and desires which they were holding onto in their hearts. These included their wanting to be independent, while at the same time, wanting to be in Christ. In addition, they wanted to have their own way, which would give them the liberty to do whatever they chose, without ever being accountable to God or man. They also wanted to have control over their destiny, and control over their circumstances, as well as the will to do as they saw fit. In other words, having their own way, across the board.

These selfish ambitions and desires, also included the possession of things, the positions that they wanted to hold, the rights which they believed that they should have, the alternatives that they wanted when they feel for one, and the liberty to have the things they desire, along with all the other things that I have previously mentioned. Yes, all of this they demanded to have, while at the same time, believing that they should also have a life in Christ. We must understand that these are demands held in the hearts to have both lives and not give up either. But coming to the Lord Jesus is to surrender our lives to Him so that He can govern them in the way He sees fit. We therefore cannot surrender, and be independent to have our own way at the same time. This cannot be.

This state of selfishness and selfish ambitions is a way of life for many, and in these they walk. But this is the reality of the heart of the church that the Lord Jesus is revealing.

These are some of the things that they refused to die to, which if they had, they would have been able to surrender their lives to their Lord Jesus on an ongoing basis. They would then have been set free from the bondage of the old life, because, by holding on to these things, indeed they were holding on to the old life. This means they were holding to the ways of the sinful nature, with all its weights, burdens, problems and sins. Therefore, through their sinful nature, they remained under the influence of the world and the devil, with all their focus on themselves and on their wants, while continuing to be in the church, for they are determined to have both worlds. In their minds, they believe that they deserve to have them both, and it seems that they are not willing to let go of their want for either, and so the struggle goes on, because what they are demanding is not possible.

> For what the law was powerless to do in that it was weakened by the sinful nature, God did by sending his own Son in the likeness of sinful man to be a sin offering. And so he condemned sin in sinful man,
> [4]in order that the righteous requirements of the law might be fully met in us, who do not live according to the sinful nature but according to the Spirit.
> [5]Those who live according to the sinful nature have their minds set on what that nature desires; but those who live in accordance with the Spirit have their

minds set on what the Spirit desires. 6The mind of sinful man is death, but the mind controlled by the Spirit is life and peace; 7the sinful mind is hostile to God. It does not submit to God's law, nor can it do so. 8Those controlled by the sinful nature cannot please God. 9You, however, are controlled not by the sinful nature but by the Spirit, if the Spirit of God lives in you. And if anyone does not have the Spirit of Christ, he does not belong to Christ. 10But if Christ is in you, your body is dead because of sin, yet your spirit is alive because of righteousness. 11And if the Spirit of him who raised Jesus from the dead is living in you, he who raised Christ from the dead will also give life to your mortal bodies through his Spirit, who lives in you. 12Therefore, brothers, we have an obligation – but it is not to the sinful nature, to live according to it. 13For if you live according to the sinful nature, you will die; but if by the Spirit you put to death the misdeeds of the body, you will live, 14because those who are led by the Spirit of God are sons of God. Rom. 8:3-14

## STUDENTS IN JAMAICA

In 1987 the Lord Jesus sent me back to Jamaica, and while there, He called a couple and had me work with them in the same way that He had me working with those in Mexico. I began finding the same problems: the same resistance, the same opposition, the same lack of love for the Lord Jesus, and the same wanting to be someone great in the flesh. I also found the same scheming and covering of their lives, hiding them from our beloved Lord Jesus, as if this were possible, believing that He would rob them of their lifestyle. They did not want to surrender their lives for fear that they would lose control over them, along with their carnal liberty and possessions. I found the same dishonesty, lies, deceit, self-defense and self-justification, while holding to the belief that they loved the Lord Jesus. Yet, at the same time, they were running and hiding from Him, while deceiving themselves to believe that they were not.

One of them even took pride in his ability to deceive me. He even spoke of it in front of me and others, but this deceit would eventually cost him and his wife their place in this work of God. I had warned them several times over the years to stop the lies, the deceit and the pretense, but they would not. One day, after approximately twenty years, I had to confront them heavily over this problem, and they chose to abandon their place in this ministry, than to turn from the ways of lies, deceit, pretense, pride, fantasies, along with the many alternatives to the Lord Jesus that filled their hearts, so that no room was left for the Lord Jesus. When you practice such things, you will fall by the wayside as they did. Their lives went downhill from there. When they left, they were in good health, but three years after they left, I heard that cancer overtook the wife and she died. I have not heard of them since then. At the same time, the Lord Jesus has sent three others to take their place, having the same attitude as the others. The Lord is really teaching me in a real way, the darkness He has been showing me over the church.

Some have the belief that they can, through deceit, hide their motivation and their choices from God to go on having their own way, but that is a lie, because no one can.

I have found that the base of all their problems was and is a profound state of dishonesty, to cover their deep hidden rejection of God, which they do not want to face, for in their eyes, good people do not reject God. This allows them to hold to all kinds of erroneous beliefs, although knowing they are lies. They do this to avoid the truth of God's Word. This allows them to escape all responsibility for the knowledge that they have of God's Word, and therefore their sins. They are therefore running and hiding from truth, for they see truth as their enemy. In this state of dishonesty, they lie to justify holding to these deceits and a prideful, exalted way of life.

> "If you love me, you will obey what I command.
> John 14:15

> Those who obey his commands live in him, and he in them. And this is how we know that he lives in us: We know it by the Spirit he gave us. 1 John 3:24

Some souls believe that they just cannot trust the Lord Jesus, for He will steal all that they have. This belief is in the hearts of many who call themselves Christians.

After a few years had gone by, the Lord Jesus called another couple and then another person. Again, their problems were identical, and in some areas even worse. After six years, the Lord called the wife of this couple home. This sister reasoned and wrestled with the Lord Jesus, so much so, that she would not hold to the simplest truth of His Word. Yet she was held in great honor in the church, to be one of the most spiritual of them all. But before she died, the beloved Lord used me, by way of a long distance telephone call from her, to bring her to repentance. She died shortly thereafter, within two days.

The problem with all of this is we cannot proclaim that we love the Lord Jesus, while at the same time we are withholding the life from Him. This is dishonesty. We are not going to love the Lord our God, while at the same time we are fearing that He will not give us that which we desire to have. We are not going to love or trust the Lord Jesus, while we are holding alternatives to Him in our hearts, because that tells us that we do not trust Him. We are not going to love or trust the Lord Jesus, while believing that He does not love us. We are not going to love or trust Him, if we are suspicious of Him, as so many are.

We are also not going to love or trust the Lord Jesus, while we believe that His intentions towards us are not good and pure. And, we definitely will not love or trust Him, if we believe that He is unjust, especially to us, and therefore we will not surrender the life to Him. Yet, with all of this happening, the mouth is saying, "I love Jesus." This is dishonesty and lies. In such a state of deceit, souls use these kinds of excuses to justify their refusal to yield and surrender their lives to the Lord Jesus, and continue to do so.

Moreover, what if we believe that the Lord Jesus should supply all our financial needs, and this does not happen, will we love Him or trust Him? What if we hold to the false right to have all the desires of our hearts met by Him, and they are not, will we then love Him? No, we will not, because we definitely do not love those who we believe we cannot depend on, or trust. While many hold to these beliefs, they continue to proclaim that they love Jesus. These are lies.

If any of us, or any member of our family gets sick, and our beliefs are that we have a right to health, and we are not healed, will we love the Lord Jesus? What if we are one of those persons with a large radio or television ministry, or a pastor of a large church with many souls, or an evangelist that is in demand, and we lose our place of ministry and are no longer in demand? Will we turn against the Lord Jesus? Will losing that place cause us to rebel and accuse the Lord Jesus, and even turn our backs on Him? If this happens, this is a clear indication that those persons did not love the Lord Jesus. You do not turn from the One you love because He chose for your highest good, and did not fulfill your carnal desires and demands, which would have destroyed you if He had.

These things happen continually on a daily basis in the church, even for something as simple as losing a position in the church. What this proves is that indeed, our so-called love for the Lord Jesus was only because of the position and possessions that we believe He gave us, or thought He was going to give us.

Most Christians do not even know if they love the Lord Jesus or not, for they were never faced with the question, or if they were, they never dealt with it in a sincere and serious way. When they came into the church, they heard everyone saying that they love the Lord Jesus, and so, they just fell in line, using those same words, "I love You Jesus." There is always someone asking if you love the Lord Jesus, and the customary answer is always yes, whether it is so or not. This then becomes a way of life for many who follow this pattern. So, they go about assuming or simply mouthing those words that they love the Lord Jesus, when this has never been taken seriously, or tested through real difficulties and losses. For many, what they call love changes as their feelings change, and that is several times per day. It changes to accuse the Lord Jesus, judge Him, murmur against Him, doubt Him and take Him for granted, even to lie on Him to justify themselves when they do not get their way or the things they wanted or when they feel bad.

I have met many Christians who, with their mouths have proclaimed love for the Lord Jesus; while on the other hand they are asking me, how do you love Jesus. What I am saying with this is there is a lot of dishonesty in the church. Indeed, many who are proclaiming love for the Lord Jesus do not even know what love for Him is. For on the one hand, they say they love Him and on the other, they simply accuse Him and give up when they do not get their way with Him.

Many practice a carnal type of love when their needs are met, or when they are satisfied or pleased with what they believe is being done for them, or with the things they believe the Lord Jesus has given to them, or with what He has done for them. But that type of selfish carnal and emotional love is not what the Lord Jesus requires. He requires love from a pure heart, a heart that accepts its place with Him in His death, demonstrating its love for Him, through the laying down of the life and surrendering it in obedience to Him, trusting Him completely with it, whether He has given them gifts or not. Love from a pure heart does not seek to get, in order to give. It simply gives without ever seeking to get anything in return, because to honor its Lord in everything and in every way is very important to it.

> For Christ's love compels us, because we are convinced that one died for all, and therefore all died. [15]And he died for all, that those who live should no longer live for themselves but for him who died for them and was raised again. 2 Cor. 5:14-15

> But whatever was to my profit I now consider loss for the sake of Christ. [8]What is more, I consider everything a loss compared to the surpassing greatness of knowing Christ Jesus my Lord, for whose sake I have lost all things. I consider them rubbish, that I may gain Christ [9]and be found in him, not having a righteousness of my own that comes from the law, but that which is through faith in Christ – the righteousness that comes from God and is by faith. [10]I want to know Christ and the power of his resurrection and the fellowship of sharing

in his sufferings, becoming like him in his death,
Phil. 3:7-10

Here are a few thoughts that flowed out of Mme. Guyon's heart of love towards her Lord, taken from her book, Final Steps in Christian Maturity (The SeedSowers – Christian Books Publishing House).

*"Let us now see a person who has surrendered his life to his Lord. I find it impossible to believe that one who places his whole happiness, his whole state, in the hands of God alone could then continue to have a list of desires for his own happiness to bring to his Lord. None but that one who dwells in God by love can place all his happiness in God alone. To seek to place your happiness in God by the strength of your will, or out of fear, or even "to please God" are all horrible states and poor motives.*

*Love alone should cause anyone to yield up his will to the Lord. If it is not love that produces submission, eventually that submission will come out as something brutish. When the believer relinquishes his soul, his will, his all to his Lord, desires nothing of himself and desires only God for the sake of God (and that, in a state of passionate love), then we see that he has made a good beginning. Why? Because here is a state where there is no enjoyment with self as an end in view!*

*The glory of heaven is not the motive. Nor can the motive be the wonderful feeling of the Lord's presence. There must be no object, earthly or heavenly, that is your ultimate desire. It is only that you have loved Him, have fallen in love with Him, and are in a state of loving Him.*

*It has been wisely said, "Motive is but the child of love." If I love God alone, I will desire God alone. If I love God alone for Himself alone, with no thought of self, then my desire will be in Him alone. Later, to be sure, whatever comes from within will be pure and without selfish motive.*

*There is no dominance of "vivaciousness" in this desire of love. Rather there is an element of quietness and rest. Pure motive and pure desire are quiet and restful, filled and satisfied. If a love is expressed toward an infinite God, and if that love itself has its origins in Him, and if the believer has no goal but the blessedness of God, then the desires within the heart of that believer could not be manifested in something as common as restlessness or unsatisfied wants. There must be present a sense of rest, a sense that "I have no ungratified wish, no unfilled personal desire."*

*Please realize that this foundation alone can be the true foundation – and the only unshakable foundation – for the believer to build his spiritual life upon. Be mindful that most believers love God with some other state than this mixed in. There is a love for God that has within it a regard for the self and its needs. Even worse, and perhaps more common, is the believer whose love for God is actually a love (and a seeking) for the gratification of his own being. He is seeking God because of what he feels when he loves his Lord. When that love dies (that is, when the feeling that goes along with that love dies), this Christian loses a great deal of interest in God!*

*This is a self-seeking state, and it must be abandoned if we are to know true spiritual growth. We must love Him without any end in view and even – as must come – without any feeling present to buttress us! We must love Him with total disregard to dry spells and to times of spiritual abundance. Our love must pass beyond the gratification that we get in loving God . . . otherwise we are built on sifting sand.*

*It is true that God may plant desires within you. He does plant motives within the heart of a believer. Paul had such a thing happen to him when he cried out, "I am in a straight between two alternatives. I desire to depart and be with Christ, which is far better, and yet I also need to be here with you."* **(pp. 9-11). Mme. Guyon's quote ends here.**

One day, as I spoke to the students, the beloved Lord Jesus revealed again that they did not love Him. It took a while for them to embrace this truth, which they have been shunning for a long time, but some did, while others left, as they could not continue pretending in the face of the light that the Lord Jesus was shining. I had to ask some to leave for this and other reasons, such as: the state of selfishness, dishonesty and the self-efforts that they chose to walk in; their hostility towards their Lord; their self-seeking ways, and their pursuit to be somebody in the flesh; their state of deceit and hypocrisy, along with a trust in self, rather than in the Lord Jesus, etc. – all of which they refused to turn from, while saying that they had. However, the principal reason for all this upheaval was the revelation that came, which exposed the reality of their rejection of God buried deep in their hearts, which keeps them on the run from the Lord Jesus – in which case, they could not love Him. Without this deceitful cover, you are naked; you are exposed, and you are therefore no longer able to use this lie to continue justifying your deceit.

Here, we must understand that without the heat of the Holy Spirit's fiery oven of purification to open the hearts of these souls, to reveal to them who they really are deep within, these things would have remained permanently hidden. And those souls would have continued as always, proclaiming love for the Lord Jesus, without ever realizing the true state of deceit in which they were walking.

In the end, these souls would have been no different from those the Lord Jesus revealed in the vision, "Loss of Hope," which I shared on in Volume 1 of this book. They were comfortable in their beliefs about themselves and their place in the church, but in the end, they were sucked into hell as I watched. Therefore, these revelations of the heart reveal the love of the Lord Jesus for those souls, through whom He is revealing these tremendous deceits held in the hearts of so many souls in the church. This is all for their benefit and highest good, and for that of the whole church, His body. I pray that through this knowledge, we will more clearly understand the state of the church as the Lord Jesus is revealing it. "Thank You beloved Lord Jesus."

The Lord sifted the student body throughout those years, and only five were chosen by Him to remain, and they are still there today, waiting, as I am. In the process, these struggles continue to occupy me.

In 2001, the Lord Jesus began to write these books through me, one who has no memory to recall anything, yet He brings all these back to me for me to write. Now, in addition to ministering to those few students, I have been assigned this responsibility by the Lord Jesus. This is what I now do full-time, while I continue to wait on my Lord for His day and time, when He will begin His work of cleansing in His church. In the meantime, we are covered and hidden, and no one, other than ourselves, knows of our existence – that we are called by the Lord Jesus for this purpose. And even if anyone should know of our call, they would not believe, because it is not yet the time of the Lord Jesus for us to be known, or to be revealed to the church, or to anyone else. If anyone should therefore believe, this would be a gift given to them by our Lord

Jesus, and it seems that the Lord Jesus has given this blessing to three persons that I know of.

There are those very few students in Jamaica whom I used to visit three times per year to teach, along with those in Mexico. I therefore travel back and forth, teaching both groups. At the same time, the writings continue, whether I am in Jamaica or in Mexico. They are now in their tenth year and have not stopped, although that which is given me to write, at times only comes in segments. So when I thought the books were finished, which I have several times, they were only partially done, because the Lord Jesus continually brings other things to be added. This has not stopped.

If you met the students before the church was closed, your impression certainly would be, "What lovely Christians; how sweet they are. Look how they love the Lord Jesus; look at their zeal for Him and for winning souls. Look how they are always reading their Bibles and praying. Look how transparent, open and free they are, for they openly share about any and all aspects of their lives without hesitation. Look how tears flow from their eyes as they sing and praise the Lord. Look how saint-like they appear as they talk about the Lord Jesus. Look how people love them, look up to them, and speak so highly of them, referring to them as examples to others. They are so sincere in their walk with their Lord, so honest, so easy going, so humble, so easy to talk to and to work with." These were the types of comments I would receive from those who met them. People would even call on the telephone and commend them.

I once asked them to attend different churches, and when they did, they received comments such as: how different they looked, and that the grace of the Lord Jesus could be seen on their faces, etc. I remember one pastor making a lot of fuss about how gracious they were and how humble they looked. He went on to say that his people did not look so godly. These comments seemed to be contradictory, for I know our people, and yes, you could say all these things about them from their external appearances, but the heart is what God looks at, and He judges according to what He sees there. That is simply the way it is, and we will not escape that reality.

Yes, there were many changes in their lives as it related to their mannerisms according to the natural and physical, and even in their responses to me, but there was no evidence of a heart change, because they would not let go control of their lives to their Lord Jesus. I often discussed these things with them, and they would agree with me that indeed, their spiritual state was bad, for the Holy Spirit had opened their eyes to their true state. Yet, they would not choose to surrender all to the Lord Jesus, and indeed they could not, as long as they continued to reject the Lord in their hearts. In spite of all of this, the Lord Jesus kept me right there showing me the depth of the rejection of Himself in the hearts of souls right there in the church, while claiming that they love the Lord Jesus. The Lord Jesus however used it all for good, as He taught us through it.

In deceit and dishonesty, the students would say that they were willing to change their pursuit from self-will and having their own way, to pursue surrendering their lives to the Lord Jesus; and I was deceived several times to believe that this was the case. However, this so-called commitment would only last sometimes for minutes, because as soon as the enemy presented them with an alternative belief or plan to what we had discussed, they would quickly take hold of it, and they would be gone again with that which they found appealing to their flesh. For anything that the enemy brings, is more preferable to their flesh than anything of the Lord Jesus, and so they would run with whatever he brought. This has continued over the years, as if without an end, and through it, the Lord Jesus has been revealing the heart of the church.

Yes, our beloved Lord Jesus kept the heart of the church before me, and I could not look away. Indeed, it is now clear to me that the Lord Jesus has used the students' lives before me, as a representation of the condition of the church. Here I am reminded of the vision of the jungle, with my forever chopping down those branches, and no matter how long I spent chopping and pulling down those branches, the darkness continued as if for a lifetime. Then finally a peep of light came breaking through – it was the light of the blessed Holy Spirit.

One day, before the chapel was closed, somebody took a picture of the students, which I still have today. As I looked at it, I recalled the setting as it took place. We were worshiping and praising the Lord. As I glanced across at the students, they looked so innocent, so saintly, so humble and so sweet. Tears were just running down their faces, and as the singing softened, I could hear them proclaiming words of love and adoration: "Jesus I love You; I give You my all; all that I am is Yours; I will withhold nothing from You; please be Lord over this life and direct its steps," etc.

The service was sweet, and everything seemed to be so clean and so holy, that you could sense the precious presence of our beloved Lord Jesus. I then thought, "Wow, these people have changed!" But it did not take long to find out that no; nobody had changed, for their conversation remained the same. Their choices were the same. No, there was no change, for their attitudes and desires were the same. The, "I will," remained dominant, while God's will did not enter the picture. There was still no decision in their hearts to surrender all of their lives to the Lord Jesus. Therefore, no change had taken place. I have found this same condition in all the places where the Lord Jesus has sent me over the years.

I pray that all who read this book will understand that these things we are looking at, are things that are buried deep within the heart. Unless the blessed Holy Spirit brings them to the surface where one can see and understand them, they will forever remain buried, where we will never be able to get in touch with them, much less to talk about them. This is the way most want it, because they do not want to see or to get in touch with these things, nor do they want to deal with the reality of who they are in their old nature.

For many, the reality of who they really are in that old nature offends them. They therefore do not want to believe that they are that ugly and wretched sinner that they are, so they escape it and create false images for themselves that say they are good, they are spiritual, they love the Lord Jesus, they are considerate, etc. Therefore, there is no intention to be in touch with who they are in that nature, for the purpose of repentance and prayer. From then on, that is where they will live – being a "good" and "innocent" person, in total denial of who they really are in their sinful nature, and therefore this denial continues also before God and man. They will therefore continue to sin and see nothing wrong with it.

Throughout this time of revelation of the depth of deceit in which the students were all living, they saw me only as their enemy, for truth is their enemy because God is their enemy. They believed that I did not want good for them, but rather evil, and that I did not love or care about them. This was because I kept the truth consistently before them. These were only some of the many accusations that were made, and I know that all of these accusations went directly to the throne of God, because they have said the same about God.

However, these accusations were made only to intimidate me and to further justify themselves, for they believed if they were able to intimidate me in this way, I would no longer be able to put the truth before them, and therefore they could remain in their present state of sin – justified, believing themselves to be good, innocent and therefore deserving of God pouring out blessings on them. When this did not happen as they expected, this gave them reason to further accuse the Lord Jesus day and night saying, "Just as I thought," for they "knew" that He would not give them anything. In this state of contradiction and confusion, they are demanding of the Lord Jesus to give them their heart's desires, although they do not believe that He will. Yet, they are asking Him so that they can use it to further accuse Him of not loving them, and therefore rejecting them. All this is to cover their rejection of God. This deceit is profound.

Nevertheless, I took a firm stand against this state of continual sinning against our beloved Lord and God, and I too became the enemy of everyone. I must say that I also became the enemy of even the one closest to me, and who would later abandon me. In all this, the hands of the Lord Jesus were firm against my defending myself, and because of that, there are many things I cannot go into or touch, for He has put them off limits to me.

Some of the students would do anything to deceive me so as to have my favor, because they believed that in deceiving me and gaining my favor, they would be able to manipulate what they were being instructed to do, and therefore have their own way. However, God was seeing the intent of their hearts in their pursuit to have my favor, instead of the favor of the Lord Jesus, and so, they were exposed. Notwithstanding this, our beloved Lord continued to extend mercy and grace to them.

To many, man's favor is preferable to God's favor, simply because when they have man's favor, they can easily deceive, and so be able to get the things they want and so have their own way. When this is allowed to happen, continual sinning against our beloved Lord Jesus becomes a way of life and is justified. This is so because, to them, having the favor of the spiritual leader means their way of life is sanctioned by God. It also is to them, a short cut to getting what they want, when they want it, through deceiving their spiritual authority, rather than having to go to the Lord Jesus; for with Him, they cannot get what they want, when they want it. They have to wait on His timing, and maybe in the end, they will not get what they want, the way they want it. Therefore, as long as they can deceive their spiritual authority to get what they want to continue having their way, this is preferable to them than going to the Lord Jesus, since they are not even believing the very prayer they are praying. This is part of the deceitful life which they live.

> nor does his word dwell in you, for you do not
> believe the one he sent. 39You diligently study the
> Scriptures because you think that by them you
> possess eternal life. These are the Scriptures that
> testify about me, 40yet you refuse to come to me to
> have life. 41"I do not accept praise from men, 42but
> I know you. I know that you do not have the love
> of God in your hearts. 43I have come in my Father's
> name, and you do not accept me; but if someone
> else comes in his own name, you will accept him.
> 44How can you believe if you accept praise from
> one another, yet make no effort to obtain the praise
> that comes from the only God? John 5:38-44

## VISION OF THE LORD JESUS IN THE CHAPEL

Shortly before some of the students left and before the church was closed, we were having choir practice one evening, when all of a sudden, I had a vision of our beloved Lord Jesus walking into the chapel. He was so gentle as He came in. As He did, everything stood still. He walked in front of all those who were present, as I stood there looking on in admiration and awe at His majestic presence.

The Lord Jesus stopped very close in front of each and every one of the students and looked intently into the face of each one, and to my surprise, although He was that close – within six to eight inches of the face of each one of them, no one looked back at Him. Indeed, they all looked away from Him. Then, when He turned and walked behind them, again stopping at each one, no one turned around to see Him. He was not welcomed or embraced by any of them. This was precisely what the beloved Lord wanted me to see – how profoundly He was rejected by them in their hearts, while their mouths were saying, I love You Jesus. Yet, they took the time to travel, some of them for miles, to attend choir practice. This is the church of the Lord Jesus Christ. We are therefore looking at the rejection of Him in the midst of His church.

When I saw this, I could no longer withstand this ugly rejection of my beloved Lord Jesus. I threw myself on the floor and wept over what I had just seen. Then the Lord Jesus left. He walked out as

He came, and everyone remained as they were before. They just continued standing there singing – they had not seen the Lord. The Lord Jesus used this to reveal to me, even more so, what their heart attitude was to Him – the hostility, the total rejection, the enmity and the hate for Him, instead of the love that their mouths had been proclaiming. This He would later reveal to each of them, and they would come to testify of it through their very mouths.

What the beloved Lord Jesus was showing me was; regardless of where He would have gone, or the congregation He would have visited, this is the same reception He would have received.

> Now while he was in Jerusalem at the Passover Feast, many people saw the miraculous signs he was doing and believed in his name. [24]But Jesus would not entrust himself to them, for he knew all men. [25]He did not need man's testimony about man, for he knew what was in a man. John 2:23-25

> Even as he spoke, many put their faith in him. [31]To the Jews who had believed him, Jesus said, "If you hold to my teaching, you are really my disciples. [32]Then you will know the truth, and the truth will set you free." John 8:30-32

The heart of the church was being put before my eyes and within my hearing, but I was slow to understand it and even slower to accept it. As I am writing, my eyes are being opened to the reality that I had not wanted to see this. I did not want to see myself in the place where I am called to be; neither did I want to face the persecution that I know is waiting for me there in the church and elsewhere. I think the truth is, in the beginning, I was scared, for I had very little understanding of what was really happening.

> Therefore, since Christ suffered in his body, arm yourselves also with the same attitude, because he who has suffered in his body is done with sin. [2]As a result, he does not live the rest of his earthly life for evil human desires, but rather for the will of God.
> 1 Peter 4:1-2

The students would say, "Jesus, I love You," but this was not the reality in their hearts. Yet, some of them continued unrepentantly to live the lie that says they love the Lord Jesus. They refused to acknowledge the truth that they did not love Him, and therefore they could not repent of not loving Him in sincerity and truth.

As long as we choose to reject the truth and embrace the lie that we deceivingly want to believe, we cannot repent. Our repentance must be in sincerity and truth, and if it is not, although God in His inestimable goodness wants to help us, He cannot, because by our insincerity we have decided that we do not want His help. To get His help, we must turn from the lie and the deceit in which we have been walking, and turn to the truth. Then, by the acknowledgement of the deceitful ways and acceptation of that truth in sincerity, we can then repent. We will then be able to receive the help that the beloved Lord Jesus is just waiting to pour out upon us.

Therefore, as long as the students believed and proclaimed that they loved the Lord Jesus, although they did not, in their minds they thought they were doing no wrong, simply because they had accepted the lie to be their truth. So then, because they refused to face the truth of what was really in their hearts, they therefore convinced themselves, or rather were deceived to believe that they really loved the Lord Jesus, when in reality, they did not. So in this deceitful belief they had nothing to repent of, because to them, they had done nothing wrong. For their "truth" was what their mouths were saying, and that is, that they loved the Lord Jesus, while in their hearts, they rejected Him. Deceitful ways and pride are two of the major reasons why the lives of most Christians are so poor.

These are some of the reasons why the Lord Jesus has chosen for us to be sanctified after we are saved. Sanctification is to cleanse our souls of those deceitful ways, so that our hearts will truly be turned to Him from those old crooked ways.

> Sanctify them by the truth; your word is truth.
> John 17:17

This is when I really began to understand this aspect of God's call on my life to the church, through Acts 26:16-18. The students would not willingly nor sincerely embrace their sanctification, therefore they could not be cleansed of the evil beliefs held to in their hearts against the Lord Jesus, and so they continued to cover them with innocence, proclaiming themselves to be good, innocent and deserving. This justified them to remain in that state.

The students had used the terms of loving the Lord Jesus for so long, that it had now become routine for them to do so. This went on to the point where they were deceived by their own words, and so they believed them. Their beliefs were therefore based on the words of their mouth, rather than in the truth of their hearts. They therefore walked according to the belief in the words of their mouths that says they loved the Lord Jesus, but there was no reality to it.

What we are understanding here is: by repeating enough times the things you deceitfully want to believe, they will eventually become your reality, although they are lies. This is what deceit does.

So, as long as the students held to the lie that they loved the Lord Jesus, for them there was no reason for repentance, because it had become their reality. However, when they faced the truth that they did not love Him, they were then able to take that step to go to the Lord Jesus and say: "Lord" or "Lord Jesus, I have been saying with my mouth that I love You, while at the same time, I have been living in resentment and hate towards You, rejecting You in my heart for a long time. As a result, I have been running and hiding from You, but I do not want to continue living in that state of continual rejection, inconformity and demand before You, out of a heart that is full of self-love and self-will, and that is always holding before You rights and demands that have no basis in reality. Indeed, they are all lies. All these things were all excuses to cover up my hate and rejection of You; all because I held to a belief that You did not love me, and so You rejected me and did not want anything good to happen for me. Based on those lies, I rejected You, resented You, and have been running from You all of my life. I no longer want to live this way, because it is wrong, and it is evil/sin against You. Lord Jesus, please forgive me and rescue me from this wickedness in which I have been living and walking, and for harboring all this lying evil in my heart against You, while at the same time, proclaiming deceitfully with my mouth that I love You, when in reality this was not so. I choose to repent of this, my wickedness against You, right now. I am sorry for living so falsely practicing evil before You, and doing so continually and therefore sinning against You unendingly. Please forgive me of these many sins, and please turn my heart from this evil, to You. Please give me a love for You. I want to love You, and right now I choose to believe Your Word and obey it, to love You. Please help me to do so. I now choose to submit myself to be cleansed by the sanctifying work of the Holy Spirit of all this evil and wickedness I have in my heart against You."

> It is God's will that you should be sanctified: that you should avoid sexual immorality; [4]that each of you should learn to control his own body in a way that is holy and honorable, [5]not in passionate lust like the heathen, who do not know God; [6]and that in this matter no one should wrong his brother or take advantage of him. The Lord will punish men for all such sins, as we have already told you and warned you. [7]For God did not call us to be impure, but to live a holy life. [8]Therefore, he who rejects this instruction does not reject man but God, who gives you his Holy Spirit. 1 Thess. 4:3-8

> May God himself, the God of peace, sanctify you through and through. May your whole spirit, soul and body be kept blameless at the coming of our

Lord Jesus Christ. 24The one who calls you is
faithful and he will do it. 1 Thess. 5:23-24

But we ought always to thank God for you,
brothers loved by the Lord, because from the
beginning God chose you to be saved through
the sanctifying work of the Spirit and through
belief in the truth. 14He called you to this through
our gospel, that you might share in the glory of
our Lord Jesus Christ. 15So then, brothers, stand
firm and hold to the teachings we passed on to
you, whether by word of mouth or by letter.
2 Thess. 2:13-15

For the grace of God that brings salvation has
appeared to all men. 12It teaches us to say "No"
to ungodliness and worldly passions, and to live
self-controlled, upright and godly lives in this
present age, 13while we wait for the blessed hope –
the glorious appearing of our great God and Savior,
Jesus Christ, 14who gave himself for us to redeem
us from all wickedness and to purify for himself a
people that are his very own, eager to do what is
good. Titus 2:11-14

Now that they have repented in this area, they are now on their way to dealing with all the other wickedness that they have been harboring in their hearts against their God and Lord, and against others, while at the same time, believing themselves to be good, innocent, righteous, deserving, etc., along with all the other evils that they have buried and are hiding from.

You can then understand how darkness multiplies when you do not face the truth about your true state before the Lord Jesus. However, when you do face the truth in sincerity before the Lord Jesus, and repent of your sins, darkness quickly unravels in that area, and the light of the Lord Jesus will then begin to shine brightly to give you more understanding of what your true state is. This now enables you to take those other areas where there are problems with sinning against your Lord, to Him in repentance, so that you can now walk before Him in the light, as He is in the light, with the confidence that comes from sincere faith.

> This is the message we have heard from him and declare to you: God is light; in him there is no darkness at all. [6]If we claim to have fellowship with him yet walk in the darkness, we lie and do not live by the truth. [7]But if we walk in the light, as he is in the light, we have fellowship with one another, and the blood of Jesus, his Son, purifies us from

> all sin. [8]If we claim to be without sin, we deceive
> ourselves and the truth is not in us. [9]If we confess
> our sins, he is faithful and just and will forgive us
> our sins and purify us from all unrighteousness. [10]If
> we claim we have not sinned, we make him out
> to be a liar and his word has no place in our lives.
> 1 John 1:5-10

The beloved Lord Jesus is leaving no stone unturned to unravel before me the darkness that is over the church. I remember when I had thought of myself as too "spiritual" (which was pure ignorance) to look at the church. Indeed, I was determined not to look, saying that I am not going to judge. Yes, I had to judge the few students who were before me, but I was not prepared to judge the church, because I really did not see myself in that place. I did not even see myself as the one in charge of the work that I was doing. Rather, I saw myself as one of the students, and indeed, I was, since I too was learning. On the other hand, I was very much afraid of pride, which, by the grace of the Lord Jesus, I had come to hate, and I did not want that ugly thing to ever again dominate my life.

The glorious and wonderful Lord Jesus then packed me off to Oklahoma City, the heart of the "Bible-belt" country. I expected to find people there who loved the Lord Jesus in ways that I had not seen. Instead, I found the same spiritual poverty with a twist that asked, "How do you love God?" This question is being asked throughout the church, by the very same souls who are saying, "I love You Jesus."

From then on, I found that this question is in the heart of the church, but many are not honest enough to face this reality in their own hearts. I am always surprised by it, because the very persons who are in the church raising their hands, and with tears flowing, praising and saying, "I love You Jesus," are the same ones who are asking questions such as, "How do you love the Lord Jesus?" "Can you really love God, although you cannot see Him?" It is shocking to hear such questions from Christians. After leaving Oklahoma, He sent me back to a church in California, where I found the same spiritual poverty, with the same questions.

Yes, the great Almighty has kept the church before me all these years, and I have hesitated to look. But now that He has made His purpose clear to me, by showing me the condition of the church, I can no longer look away or hide from it. By the grace of the Lord Jesus, I have now chosen to look into the church, and to proclaim what the beloved Lord Jesus is showing me, and that is – the deep darkness that is over the church.

For this reason, the Lord Jesus held my feet to the fire over all those years, and would not release the students or me from the furnace

He has chosen to place us in, to teach us this simple message, and that is: you need to be sanctified from the ways of the sinful nature after you are saved. For lack of sanctification, the people of God are covered in darkness and are struggling with uncertainty of who God is and who they are, and the devil is having a field day with it all.

> . . .I have appeared to you to appoint you as a servant and as a witness of what you have seen of me and what I will show you. Acts 26:16

I am therefore a servant and a witness of the living God, and an apostle of the Lord Jesus Christ to His church, for the very last of days. I must therefore look at what the Lord Jesus is showing me.

I must confess that I have not touched most of the sins that the church is in, for they are too many and too depraved. These run the gamut from A to Z. There is every type of sexual activity and immorality, ranging from adultery and homosexuality, to pedophilia, to bestiality, and from petty theft to major robbery. All this is a result of the rejection of God in the hearts of His people, the church. Let me not go any farther, so that you will not be further discouraged.

So yes, we can have negative feelings and thoughts, but faith in the true and living God and Christ is not negative. It is always positive. When negative feelings hit me, I simply hold to faith in the knowledge of God's Word, knowing that God is, and who He is, and always will be, and not only that, but He is also always present with each of His children. If only we would hold to knowledge, and by it acknowledge Him and hold to the truth of who God is, knowing that He is inestimably good at all times, from the beginning of time; those negative feelings would have to let go, because we need to come to know and believe who God truly is, and hold to that knowledge – meaning, that He is inestimable good through and through, and from the inside out. This means that His very essence is inestimable good. Therefore nothing bad can come from God.

> Every good and perfect gift is from above, coming down from the Father of the heavenly lights, who does not change like shifting shadows. James 1:17

> God saw all that he had made, and it was very good. And there was evening, and there was morning – the sixth day. Gen. 1:31

> For everything God created is good. . . 1 Tim. 4:4

> To the Jews who had believed him, Jesus said, "If you hold to my teaching, you are really my disciples. [32]Then you will know the truth, and the truth will set you free." John 8:31-32

The Lord Jesus has revealed the reason why people are suspicious of Him, resent Him, hate Him, doubt Him, withdraw from Him, and do everything possible to escape Him, His ways and His will, and then to reject Him. This is because after coming to Him, they have not sincerely faced and dealt with the deceitful, lying beliefs about God held in their hearts from their childhood, such as blaming and hating Him and the way they look, which they rejected, and believed He deliberately did them wrong by making them the way they are, and for their circumstances. They believed these lies, along with those which they picked up in their youth and as they continued to grow. As they grew, all the negative things that happened to them along life's path, were and are used to confirm and reaffirm those negative beliefs already held in their hearts against the Lord. This continues to drive them even further away from the Lord Jesus, leaving no room for even trusting Him.

The reason this state continues to be a problem is because of persons coming to the Lord Jesus and remaining stagnant, never growing up in their salvation. This tells us that such souls have never submitted themselves to be cleansed by the sanctifying work of the Holy Spirit, therefore all the evil of the heart is still with them. The result is stagnation.

Therefore, because of the base of those evil lying negative beliefs about God and the Lord Jesus, it makes it easy to embrace further negative beliefs as they come to them along life's path, affirming those that they have already held in their hearts against the Lord Jesus. These tendencies have the effect of causing a continual moving away from the Lord Jesus, instead of towards Him, which has the further effect of a continual hardening of their heart towards Him, although they do not believe these things are happening.

They see receiving those negative beliefs and thoughts as a natural part of their daily lives, and many see nothing wrong with receiving them. So, instead of becoming more spiritually satisfied, they become increasingly more dissatisfied with the spiritual life, and therefore empty spiritually, to the point where they become spiritually dried up, and are further open to even more negative beliefs, thoughts, feelings and impressions that the devil brings to them. They therefore easily and quickly embrace these negatives, because they are in line with the beliefs already held in their hearts against the Lord Jesus. Therefore, those negative beliefs remain their reality.

Some of these beliefs are to always be in suspicion of the Lord Jesus and God the Father, with very subtle questions and comments like, "What if God is not what the Bible says He is?" and, "Be careful of how you trust Him, because you might be disappointed because His Word doesn't always mean what it says, so you can't believe it or depend on it." There is also resistance to believe that God is good, impressions of uncertainty and doubt about God and His Word, and at times there is fear to think of embracing His Word and His ways. There are even the beliefs that He will not forgive you if you sin, and so you are always hiding and covering your sins, while being on guard against Him whacking you. There is the belief that He is not just, therefore you need to be afraid of what He will do to you. There is even the belief that God does not love you, to justify continuing in sin against Him. There is also the belief that God has wronged you, and will even rob you if you should get too close to Him. Therefore, be sure not to get close to Him. There are the beliefs that God will not let you have the things you desire or would like to have, or should have, or even the things that you need, and so there is a subtle fear to come close to the Lord Jesus and trust Him, for He is not trustworthy; they also believe that He is not a good God, etc.

These are just a few of the lighter deceitful beliefs to which the devil deceives and holds many souls in the church captive to. The souls that hold to these beliefs will not sincerely come to the Lord Jesus, for these beliefs are a barrier between them and the Lord Jesus, which separates them from Him, and completely blocks them from sincerely yielding to Him. And since they are apparently ignorant of the sanctifying work of the Holy Spirit, they continue to live in a state of misery, believing that this life is all that Christianity is and offers.

However, these are only the beginning of sorrows and misery for those who follow such thoughts, for they will only get worse, to the point where they see God as evil, unjust, unloving, unforgiving, etc., and so you find such souls always running and hiding, believing that they need to escape the Lord Jesus, otherwise He will catch up with them and cause them further suffering, although they are right there in the church proclaiming that they love the Lord Jesus.

These are some of the reasons why people doubt God. Without this base of evil beliefs held in the heart, one could easily see these negative thoughts about their God and Lord as foolishness and demonic, and so reject them. But because they hold to those beliefs, they easily embrace the negative thoughts and feelings that the enemy brings, because they are reinforced by the lying beliefs that are already held in their heart, instead of holding to knowledge of who God is.

Grace and peace be yours in abundance through
the knowledge of God and of Jesus our Lord. 3His
divine power has given us everything we need for
life and godliness through our knowledge of him
who called us by his own glory and goodness.
4Through these he has given us his very great and
precious promises, so that through them you may
participate in the divine nature and escape the
corruption in the world caused by evil desires. 5For
this very reason, make every effort to add to your
faith goodness; and to goodness, knowledge; 6and
to knowledge, self-control; and to self-control,
perseverance; and to perseverance, godliness; 7and
to godliness, brotherly kindness; and to brotherly
kindness, love. 8For if you possess these qualities
in increasing measure, they will keep you from
being ineffective and unproductive in your knowledge of our Lord Jesus Christ. 9But if anyone does
not have them, he is nearsighted and blind, and has
forgotten that he has been cleansed from his past
sins. 10Therefore, my brothers, be all the more eager
to make your calling and election sure. For if you
do these things, you will never fall, 11and you will
receive a rich welcome into the eternal kingdom of
our Lord and Savior Jesus Christ. 2 Peter 1:2-11

So, the negative beliefs and thoughts become their reality, rather than the knowledge they had or should have had about the inestimably good, kind, loving and forgiving God – His Word, His will and His ways, for He is faithful in all His ways. But because of that negative base of evil beliefs held in the heart, which indeed are the foundation of their belief system about God, they quickly embrace the negative that comes to them about God, and that indeed is their ongoing reality. These are the reasons for suspicions, accusations, fears and doubts, along with all the other evil, lying beliefs held there in the hearts about God.

> But we ought always to thank God for you, brothers loved by the Lord, because from the beginning God chose you to be saved through the sanctifying work of the Spirit and through belief in the truth. [14]He called you to this through our gospel, that you might share in the glory of our Lord Jesus Christ. [15]So then, brothers, stand firm and hold to the teachings we passed on to you, whether by word of mouth or by letter. 2 Thess. 2:13-15

One such person in a prominent leadership position in the church, when anything negative or bad happens to them, their response to the Lord would be, "What else are you going to do to me now?"

This person openly says what is in their heart, but most will not openly speak what they are believing or thinking in this way, but rather, they cover them deep in their heart, and pretend they are not believing or thinking these things. Therefore they refuse to face them, and will even vehemently deny that they are doing these things, to keep projecting an image of spirituality. When such wrong beliefs are acknowledged, one could easily repent of them, but because they are not, their misery continues.

Therefore, whatever problem we might have in coming close to the Lord Jesus, and embracing Him wholeheartedly, would be caused by that base of evil beliefs held in the heart about God. Without those evil beliefs being there in the heart, it would be very easy to believe the Word of the Lord Jesus. If they did, such souls would run to the Lord Jesus and embrace Him, as He has embraced them, and therefore there would be no doubts or fears to contend with. But because of such lying evil beliefs, they cannot believe or receive the loving embrace of their beloved God and Lord, and therefore their uncertainties, suspicions, doubt and misery continue.

However, why would anyone want to hold any negative or evil belief in their heart about the inestimably good God? Therefore, these evil beliefs about God the Father and the Lord Jesus that are held in the heart, must be faced and acknowledged, repented of and surrendered to be cleansed by the Holy Spirit through His sanctifying work. This cleansing needs to continue until you are free to embrace your Lord completely without any opposition to Him, His Word, His ways and His will for your life. Also, without any hesitation, any accusation, any resistance, any reluctance, any withdrawal, any laziness or giving-up to believing the Lord Jesus, or any opposition to coming in agreement with the Lord Jesus, trusting Him completely, obeying Him unreservedly, submitting to Him completely and embracing His Word, His ways and His will, in complete submission and obedience to Him faithfully, because you want to, out of love for Him.

The negative beliefs held in the heart against the Lord Jesus, are the culprit that stands between you and your Lord, because they make it easy for you to take all the evil thoughts that the enemy brings to your mind against the Lord Jesus, for they are all in line with those evil beliefs you hold in your heart.

If you encounter any of these negative beliefs, thoughts, feelings or impressions that are just mentioned, please come out of agreement with them, repent of them and oppose them, yielding them up to the Holy Spirit to be cleansed/sanctified, until you are totally free of them.

> This is good, and pleases God our Savior, [4]who wants all men to be saved and to come to a knowledge of the truth. 1 Tim. 2:3-4

> He who conceals his sins does not prosper, but whoever confesses and renounces them finds mercy. Prov. 28:13

If at any time anyone of us chooses to believe and follow after any of those negative, accusatory thoughts and feelings, then indeed, the result will be according to the choice that we have made. And yes, if we make the wrong choice and believe those negative thoughts and feelings, instead of choosing to make our choices based on knowledge, truth and faith, then those negative feelings and thoughts are what will dominate our minds. I believe that if we would choose the way of knowledge, truth and faith, to deal with those negative beliefs held against the Lord Jesus, and surrender them in repentance to be sanctified, there would not and could not be any doubt or accusation against the loving and inestimably good God, because He purifies our hearts by faith. (**Acts 15:9**)

When knowledge that is based in truth and sincerity in God's Word is held in the heart, there can be no accusation in our hearts against our God and Lord. However, when we let go of God's Word/Truth, and hold to the lies of the enemy in the hearts, there will definitely be suspicions, accusations, fears and doubts, along with all the other lying beliefs held there in our hearts against our Lord.

> For the grace of God that brings salvation has
> appeared to all men. [12]It teaches us to say "No"
> to ungodliness and worldly passions, and to live
> self-controlled, upright and godly lives in this
> present age, [13]while we wait for the blessed hope –
> the glorious appearing of our great God and Savior,
> Jesus Christ, [14]who gave himself for us to redeem
> us from all wickedness and to purify for himself
> a people that are his very own, eager to do what
> is good. [15]These, then, are the things you should
> teach. Encourage and rebuke with all authority. Do
> not let anyone despise you. Titus 2:11-15

# CHAPTER 16

# THE DILEMMA

After the revelation of Abraham and the roots came, I barely had time to reflect on it, when within four or so hours, the beloved Lord Jesus brought before me the one thing that I am still ashamed of to this very day, and that is my marriages and divorces. I suspected that one of the reasons why the Lord Jesus brought all this before me at this time, was to keep me conscious of who I am in my carnal nature, so that I will never be tempted to forget or to go back there and deny my Lord. I give the beloved Lord Jesus thanks for this. I will now try, with His help, to lay them out as much as I am permitted to at this time.

When I was twenty-one years old and not yet a Christian, I got married. That marriage lasted seven years. I was very empty and lonely before I got married. After marriage, not only did my state of emptiness and loneliness continue, but it actually became even worse. After a short time, I got very frustrated with the marriage, as I was with life. I was therefore deceived to believe that it was the source of my problem. My state got so bad, that several times, rather than to go home, I tried to run the vehicle I drove off the road to kill myself. At this point, I did not want to live.

Finally, after seven years of marriage, I asked her for a divorce. However, she did not agree for a time, but after seeing my deteriorating state she relented, and agreed to give me the divorce. I gave her the home with all the furniture, and the car. I was left empty-handed except for the van, and I started from scratch all over again. We had no children, thanks to my dear Lord Jesus. I later found out that I am not able to have children.

I left that marriage with high hopes that now that I was free, I would finally be happy. However, this was not to be. The emptiness and loneliness continued, as if I was not free from the marriage, which I had believed was the cause of all my problems. Additionally, I was quickly deceived to believe that these problems existed because I had married the wrong person. Now, if I could only find the right person, I would then be fulfilled. In this deceit, I began to pursue that goal.

I finally met a young lady who was upright, decent and very unselfish. I respected her very much. She gave me the very first birthday party that I ever had. It was held in a restaurant and she even hired a band to play. I quickly began to believe that this was the right woman for me who would make me happy, and with her, I thought I would no longer be lonely or empty. As you can see, all my motives were totally selfish – it was all about me and my happiness. So within a short time, I asked her to marry me. She agreed, and shortly thereafter, we were married.

It did not take long before I found out that this marriage also did not resolve my problem of emptiness, loneliness and restlessness, and I quickly became discouraged, because here again I had failed. What was worse this time, here was this decent lady who I was going to hurt very badly if I divorced her, as we were only married for a short time. Yet, on the other hand, I knew that I should not be living with her in my miserable and wretched state, knowing that I would not be able to make her happy, but rather miserable.

The beloved Lord is now opening my eyes as I write, for me to see how I was being deceived right and left, believing that I could resolve my own problems by those foolish choices that I was making. I can now see that my whole problem was caused by my escaping the Lord Jesus, to continue having my own way. This I did, deceived by the enemy, by attempting to resolve the emptiness and loneliness that I was experiencing on my own terms, so that I could feel good about myself and my accomplishments. I understand this now, but at the time I was so blind, selfish and ignorant, that I really could not see beyond my nose.

Added to my dilemma was the condemnation I felt over the previous divorce, and now, to face another divorce was torment in my soul. Yet I knew that it was before me. I felt condemned, and at the same time, I saw myself as a hypocrite, living with such a wonderful person who I did not deserve; yet unable to make her happy, because before me was me and me alone.

Now I can see the self-righteous state in which I was living, and the evil that self-righteousness is. I was doing evil and calling it good by wanting to divorce her, while thinking I was doing her a favor by doing so. But I was only justifying myself by believing that I was divorcing her because I did not want to see her suffer if she continued with me. This of course is hypocrisy at its best, but being in the world at the time I saw none of this, and neither do I believe that such things would have mattered to me then, even if I did see them since I was so much into me.

The fact that I did not deserve this wonderful person was secondary to my true motive and pursuit; which was seeking my own happiness and to resolve my problems – the problems of "number one." Yet I knew that whatever I did, I had a problem. If I remained with her, I would only hurt her as I was hurting, and that would be wrong. Likewise, I knew that if I left her, she would be hurt, and this was also wrong. All this added to my state of guilt, misery and frustration. I had a dilemma.

I remember that I could not sleep at nights, wrestling over this matter, but being in the world at that time, the options seemed clear before me. They were to divorce her, or to stay with her, or to kill myself, but whichever one I chose, I would make her life miserable. All these were terrible options. Yet I remembered thinking that if I continued with her, I would only cause her more pain in the long run. And yes, although this was so, this was not the reason for my wanting a divorce – rather, being at peace with myself, was. I finally laid out my situation to her and asked her for a divorce. She was very hurt, but finally she agreed, and we were divorced, after I think, one year or less of marriage; I do not remember exactly. Thanks to the Lord, we had no children.

This divorce left me feeling less than human. I felt condemned, confused, dirty, ashamed and suicidal; for divorce was against all that I was taught and believed. It rubs me the wrong way. I looked down on it. It did not seem right. Yet now, I had done it twice. How am I going to live with it?

I can now see how the devil was trying to destroy me before I could turn from that selfish, miserable, tormenting and sinful way of life to the Lord Jesus, for I continued throughout all those years trying to commit suicide by attempting to run the vehicle I drove off the road. But each time I would drive to the edge of the road, fear would grip me, and I would swing the vehicle back again on the road. And so, I failed at every attempt. I just did not want to live; yet as badly as I wanted to, I could not kill myself. However, the suicidal thoughts and desires never left me throughout all those years.

I believe what the Lord Jesus used to save me was the fear, and the fact that I was a coward. I kept thinking, "What if I fail and end up in a wheelchair and cannot finish the job? Someone would then have to take care of me." I thought I could not live with that, and I believe that the Lord used this, more than anything else, to keep me from killing myself, and so although I continued to try, I failed at every attempt because such thoughts would always be there. "Thank You Lord Jesus, for those thoughts along with the fear. I can now see as I write, how You have used them over the years to rescue me from that fatal act each time."

I can now see the hands of the beloved Lord Jesus in all those situations protecting me from every kind of danger. I am now understanding as I write, that my real problem was the fact that

I was running from my Heavenly Father and Lord, and though I was in misery doing it, yet there I was, running from a wonderful heavenly Father and the beloved Lord Jesus, who love me. The consequences of this were continuous disasters, yet I would not stop. All this took place during the decade of the nineteen sixties and into the early nineteen seventies. I guess by now you know what is going to happen next.

My state of emptiness and loneliness never seemed to cease, it only kept getting worse. I desired female company, and although I could have had a lady live with me, I just could not do that because, within me, I found that idea to be detestable. I just could not bring myself to do that. In my make-up and belief system, for me to live with a woman, she would have to be my wife. I can now see that my sense of morality, foul as it was, did not permit it, yet it permitted divorces. I can also see that this sense of morality, without the Lord Jesus Christ reigning as Lord over my life, was only self-righteousness. In this belief, and in my state of tremendous darkness, emptines, and loneliness – here I go again!

It was now 1969, and I met a young lady from Mexico. Within three months, we were married. Again, this marriage did nothing for my state of emptiness and loneliness, but rather, my state continued to deteriorate at an accelerated rate. My attempts at suicide increased. My nights became nights of torment, with fantasies of all kinds. I would soak the bed with sweat from anxiety and worry. I worried about everything, with continual desires and thoughts of ways to kill myself.

In this state, masturbation became a ritual, and after each time, I would be condemned that I had done so. I even began to buy pornographic magazines to satisfy my lust, but they did not. All that this did was to add to the state of shame over me. I bought the magazines in secret, because I was ashamed of what I was doing.

By now, I was thinking of getting another divorce, when the beloved Lord Jesus saw my dilemma and intervened. He turned things around for me by putting me on the road to pursue Him, instead of another divorce. In the process He forgave my sins – yes, even the sins of divorce. He gave me a new life, and filled my emptiness and loneliness with Himself. Now I was no longer alone, for the Lord Jesus is with me, and I have never been empty or lonely since. Thanks to the Lord Jesus He saved me from another divorce. But even more than that, He rescued and saved me from that miserable, tormenting, filthy state of sin, in which the devil had me bound to do his will, which I fully and willingly did. My Lord rescued me from the trap of the enemy, my flesh, the world and from hell, to instead live for Him and do His will, while waiting for Him to return to take me to be with Him eternally in heaven. This is the hope He has placed in my heart.

From that day onward, my dearly beloved Lord Jesus gave me a state of contentment, and an acceptation that I had never known in life or in marriage before. I was also very thankful to the Lord Jesus for this, and for His delivering me from that ugly sinful state of evil against Him. From that day to this, I have never again fallen back into those things He has delivered me from. The Lord Jesus also delivered me from the pornographic magazines, from masturbation, adultery and cigarettes, along with so many other things, that I could go on and on. These things just made me feel filthy and terrible. They humiliated and belittled me. They made me feel like I was nothing. Indeed, you could say they demoralized me. They were very dehumanizing. Yet, there was always a compulsion to be doing these things, although I never enjoyed them. However, after some years in the Lord Jesus, I came to knowledge that it was the devil who had me deceived, and bound me in that terrible lifestyle so that I would continue running from and escaping the Lord Jesus.

Thirty-nine years have now passed, and I have never again done any of those things. The Lord Jesus has removed them from me permanently. His grace is indeed sufficient in all situations. I give my beloved Lord Jesus thanks for keeping me free throughout all of these years, and by His precious grace, enabling me to never again be involved in any of those demoralizing, demonic indulgences. Thanksgiving to the glorious and wonderful name of the Lord Jesus.

After coming to the Lord Jesus, I persuaded my wife to give her life to Him also. She said that she did, but over the years her commitment to the Lord Jesus (if there was one) seemed to be somewhat weak and questionable at best, as if she had only done so because of me. This became a source of concern and many problems, because it was not easy for her to live with me based on our different convictions and beliefs.

For this reason, at times she would struggle and work to undermine the work of the Lord Jesus through me. She had a difficult time understanding my commitment to the Lord Jesus. I believe it might even have seemed strange to her, and indeed to everyone else. I could understand that, for my life is totally controlled by the Lord Jesus, which she either did not understand or want to accept. When I explained, this could have been a source of struggle for her also, especially if her commitment was not complete or real. I could therefore see how that in itself would frustrate her. She also did not like living in Mexico. Additionally, she did not like to live in the same house with the students, although our apartment was apart from the house, and therefore she wanted to return to California where we lived before. However, I could not leave Mexico, for that would have been disobedience to the Lord Jesus who sent me there, as I would be walking away from His will for my life. I simply could not do that.

She was also affected by the fact that I could not have children, and so we adopted a child in Mexico. We were both very happy with our son, but external things only satisfy for a short time, especially if the Lord Jesus is not Lord of your life.

I was sick very often, and I suffered from weakness in my body. I believe that these things would have also added to her problems, and they might even have scared her. I guess she just could not cope with the pressure of it all.

Additionally, it seemed to her that our state would never change, and that I would remain forever "waiting on the Lord Jesus," which she believed to be deceptive on my part and in vain. This was another source of problem for her, as what she saw was this forever waiting, believing in the process that her life was being wasted away, especially since she had no children of her own.

To make things worse, there was no visible or external sign that anything was happening in the ministry. Indeed, there was no tangible, physical evidence of any kind of success in the ministry. There was simply none, and neither did it seem to her or anyone else that there would be any in the future, for by now it had diminished to almost nothing. The Lord was testing hearts, and sifting us all.

The ministry now consisted of only ten souls – five in Mexico and four in Jamaica, together with myself, and that is where it is after thirty plus years, but I know that this was and is the will of God for me, and so I choose to be contented in that place with my Lord.

As a result of this, it therefore appeared to everyone that I was a deceiver. Someone once said to me, "Brother, where is the fruit of your ministry? I see none." And he was right, according to the natural, because the ministry had diminished to the point where nothing could be seen. Indeed, it was a joke to use the word ministry. My wife was the choir director, but because the church and school were now closed there was no ministry, and therefore no choir to direct.

So as far as the eyes could see, the ministry had diminished to nothing, and I imagine that this embarrassed her a lot. Yet, the life of the Lord Jesus was being expanded within me, although externally, there was nothing to see. So I looked like a fool to her and to everyone else, and I was looked upon with much suspicion and disdain. Indeed, I was seen as a deceiver, but what I did not know until it was too late, was that my wife also saw me in that light.

This is the life my beloved Lord Jesus permitted me to have for His purposes, and I am thankful to Him for all these different types of experiences which He has allowed me to have. He used them to put an end to my preoccupation with what people think about me. He has also used them all to strengthen me more and more in faith, and to build character in me, for I had none. He also used them to draw me closer to Him, for which I am grateful, and I give my Lord many thanks for them all. "Thank You beloved Lord Jesus."

At a point, she began to give up, and was not willing to believe me any longer when I would tell her that I am waiting on the Lord Jesus, and that she also needed to wait. All that she could see was how much she had given up and lost (while at the same time, getting on in years). Therefore, in her mind-set, she was not willing to give up anymore, and so in 1997, she abandoned the ministry and me. After twenty-eight and a half years of marriage, she left, and a year later, she got a divorce. She remarried shortly thereafter.

People were told that she had to leave because I was committing adultery with one of the students, and that I was leading a cult. So many have used these same tactics for self-justification, and also to save face and at the same time to gain sympathy for themselves from family, friends and others.

I do understand her difficulty and frustration according to the flesh, and I empathize with her, because I believe that it was tough for her based on her choices and her spiritual state. As a result of this, the Lord's call on my life would have caused her major difficulty if she was not equally committed to the Lord Jesus.

When she left, we had been married for twenty-eight and a half years. I was shocked by this, because I did not know that things were moving in this direction. I had believed that never again would I ever be divorcing anyone, or be divorced by another. I had thought that aspect of my life was over, but I was wrong. The enemy was and is still determined to slay me, but by the grace of God, he is not going to succeed.

At this stage of my life, this was the last thing I thought could have ever happened. Indeed, such things were just not in my mind, and how could they be? After all, we are Christians, and so where would there be room for such a thing as divorce? This is the church of the Lord Jesus Christ. Divorce is out there in the world, and should not be in His body, His church. It should not be found among God's children, for God hates divorce. So I was torn, and I was hurt. I think the best way to describe it is I felt like I was in a state of unreality, as if I was dreaming, and that I would soon awake and find that none of this was really happening.

I had felt very comfortable with my wife, and I thought that likewise she was comfortable with me. At no time was there ever a desire or even a thought on my part of having anyone else in my life. So then, why would this happen now, at such a critical time, when it seemed that God was about to move in our lives and in the ministry? Yes, we had spiritual differences, but they never seemed to surface long enough so that they could be dealt with and therefore resolved. They always seemed to disappear back into darkness, and there they remained covered. Nevertheless, those were not reasons for such an action.

I must confess that I felt very much ashamed as a man of God to face and go through a divorce. The enemy's intent, through this shame, was to get me to abandon God's will and therefore His call on my life and go with her to California to save face. But thanks to the beloved Lord Jesus, it backfired, because my Lord sustained me strong in faith in Him throughout.

Then my beloved Lord Jesus again brought back to my mind that He had opened up the black covering of the heavens over the House of Life, and showed me the double-headed snake looking down on us. I could then clearly see the enemy in this. That double-headed snake has been working havoc in the church over all these centuries.

The devil's purpose was to discredit any of God's further work through me, and to make sure that nobody in the present or future would ever want to hear from me. His plan to bring about a permanent discreditation and destruction of me was so real, even before I came to the Lord Jesus. It was also his plan to humiliate and destroy me, and to get the few remaining students to leave, for they had been told several times, "What are you doing here? You should leave, and if you don't you will be destroyed here, for nothing good will ever happen here."

In the process, it was also to wear me down, discourage me, and get me to give up and accuse God, and by this, to destroy God's purpose for His church through me, if that were possible. However, the enemy failed in his plan, for the Lord sustained me. I give thanks to my blessed God and Lord that His purpose cannot be thwarted, and that whatever He has willed to happen, shall happen, just as He designed it.

> The LORD Almighty has sworn, "Surely, as I have planned, so it will be, and as I have purposed, so it will stand. Isa. 14:24

At this time, the beloved Lord opened my eyes to a lot of things that had been happening throughout the years to destroy His work, which I had been blind to. Many times in these later years, I have heard demons say, as I cast them out by the Spirit of the living God and Christ, that they are here to frustrate me, drain me, wear me down, cause me to give up, discourage me, oppose me, oppose God's work in and through me, oppose my apostleship, etc. And yes, they have tried, and tried hard over all these years, but without success, thanks be to the beloved Lord Jesus. Yet, they have not ceased in their attempts in doing all these things and more.

I remember that the blessed Holy Spirit, through that little old lady (or was she an angel?) in the church in California, had said, "Young man, God has His hand on you, and He will never take it off." He has proven this to be so throughout all these years. It is not once or twice that the enemy has tried to discourage me over these many years, but has not succeeded, because the glorious Lord Jesus has never failed to sustain me, uphold me, protect me, defend me, love me and to keep me close to Himself, through the wonderful and blessed Holy Spirit. "Thank You blessed Father and Lord."

When I was asked for the divorce, just hearing those words was enough to wipe me out. It was hard to deal with it mentally, and even harder to deal with it from a spiritual perspective. In my own state of darkness, I just could not find anything in the Word of the Lord Jesus that I was comfortable with, that would permit me to get involved in a divorce. Indeed, I was scared even to touch the subject. I then told her that if she wanted a divorce, she was on her own. I would not be involved. She said okay to that.

Before things got this far, I had made three attempts to reconcile our differences so that we could get back together. However, the only door that was open for reconciliation as far as she was concerned, was if I moved back to the US – to California. That was a compromise I could not make, for then I would have had to abandon God's will to be able to do so. He had sent me to Mexico, and that is where I must stay until He, and only He, changes that. So she proceeded with her divorce.

I realize that I would have done almost anything, short of abandoning God's will for my life, to avoid the shame that I felt of going through a divorce as a man of God – a Christian.

I did all that was possible to slow down and delay the process of the divorce, while waiting to hear from the Lord Jesus. About this time, the Lord sent me off to Jamaica. This trip would give me two months more to wait on my Lord for the understanding of what He required of me in such a situation, because the truth was, I did not know what to do.

I left for Jamaica still feeling somewhat numb, as if what was happening was still not real. All during my stay in Jamaica, I was concerned with the dilemma of this divorce, which at times occupied my mind. I kept it before my Lord, but no utterance was given to me to talk to Him about it, apart from saying, "Lord, what must I do in this situation?"

But glory to His holy name, after spending seven weeks in Jamaica, and it was almost time to return to the US and Mexico, my Lord intervened one night as I sat to read my Bible. I opened the Bible, which was in my lap, and left it there for a while. I had unintentionally opened it at 1 Corinthians, Chapter 7, where obviously the beloved Lord had intended for it to be opened. I then looked up to my dearly beloved Lord, again asking, "What must I do Lord Jesus?"

I remained in this position of holding up my head for quite a while, as I continued to look up to Him. Nothing was happening; all was quiet; no answer was given. But, as I lowered my head, instead of my turning the pages to find the passage that I was to read that night, the Lord fixed my eyes on verse 15 of 1 Corinthians, Chapter 7, where the Bible was still opened. So instead of turning the pages, I had to read that which He had fixed my eyes on, for He had so illuminated it that I could not miss it.

My eyes were fixed by the Lord Jesus, and focused right on that verse alone. It was amazing what was about to happen when I read this Scripture. I must state here that I have read this Scripture hundreds of times, but it was never opened to me before like it was that night. It was as if it was closed to me before. The Scripture says, **"But if the unbeliever leaves, let him do so. A believing man or woman is not bound in such circumstances; God has called us to live in peace."** 1 Cor. 7:15

As I read these words, I was instantly set free from all concern, all contemplation and the pressure of the dilemma I was facing. I felt refreshed internally, as if I had just been washed. His Word washed me, and I felt clean and light within. That night, I felt the power of God's Word in action within me. Papa had freed me from another demonic bondage – the dilemma I was facing, by His Word.

The loving living God and Lord washed me that night with His Word. I was washed spotlessly clean that night by the Word of our God and Lord.

> Sanctify them by the truth; your word is truth.
> John 17:17

The other word He gave me that night was, "facilitate" – meaning that I was to facilitate her. It came with the understanding that I was to help her in every way, and to make it easy for her to do what she wanted to do, rather than to be an obstacle in her path. Also,

I was to get her on her way in peace. This I did, although there was not much I could do for her at this point, as twelve months prior to this, she had already moved out and had gone back to live in the USA.

The only thing I could now help her with would be the divorce, which I was avoiding like the plague. My Lord had now freed me to help her, even in that, by making it clear that night, that yes, He hates divorce, but He also hates every evil belief, along with pride, lies, deceit, dishonesty, pretense, falsehood, envy, jealousy, fornication, adultery and every evil practice as well, because love hates evil. Nevertheless, many practice these things and justify themselves when they do so. Yet, they take a firm stand against divorce, because it is an external act which can be seen and judged by men all around. However, the pride of life, the lies, deceit and falsehood, the disobedience, the lack of submission, the rebellion, the dishonesty, along with all the other evil motivations and things that God hates, tend to go on unabated every day before Him, and they are justified because they are not open to scrutiny as divorce is before men, and so they can practice and cover these evils because they are not seen by men.

> There are six things the LORD hates, seven that are detestable to him: [17]haughty eyes, a lying tongue, hands that shed innocent blood, [18]a heart

that devises wicked schemes, feet that are quick to rush into evil, [19]a false witness who pours out lies and a man who stirs up dissension among brothers. Prov. 6:16-19

To fear the LORD is to hate evil; I hate pride and arrogance, evil behavior and perverse speech. Prov. 8:13

"For I, the LORD, love justice; I hate robbery and iniquity. . . Isa. 61:8

These are the things you are to do: Speak the truth to each other, and render true and sound judgment in your courts; [17]do not plot evil against your neighbor, and do not love to swear falsely. I hate all this," declares the LORD. Zech. 8:16-17

"Blessed are those who wash their robes, that they may have the right to the tree of life and may go through the gates into the city. [15]Outside are the dogs, those who practice magic arts, the sexually immoral, the murderers, the idolaters and everyone who loves and practices falsehood. Rev. 22:14-15

God is saying to us through all of this, that when we come to hate falsehood, along with all the other detestable things that He hates, which include divorce, then this will be acceptable to Him. For many, the hating of divorce, while accepting falsehood, pride, lies, deceit, etc., is part of their spiritual façade. Rejecting one, while covering the other, is not acceptable to God. When we are justified by faith, we are therefore justified before God, because faith purifies the heart, but when we choose to justify ourselves in this way, we are only justified before men.

Someone who was assisting me, said to me, "Aren't you justifying your being divorced by what you have just written?" My answer to him was, "I have no such motivation. All I have written in this book, I have done so by the strict guidance and leading of the blessed Holy Spirit, and I am sure that He will confirm this fact in the hearts of all those who are His who will read these writings, because God is serious about putting an end, not only to divorce, but to all other evil that is before His eyes." This too would be my answer to all who would question what I have written by the strict guidance of the blessed Holy Spirit. "Thank You Lord Jesus."

> After he had left the crowd and entered the house, his disciples asked him about this parable. [18]"Are you so dull?" he asked. "Don't you see that nothing that enters a man from the outside can make him

> 'unclean'? [19]For it doesn't go into his heart but into
> his stomach, and then out of his body." (In saying
> this, Jesus declared all foods "clean.") [20]He went
> on: "What comes out of a man is what makes him
> 'unclean.' [21]For from within, out of men's hearts,
> come evil thoughts, sexual immorality, theft,
> murder, adultery, [22]greed, malice, deceit, lewdness,
> envy, slander, arrogance and folly. [23]All these evils
> come from inside and make a man 'unclean.'"
> Mark 7:17-23

Ever since the beloved Lord Jesus put me to write about my divorces, He has given me the understanding that He has purposed to use them to speak to His church. Because, apart from the hypocrisy that is being practiced in this area of so many lives, which God is speaking to, there is so much confusion in and among many of the denominations and different congregations. For instance, one large denomination has for decades covered up and tolerates every kind of illicit, immoral sexual activity – from adultery, homosexuality, pedophilia to the raping of women and small girls. Yet their stand against divorce is immoveable – no tolerance is allowed here. God is speaking to these and other types of hypocrisy.

That night, Papa also gave me a clear figure of how much money I was to give her, which He had provided before. With this in mind, I went home with zeal to facilitate her in every way possible. We met at her lawyer's office, and I accompanied her to the courthouse, where I signed the divorce papers with a God-given liberty that surprised me. These are things that I just could not contemplate doing before. I found that I was freely talking and joking with her in the courthouse, as if nothing had happened. Her lawyer remarked, "You two are talking as if nothing is wrong." I responded, "As far as I am concerned, nothing is wrong." This is liberty that only the beloved Lord Jesus can give.

This experience further reinforced the fact to me that it is only God, the Holy Spirit, who truly knows His Word, and it is only He who is able to reveal its true contents and meaning, for He is the Author and Revealer of it. I praise Him for so leading me through such a difficult time and process.

That night, my blessed Father and Lord used these words, **". . .A believing man or woman is not bound in such circumstances. . ."** (1 Cor. 7:15) to free me. When I read this portion of the Scripture, I was given clear knowledge through it that my God, Lord and Father had freed me to remarry, if I so chose. All this happened that night, by His Word. Only His Word and nothing else has the power to wash us, to transform us and to light our path. Shortly after the divorce, the Lord moved me to begin writing these books, revealing the purpose for His call on my life.

Previously, by the leading of the Lord Jesus, I had deliberately left out of this book, any discourse about my marriages and divorces, while not realizing that the beloved Lord Jesus had it planned for the ending of this book. It is only because of God's will and guidance why I have touched the subject, although with some hesitation. However, I choose to obey my beloved Lord Jesus in going wherever He leads, and doing whatever He chooses, and I give Him thanks for that. "Thank You dearest, beloved Lord Jesus."

# CHAPTER 17

# DECEIVED

I have spent thirty-six years teaching the brethren – encouraging, correcting, rebuking and instructing – to turn them from sin and to a life in the Lord Jesus, but today it all seems as if all has been in vain. At times, I have gotten angry with them, especially over the dishonesty in which they walk, which always leads to their rejection of God, while saying that they want the Lord Jesus. This caused much pain, as I watched them continue in this state over all these thirty-six years.

At the beginning of the year 2006, the beloved Lord Jesus began to pour out knowledge on us as never before. He also poured out grace in abundance that so transformed the brethren, to the point where even their facial appearances were changed. This I had seen several times before, but not to this extent.

In one particular case, we had all returned to the dining table, only to see the grace of our Lord Jesus poured out in such a way, that a dramatic change had taken place which manifested on their faces, but especially on the face of one of the brethren. The transformation was so radical and her face became so bright and beautiful, that all of us who were there began to admire the beauty that was upon her face. It was evident to us that this inestimable goodness of our God and Lord was being poured out on us all.

Three times during the first eight months of the year 2006, this kind of radical transformation took place in the lives of all the brethren. Each time that this happened, they would be so happy and so thrilled to be at peace with their God and Lord that they would be giving Him thanks and worshiping Him. Also, tears would be flowing it seemed from grateful hearts. They would look ten years younger each time that this happened. However, none of this lasted, because they enjoyed their new-found happiness carnally for a short time, and were again deceived to believe that they had deserved this act of grace. In these beliefs, they began to reason even more, that they should always be this way – happy, carefree and beautiful – feeling good about themselves.

In one case, all that one of the brethren wanted to do was to be in front of the mirror admiring herself. She believed that she deserved this and it was long overdue. She was determined to enjoy this in a carnal way and use it to show-off. With such a heart attitude, the beauty left her face, and her face returned to what it was before.

## LATER WRITINGS

> Those who oppose him he must gently instruct, in the hope that God will grant them repentance leading them to a knowledge of the truth, [26]and that they will come to their senses and escape from the trap of the devil, who has taken them captive to do his will. 2 Tim.2:25-26

The Lord Jesus continues to show me the things He said He would. For instance, two of the students after receiving such a great deliverance, one of them out of pride and therefore shame, chose not to acknowledge the sinful way they have lived rejecting God's grace, accusing Him, lying on Him, living in a continual state of rebellion against Him. While at the same time chose to fix their eyes on others, judging them with evil intent to tear them down while exalting themselves over them, belittling them. This, along with all the other evils they have practiced over the years. They simply refused to acknowledge and face any of these truths so that they could repent before the Lord for Him to cleanse them of their wicked ways, and therefore be enabled to draw close to their Lord since sin separates us from the Lord.

This lack of acknowledgement and repentance blocks them from embracing the liberty of the deliverance the Lord Jesus had given them. Because of this lack of repentance, they just drift right back into the old ways, as if they have never been delivered; now to envy the others who have continued to rejoice in their liberty in the Lord Jesus, because their deliverance has been very great.

The other student used their deliverance to begin to plan out a great future for themselves, filling their heart with carnal, worldly desires to be great and exalted before family, old friends, and people in general. They did not use their deliverance to choose to repent and turn from their old ways and choose to fill their hearts with desires for the Lord Jesus and His ways; laying down and surrendering their lives to Him. Because of this lack, they both threw away their liberty by trampling on the grace of the Lord Jesus, just like the pig returning to its wallowing in the mud, and the dog returning to consuming its vomit.

What is the Lord Jesus showing me here? He is showing me some of the reasons for the state of poverty that exists in the church. These are all signs of the darkness that is over the church that we are not recognizing, yet it is all around us. The next thing He is showing me is that God and His grace to us should not be taken for granted, or be disregarded as have been done by these students.

I have confronted these students with what they have done with this great out pouring of God's grace to deliver them. It took a few days to bring them to their senses for them to acknowledge what they have done with such a blessed deliverance. After lying and justifying themselves, they finally faced up to what they have done, and chose to repent. I then prayed and asked the Lord Jesus to restore them. I then commanded those demons that deceived them to come out and go from them. They did, and they again began to enjoy their deliverance and the liberty it brings. The next day one of them told me that they feel over them a sense of wanting to die, and so the appreciation and gratitude to the Lord Jesus could not come forth. This is when she told me that all her life she has felt this way and took it for granted, believing that this is the way she is and so she lived with it, seeing it as a normal part of her life. When I heard this, I realized that this is another demon that evaded coming out, and how many others could there be? Thanks to the Lord Jesus who has permitted this demon to be identified so I can drive it out by the power of the Holy Spirit.

The Lord Jesus is now revealing Christians in a way that most Christians will not entertain, much less to believe that such things as these that are being revealed could be possible, much less happening in the lives of Christians all over the world. The answer of the church to these things is to believe that such souls are out of their minds, and need professional help such a psychiatrist, and so they pack them off to one, or recommend one. I must confess, this once was my belief, but God has kept my feet to the fire for all these years by keeping me locked down in this place with a few students showing me these things, and would not stop until He thoroughly convinces me, to then write about it.

This causes many souls to wonder about their Salvation. Some will ask are they really saved, or is Salvation really what the Bible reveals it to be? With such wondering thoughts, doors will then be open in those souls for the devil to torture such souls with uncertainty; reasoning with devils, fears, anxiety, worries of all kinds and doubts. This is much of what is happening in the church today and the Lord Jesus is revealing it by His Spirit through these writings. This is all a part of the darkness that is over the church.

Back to the spirit of death. I prayed and commanded the spirit of death that had possessed the student to come out. It first struggled for seemingly five seconds or so, and came out along with several others with it. Following this, the student testified that where she felt death within and without her, now she feels life and a desire to live. With this and all the other deliverance she had received, one would think that she would be jubilant, filled with apprecia-tion, gratitude, joy and thanksgiving to the Lord Jesus. But no! Instead there was a profound state of sadness upon her face. This puzzled me for a moment. After speaking with her for a moment,

I was made conscious that this was a spirit of sadness within her. I therefore commanded the spirit to come out and it did, along with others, and the depth of sadness left her. Still there was some sadness remaining on her face.

As a result of these kinds of beliefs, attitudes and thoughts, you could immediately see the precious, unmerited grace of God begin to disappear from their faces. As this happened, they began to perform so as to deceive me and others that this was not the case, but rather, all was going well with them spiritually.

The brethren literally began to act out a "spiritual" life. Self-righteousness and self-efforts had now become a way of life for them – again. They strived, they struggled, and they offered sacrifices through works of all kinds, such as doing favors for others. They tried to out-perform themselves and everyone else, with the intent to deceive everyone around them. They pretended to be other than they were; doing what they call good works. They did all this to demonstrate spirituality, instead of being spiritual. But then again, how does one become spiritual when the life and ways the Lord Jesus gives are not embraced, and how can you embrace His ways, when He Himself is not embraced?

Yes, they did all this to make themselves and others believe that they were doing good spiritually. But as we all know, you cannot keep this kind of self-effort going for long, because such acts take great sacrifices, efforts, hard work and consistency, which none of us are able to sustain for any length of time. For in a short while you are worn out, tired and frustrated in your self-efforts, while having your heart full of accusations against the Lord Jesus, blaming Him for all your frustrations and problems.

In such a case, all that is happening is that you are being further corrupted, but in these cases they do not care, for their interest is to deceive to win man's favor to have them believe that all is well with their soul. And because they are not successful in their deceit, they are now filled with accusation against the beloved Lord Jesus and everyone else, for their state of misery and frustration. This is so because, according to them, they are innocent and therefore they had nothing to do with their present state of misery. So then, whose fault is it? Of course, it is God's fault. They believe that He caused this to happen to them, and therefore the accusations and resentments against Him multiply, and so does their misery.

Over the last thirty-six years, I have watched this very thing happen over and over again. Each time, I have had to stand by and watch God's grace trampled on, through those demonic lies that say they deserve to have a spiritual life, while at the same time believing that they should be able to continue having those carnal liberties that they had always enjoyed. These are beliefs which many have come into agreement with, and have held to. The result of embracing these lies is always the same – darkness multiplies in that life. However, such souls believe this to be God's doing, even though He was never in the picture of their lives in the first place, for He was never embraced by them. In this state, the beliefs are: "God does not love me, He rejects me, He hates me, He does not want me, He is not a good God, He does nothing for me."

All these were lies to cover the reality of their hearts against God, which was nothing but hate, hostility and rejection of God, which they did not want to face. So they covered them with all these lies against God.

After witnessing this profound rejection of the beloved Lord Jesus for the third time that year, in August of 2006, I found myself in a state where I began to shut down. I was angry towards the brethren, to the point where it was difficult for me to deal with them any longer. Even to speak to them became a problem for me. So finally, I told them that since they had demonstrated over and over again that the Lord Jesus was not their interest, they should plan to leave after those other brethren, who were scheduled to come from Jamaica, had come and returned home.

On the morning of the 5th of November, 2006, while I was still in bed, the beloved Lord Jesus brought back to my mind something

He had placed before me over twenty-five years earlier, which was: He is going to make me an example before others. At that time, when I realized what the Lord Jesus had said to me, I was stunned. I remember that fear took hold of me, to the point where I wanted to run and hide. I did not want this assignment. This was something I did not want to do, for I just could not see myself in that place. When I looked at my life, I did not see anything there in me to be placed before anyone as an example. I therefore believed that this place was simply not for me.

That was the first time that I almost said no to my beloved Lord Jesus, but I am so glad that I did not. Yet, I struggled and I labored with this dilemma for a while, but because of His grace to me I did not say no, although it was difficult for me to handle. By His blessed grace given to me, I finally surrendered to the will of my Lord saying, "Thy will be done." However, I did this with much heaviness of heart.

Over all these years, nothing further was said to me by the Lord Jesus about my being made an example before others, until that morning of the 5th of November, 2006, when I was awakened with this before me. The beloved Lord Jesus brought it back to me at this time, reminding me that He had placed this before me many years prior to this. This time, however, there was a welcome embrace of it all, knowing full well that it is not in me to be an example for anyone, but it is my beloved Lord Jesus in me, and He is able to make me one. He can and will perform that which He chooses to do in and through me, as He so wills. I then realized that the Holy Spirit must have put more of me to death than I had realized – meaning, to my sinful nature.

Immediately after this, in fact you could say in the next moment, my Beloved brought the brethren before me – their state, and my anger towards them. He used this as a background to put before me my need to live the abundant life here on this earth in the flesh. This was followed by the knowledge that I am to love the brethren unconditionally, whom I could easily reject because of their continual rejection of the Lord Jesus.

Initially, this was a little difficult for me to swallow, because of all the evil that they had done in their hate and rejection of God. They frown on His Word, and close their ears to all that I had taught them, and constantly so. Up to that point, throughout the thirty-odd years of my working with them, they were very successful in their opposition to me. These are the same ones, who the Lord Jesus was now saying that I am to love unconditionally.

The question is; how does a human being love unconditionally? Can it be done? After pondering this for a short time, I realized that no, a human being in himself cannot love unconditionally, but the Lord Jesus can, and does do this on a continual basis, for He is the only inestimably Good One. He has been loving me unconditionally all of my life, and because He is in me, I can therefore yield myself to Him to be used of Him to love even the unlovable – unconditionally – as He wills.

So, I yielded to my Lord with an open and sincere heart, saying yes to Him. "Yes my Beloved; I am willing to love all my fellow human beings unconditionally, beginning with my brethren here with me." This I will do in full dependency on my beloved Lord Jesus to lead me, and do His work in and through me, knowing that if He is not in me by His blessed Holy Spirit to carry it out, my "Yes" to Him is in vain, for it is merely words. I did all this in faith, and there was no sensing of the Lord's presence, there was only a continual state of negative feelings to oppose me.

After all this had happened, I got out of bed, took my shower, etc. Then I began to feel in my flesh, all kinds of opposition against my agreement with my Lord Jesus about that which He had put before me. I felt resentment, anger and wrath, as if this was now my new state. The enemy was hitting me and opposing me from all sides through these kinds of feelings. But thanks be to the beloved Lord Jesus, He gave me the grace to take a firm stand against those negative thoughts and feelings that the enemy brought against me, which continued throughout the day and all that evening.

It was a Sunday, and at about 7 p.m. that evening, I took the step of faith against those feelings and sat down with the brethren, and shared with them the process the Lord Jesus had led me through that morning. After sharing with them, I told them that I forgave them, and all that they had done was now forgotten. I also told them that as of that very day, a new leaf had been turned, and we would begin anew. Yet those sins must be dealt with in repentance before the Lord Jesus, for them to truly and sincerely begin anew.

The opposition was still there in my flesh as I shared with the brethren, but as I continued to share with them, it began to diminish. I also asked them to forgive me for my anger against them, along with words that I had used in anger, such as "wicked" and "miserable sinners," who have continued to reject the Lord Jesus, and of which I quickly repented. They said they forgave me. After all had been said, some deep breathing, which I wrote about in this book took place, and continued throughout that night and for some days that followed.

That very Sunday evening and into the night, I began to feel the hands of the Lord deep within me, along with the deep breathing. A profound work of God's hands/grace had begun, destroying that stronghold of anger, along with all the other negative feelings in relation to what the students had been doing. I was freed to love my brethren unconditionally.

It is now a week later that I am recording this, and the deep work of my Lord has continued non-stop. Already, a radical change has taken place in my life. My attitude, responses, speech and actions have all begun to be changed. I feel new in all my thinking and ways. "Thank You, beloved Lord Jesus." He has been giving me a taste of this precious life over time, although rarely, and only for short periods. This has been the longest I have ever experienced it. Still, this also will not last; this is a taste He is permitting me to experience of the abundant life that is to come.

After I had completed the above writings, as I woke the following morning, my Lord brought before me something He had said to me twenty-five years earlier. This had happened as I sat enjoying the beauty of the coves at a seashore I had visited. There, right at the water's edge, were these tall trees shooting upwards to the sky. There was also a variety of plants which hung over the cliffs and into the sea. The scenery was so calm, tranquil and breathtakingly beautiful. I was pleased with what I was seeing and enjoying every bit of it, when out of my spirit came, "From now on, your enjoyment must only be Me."

However, I had never taken this seriously before, simply because my mind could not capture it. It had seemed so far from where I lived, and so, even after this experience, I continued believing and expecting that one day, I would find even a little enjoyment and maybe a little pleasure while I am still in the flesh on this earth. And, although from a child I have never found any, I still had this hope, slight as it may have been. This tells me, as slight as this hope was, how deep my longing was.

At this point as I wrote, I began to wake up to the fact that I am the Lord's. Before I entered the womb He knew me, and took delight in me and chose me to be His and His alone. Only, I did not know this, and so I strayed from my Beloved and sinned heavily against Him.

"I am sorry my Beloved. No wonder I have never been loved by another. Now that I know this, I repent of all my wondering and seeking to find love and some enjoyment here on this earth, to have pleasure according to my flesh. Forgive me my Beloved One. I do turn from this expectation to embrace only You, and to be happy only in You and with You. Thank You for so choosing me and loving me as only You can. I now choose to be satisfied and to be contented in this blessed, precious knowledge of You. I love You dearly, my Beloved."

Following these experiences, the Lord Jesus again poured out His precious grace on all the brethren, for they had already trampled on the latest outpouring of His grace. Again, the result was the same as always – it only lasted for a few days. This surprised and bewildered me even more. How could this be? It has now been thirty-five years. What is going on here? And so I became angry with them again, as they sought to deceive me, as has been their pattern, by pretending that all was well with them, when it was not. They could as easily have come to me with their problems in truth and sincerity, and the Lord would have helped them through me, but they chose deceit instead. Therefore, the consequences of their deceit are theirs.

At this point, the Holy Spirit brought back to my mind Acts 26:16-18. Through verse 16, the Lord Jesus had said to me that He has appeared to me to appoint me, **"as a servant and as a witness of what you have seen of Me and what I will show you."** With this, I began to understand that I was being shown unusual things, hidden things, things that are covered deeply – deeper than any of us want to know. Indeed, many run from knowing that these deceits exist, and are there in their hearts. For I could see in some of the brethren, how resentful they were to come face to face with who they really are deep down; how they have lived before the Lord Jesus in a state of innocence to cover all the evil they are practicing against the Lord, and how they are living, blaming Him for all the evil and wickedness they see in themselves.

The Holy Spirit had begun to open my eyes to what was really going on with the brethren, and why the continual abandoning of a life in the Lord Jesus, for a worldly life where they can carry out their own will and have their own way – do what they want, when they want, and how they want, with no one to interfere with their choices or actions. Fantasies are a big part of that world.

But what was more than fantasy, was their hate, bitterness, resentment and profound hostility towards God which had been covered. Although the Lord Jesus had revealed all this before in many ways, and this was verbally accepted by them, in their hearts they had rejected it, and steadfastly refused to believe that they were practicing any such evil against their God. For according to the lies they held in their hearts, they love God, and could not have hated Him since they are good people, good Christians, etc.

When I began to share these things with the brethren, some rose up in rebellion and hostility against facing the reality of who they are in their sinful nature, and the way that they have chosen to live. At the same time, there were tremendous accusations, which were all lies, pouring out against God. The devil was angry that he was being found out. Obviously, I had not escaped these same abuses held covered in the hearts.

I was discovering, by the blessed Holy Spirit, how the devil deceives people about who God is, and traps them in those lies. This happens partly because of their rejection of the Lord Jesus and therefore of their lack of commitment to Him. In this state, they are easily deceived.

Then the Lord Jesus brought to my mind the following Scripture in John 2:23-25.

> Now while he was in Jerusalem at the Passover Feast, many people saw the miraculous signs he was doing and believed in his name. [24]But Jesus would not entrust himself to them, for he knew all men. [25]He did not need man's testimony about man, for he knew what was in a man. John 2:23-25

Here the Scripture says that although they believed in Him, He would not entrust Himself to them, **"for He knew what was in a man."** I pondered over this Scripture for years, but now I can see clearly what the Lord Jesus is saying. There is much hidden evil in the heart of man, even in those who believe, that we do not want to know about, and there is great hostility and resentment towards anyone who would dare try to reveal these things to us, so as to bring us face to face with that which is hidden deep within. The devil violently opposes such revelations, because when they are revealed, and the light of the Lord Jesus shines into those dark crevices of the hearts, the enemy will then lose his hold on those souls.

For those reasons, the sanctifying/cleansing work of the Holy Spirit is absolutely necessary, indeed it is a must for every soul that comes to the Lord Jesus. When the souls are not cleansed, those souls will easily betray the Lord Jesus and each other, or easily turn away from Him.

> It is God's will that you should be sanctified: that you should avoid sexual immorality; [4] that each of you should learn to control his own body in a way that is holy and honorable, [5]not in passionate lust like the heathen, who do not know God; [6]and that in this matter no one should wrong his brother or take advantage of him. The Lord will punish men for all such sins, as we have already told you and warned you. [7] For God did not call us to be impure, but to live a holy life. [8]Therefore, he who rejects this instruction does not reject man but God, who gives you his Holy Spirit. 1 Thess. 4:3-8

After this, the Lord Jesus began to reveal the darkest secrets of the hearts of the brethren, revealing why, no matter how much grace He pours out on them, His Word cannot take hold. This is because there is simply no room in their hearts for Him, for they are filled with lies and accusations, hate and hostility towards God. They are above it all, even above being a sinner, and so they refuse to acknowledge any sin. They simply cover them and pretend that they do not exist, because they are still holding on to the belief that they are good and innocent in the face of God's truth. Some even see nothing wrong with holding sin in their hearts against their God.

> This is the verdict: Light has come into the world, but men loved darkness instead of light because their deeds were evil. [20]Everyone who does evil hates the light, and will not come into the light for fear that his deeds will be exposed. [21]But whoever lives by the truth comes into the light, so that it may be seen plainly that what he has done has been done through God." John 3:19-21

This is evil, yet they delight in it and practice it day and night. They choose to live in hate, hostility, resentment and vindictiveness against God, covering it all in a state of total dishonesty, where lies and deceit are practiced on a continual basis. In this state of dishonesty, the truth of who they really are in their sinful nature, along with the way they are living, is buried deep within their hearts, and they have not been willing to face this in truth and sincerity to be able to repent. For if they did, they could no longer justify the beliefs that they are deserving to have the things they desire, both in the spiritual and the natural world, based on their goodness. They are therefore blinded by self-goodness to reality, and so these truths are hidden from them.

I remembered just now, a theme the Lord Jesus gave me way back, when He began to open His Word to me. The theme was, "The lies in which we live." At that time, He revealed that all of Adam's descendants live in a state of lies, and naturally so, because the sinful nature by which we live is of the devil, and since he is the father of lies and deceit, we could do no different from him, but it is mostly covered and hidden. The Lord Jesus is now revealing the truth of that revelation through these students, and those others He has sent to me over the years, showing me how deeply covered these things are. However, unless you are given the setting that we are blessed to have, with the Holy Spirit leading the way with the purpose of excavating the deep recesses of the heart, these things will never be brought to the surface to be faced, for they are buried deep in the heart, covered in deceit and pride and fear to face them. This is all a part of the chopping down of trees that the Lord Jesus showed me in the Vision of the Jungle, which I wrote about in Volume 1 of this book.

Part of this dark place is the world of fantasy. Christians should not deliberately choose to do that which is wrong/sin and enter into obvious darkness, for we are the children of the light. Yet many have chosen to sin and enter into this dark place, which is the world of fantasy. This is where many spend their time and live out most of their lives. This is a world where a child of God should not deliberately choose to go. For there you are a tool of the devil to be used in whatever way he chooses, especially to be used against the Lord Jesus.

If you should fall into fantasy, or for any reason find yourself there, you should quickly turn to your Lord and repent, because all you can do there is to sin. You should also pray and ask the Lord Jesus to please keep you from falling into that dark place again. You should also ask Him to please remove from you all desires to go there, and all the curiosity to take a look at, or a thought of anything that is there. For once you do, you will most likely be trapped, because that world of fantasies can be very seductive and therefore desirable.

For many it is worse than drugs and more dangerous, for unlike drug addiction, those who are addicted to fantasy do not believe that they are doing anything wrong, and therefore in their opinion, they are not in danger. Yet, they are in greater danger. Let us be serious about this.

The pull to go to that place of fantasy can be tremendous. Therefore, once you have tasted that life, you will most likely want to continue in it. The solution then, is to die with Christ to your sinful nature, and then begin to deny it in dependency upon the Lord Jesus, and stop taking the bait, for when you do you will be hooked. It is only your commitment to our beloved Lord Jesus that can sustain you, where your gaze is upon Him and Him alone, and so you can trust Him to keep you from falling into these dark holes of that undercurrent and false life of fantasy.

In that dark place, deceit, lies, pretense, falsehood and manipulation reign, where self is deceived to believe he is king – the authority and is in charge – the center of it all. Here, arrogance and pride are the way of life, and you are free to do all that your heart desires. This is the secret world of many who call themselves Christians. You will not be able to live for the Lord Jesus, while living in that dark world of fantasy. Some people have accidents while driving because they fantasize. Even while driving, they are fully involved in that world where they are king, and so there is no room for another king, not even for the Lord Jesus. For them, He is always in their way, and so they are always having to escape Him. The world of fantasy is one of the ways souls use to rid themselves of the Lord Jesus, as they continue to hold resentment in their hearts against Him.

The reason the beloved Lord Jesus opened up this dark hole for us to look into, is because this is a huge trap of the enemy, which he uses to deceive and lure the children of God away to satisfy their flesh. In that place, the enemy offers them every kind of pleasure and entertainment that one can imagine.

In this world of fantasy, there is every kind of greed, selfish ambition, immorality, sexual enjoyment and pleasure imaginable. There, through fantasies, you can have the highest position in the world or in the universe. You can be better and greater than everyone else – number one, the greatest and the best. There you can be the authority – the boss. You can have your own business, power, wealth and fame. You can possess your heart's desire. Anything and everything you want, you can have there. You can destroy all those who are in your way, those you hate – even God! You can be the first – your own man, where no one can tell you anything, which most yearn for. There you are free to tell others what they are to do, for there you have no God, you are "god." There you can be the good person you desire to be, believing that you can be as good as God or even better – more merciful, kind, forgiving, loving, just and having a "holier-than-thou" attitude. You can even compete with God to be the best, or even believe yourself to be God, as so many have done.

This is the heart of arrogance that many are not willing to turn from. This is the way of the sinful nature, and therefore the devil. There is no limit to who you can be or what you can do in that world of fantasies. Indeed, as you choose, you can even believe that you can create your own universe, because there you are "god."

In this undercurrent life or underworld, you can be a pedophile, a rapist, a murderer; you can be the vilest and the wickedest person. There you can envy, be jealous, be vindictive, be malicious, tear down others, lie on them for their destruction, and you can deceive and lie without limit. You can also criticize, judge, accuse and belittle others. You can look down on them, exalt yourself over them, and believe that you are better than they are, all that you want. Because you have done these things, you believe this gives you the right and the liberty to think all the evil that you want to think about them. There you can betray, slander or undermine whoever you want to. You can be the villain, the victim or the victimizer.

In this fantasy world, you can justify yourself in everything that you do. You can defend and protect yourself, and be innocent all that you want, for there you can easily secure yourself. There you can carry out all the devious and crooked schemes you choose to, while smiling in the face of those you are tearing down and destroying.

> All day long I have held out my hands to an obstinate people, who walk in ways not good, pursuing

> their own imaginations– [3]a people who continually provoke me to my very face,. . . Isa. 65:2-3

This evil does not always begin with bad thoughts and images. At times it begins with good thoughts and good images to get you to take the bait, but once you do, you will be hooked. Yes, you will be trapped by the devil in this way, unless you are really finished with that life of fantasy/sin. This you choose to do, by repenting of that sinful way of life, and denying your flesh such liberty to go its own way, and therefore the way of the sinful nature. Then you will be enabled by the blessed Holy Spirit to take your stand against it by the grace given you, in obedience to the Lord Jesus in His Word which says:

> Then he said to them all: "If anyone would come after me, he must deny himself and take up his cross daily and follow me. [24]For whoever wants to save his life will lose it, but whoever loses his life for me will save it. [25]What good is it for a man to gain the whole world, and yet lose or forfeit his very self? Luke 9:23-25

If you live in this dark world of fantasy, you will not walk with the Lord Jesus. Why? Because living in this dark place is like being hooked on drugs, and maybe even worse. It is seductive, and it will trap you where you cannot escape, since it possesses your mind and body. It is only by the grace of the Lord Jesus, who destroyed the works of the devil that was against you, and who took your place on the Cross, putting your sinful nature to death there, that you can be set free from this trap. He paid the price for your sins, forgave you, and set you free to live for God, that is, if a life in Christ is really what you want, because in the life of fantasy, you are the king, and maybe that is the life you want. If this is so, you will not want to give up your place as king, to submit to the King of kings, the Lord Jesus Christ.

> He himself bore our sins in his body on the tree, so that we might die to sins and live for righteousness; by his wounds you have been healed. 1 Peter 2:24

However, although the Lord Jesus freed us to live for righteousness, we are also free to live for unrighteousness. Freewill choice – this is how it works. By the freewill given us by God, many have taken the grace of the Lord Jesus given to them, and seek to subject it to a life of self-will. Thanks be to God that this cannot be done. They have created their own way of living, and their own world of entertainment, with its carnal pleasures and self-aggrandizement. In that dark world of fantasy that so many call their own creation, the devil is the owner and the managing director, the instructor and teacher. There, we are either degraded to nothing – to feel dirty, filthy, empty, lonely and good for nothing, or we are made to feel that we are everything – big, prideful and exalted.

Many Christians who have escaped to that world, actually believe and expect that they can take the Lord Jesus, who is in them, to that dark place of self-will. They literally expect Him to remain with them while they entertain themselves, and indulge themselves with every kind of wickedness – every depraved and lewd desire, pleasure, thought and conduct – all to their satisfaction. At the same time, they also expect to come out of that place, enter the church and praise the Lord, as if nothing has happened, as if they did not sin, while having every intention to continue this evil behavior. Indeed, there are those who even practice their fantasizing while sitting in church pews.

Why would anyone who has been bought with the precious Blood of the blessed Savior and Lord, even think that you could subject the Holy Lord in you to such degradation and depravity, and then after you have done these things, to really expect the Lord Jesus to submit to your carnal way of life and remain with you in a subservient way? No! This is tremendous arrogance. This is not how it works. We are the ones who must conform to the ways of the Lord our God, and not He to ours. When you choose to live according to your old way of life – the ways of your sinful nature, from which you were saved, please understand that there will be consequences, for God is a holy God. His Word tells us that we are to remain in Him and He will remain in us.

> "I am the true vine, and my Father is the gardener. [2]He cuts off every branch in me that bears no fruit, while every branch that does bear fruit he prunes so that it will be even more fruitful. [3]You are already clean because of the word I have spoken to you.[4] Remain in me, and I will remain in you. No branch can bear fruit by itself; it must remain in the vine. Neither can you bear fruit unless you remain in me. [5]"I am the vine; you are the branches. If a man remains in me and I in him, he will bear much fruit; apart from me you can do nothing. [6]If anyone does not remain in me, he is like a branch that is thrown away and withers; such branches are picked up, thrown into the fire and burned. John 15:1-6

We must understand then, that once we have agreed with that undercurrent way of life and have therefore made it our reality, and have embraced its ways to live according to it, we have turned from the Lord Jesus. We have again returned to our sinful nature in full agreement with it, and in full submission to the devil, to once again fill our hearts with all the evil that the Lord Jesus washed us of on Calvary's Cross, and to again carry out the devil's will.

The Scriptures clearly tell us that if we live according to the sinful nature, we will die.

> Therefore, brothers, we have an obligation–but it is not to the sinful nature, to live according to it. [13]For if you live according to the sinful nature, you will die; but if by the Spirit you put to death the misdeeds of the body, you will live, Rom. 8:12-13

You need to understand that when you choose to live this way, you have chosen to send the Lord a clear statement as to where you want to spend eternity, and it's not with Him! Rather, it is in your own kingdom that you have created with the devil's help, or rather, the devil created with your agreement.

> "Behold, I am coming soon! My reward is with me, and I will give to everyone according to what he has done. [13] am the Alpha and the Omega, the First and the Last, the Beginning and the End. [14]"Blessed are those who wash their robes, that they may have the right to the tree of life and may go through the gates into the city. [15]Outside are the dogs, those who practice magic arts, the sexually immoral, the murderers, the idolaters and everyone who loves and practices falsehood." Rev. 22:12-15

The Lord Jesus has revealed to us through His Word, that hell is the destination of all who practice falsehood. Fantasy is falsehood. May we know then that falsehood is sin against God, and let it be known also, that the life of fantasy is a life of falsehood; it is a life of defiance in the face of the Lord Jesus. Please be warned, so that you will not continue in that evil lifestyle, but rather, will turn from it in repentance, and surrender your all to the only One who can cleanse you of such lewdness and wickedness/sin, which is against the beloved Lord Jesus.

It is obvious that some love this false life more than they love the Lord Jesus, and even more so, than the life He has called them to live. I say this because so many do not spend time with the Lord Jesus to come to know Him, and to learn of Him and His ways. Rather, they go off to the world they have created and love – the fantasy world, to escape all reality. The sad thing is, when we have escaped reality, indeed we have escaped God.

The real world demands responsibility from responsible souls. However, many do not want this, and so they go off to the false world where responsibility is not a requirement. To have a life in the Lord Jesus, you must want reality, and therefore you will choose to be responsible, according to the truth of God's Word.

> These are a shadow of the things that were to come;
> the reality, however, is found in Christ. Col. 2:17

As one of the brethren said, "I abandoned my life and gave up, because I did not want to take any responsibility for the disaster I suspected might be ahead waiting for me, as a result of the choices I was making. In order to escape responsibility for those bad choices I made, along with the fact that I abandoned my life, I blamed God for robbing me of my life so as to cover my having abandoned it. In the lies in which I lived, I believed that I had given my life to the Lord Jesus, and He gave me nothing in return, so this gave me the right to demand of Him anything I desired. And because I did not get what I demanded, I rebelled even more. This also allowed me the liberty to sin beyond measure, and to continue accusing the Lord Jesus for not loving me; of never doing anything for me; that He does not want me; that because of Him I have no one, and that He robbed me of everyone and everything, and now I have nothing. It is all His fault – look how He makes me suffer. He is selfish, I hate Him." On and on it goes. These are the things that I hear, and I am afraid there is more to come.

These types of accusations are always the result for everyone who chooses to escape responsibility for their life and their choices to remain innocent, and therefore truth/reality eludes them – they are deceived! For instance, look at the following two testimonies. They are loaded with accusation against God.

## THE KING FISH

Someone told me about what they called the king fish; meaning the dominant fish of the sea (as they see it) which no other fish can challenge. In their understanding, king fish had nothing to do but to push the other fish around, bullying them, eating the ones it chooses to eat, and letting the ones it did not choose to eat to continue living in fear of him.

When they told me this story, the Holy Spirit immediately gave me understanding of its meaning, and so I said to the person, "Isn't this the way you see God? Isn't He the king fish you told me about, and aren't you one of the little fish always running in fear, hiding in holes and under rocks in the sea to keep from being gobbled up by the king fish?" When I said this they denied it, and gave me every argument and reason necessary to convince me that this was not their motive or intention, but I insisted. Then after a few days had gone by, they broke, and in tears confessed that this was how they see God. Yet this person was highly respected and honored in the church. People looked to that person for council, and they called their house daily to receive words of encouragement and comfort from God, yet hidden deep in their heart was this and many other evil beliefs about God.

Living in such a state is misery. Added to this was the additional weight they had to carry caused by this false life; pretending to be this good and great spiritual giant that is always there for everyone else, while they themselves were dying – being dried up and empty inside. All this, while putting on this front before people, murmuring every step of the way, and accusing God that it is His fault that they have to live like this. For these many reasons, people refuse to sincerely go to the Lord Jesus and surrender their lives to Him.

## THE CAT AND THE MOUSE

The Lord Jesus has mercy on us always, as demonstrated by His grace to us. Following His last outpouring of grace, the students became more open. One of them shared with me that before this outpouring of grace, all their lives they saw themselves as a mouse, and saw the Lord as a cat. The cat would chase the mouse, catch it in its mouth, bite down on it just enough to hurt it, and then let it go. This it would repeat several times until it had enough fun. In the meantime, the poor little mouse would be so afraid, knowing that it was at the mercy of the cat, and at the same time knowing that the cat has no mercy whatsoever. For, when he is finished having his fun, he is going to catch the mouse, put it in his mouth, and crush it with his teeth, breaking every bone in its body, without a thought or the slightest concern for the value of the life he has just crushed, and definitely no concern for the fear or the pain he has caused that mouse while treating it like a toy. Then after he crushed it, he swallowed it – all to satisfy his selfish greed. From there he moves on to find the next mouse, and repeats this all over again.

This is who God was to that student, and obviously to many in the church of today as well. Since then, other students have told me that they see God in this same light. Then I began to understand that no wonder we have been here for thirty-six years and could not breakthrough. And how can any human breakthrough such a barrier of solid beliefs held in their hearts since childhood, while adding to it daily? How do you breakthrough? You cannot. Only the Holy Spirit can.

But the Lord is showing us the heart of the church and what He sees there, and to know that yes, with man it is impossible, but not with God, for with God, nothing is impossible, rather all things are possible. Therefore in faith, we wait for the Lord Jesus to do the impossible. These are some of the experiences and therefore preparation He is permitting me to have before sending me into His church.

> For nothing is impossible with God." Luke 1:37

I am also told by some that they could not receive anything from the Lord Jesus, because they could not do anything to earn it; meaning, since they did not earn His favor – His free gifts of grace, they could not receive them. They therefore see His gifts to them as without value, because they are free. They see themselves as being belittled to be given something for free, and this does not matter whether it is for the spiritual or the natural. Now I understand why they are always wanting to work and earn their way, and why grace has been poured out on them so many times in powerful ways, and it always comes to nothing – it is because it was not received, since it was free.

We know that people come to the Lord Jesus with a lot of negative beliefs, desires, thoughts and problems of various kinds. Indeed, we could say that we all have come to the Lord Jesus loaded down in sin of all kinds. This is how it is. But what I did not know before my years with the students, is after coming to the Lord Jesus, many souls actually continue holding to the same old beliefs they had, as if nothing has ever happened, nothing has changed. And so the life goes on as always, because the sanctifying work of the Holy Spirit has been given no room in such lives. The reason for this is because it has not been taught as a must for all who come to the Lord Jesus and are saved, and so this is the result of this neglect.

The Christian life is a life led by the Holy Spirit, and if He is not leading it, that life is going nowhere, since none of us can live the Christian life on our own. To try to do so, is to live in frustration and misery, accusing God.

> "I have much more to say to you, more than you
> can now bear. [13]But when he, the Spirit of truth,
> comes, he will guide you into all truth. He will not
> speak on his own; he will speak only what he hears,
> and he will tell you what is yet to come.[14]He will
> bring glory to me by taking from what is mine and
> making it known to you.[15]All that belongs to the
> Father is mine. That is why I said the Spirit will
> take from what is mine and make it known to you.
> John 16:12-15

> [9]You, however, are controlled not by the sinful nature
> but by the Spirit, if the Spirit of God lives in you.
> And if anyone does not have the Spirit of Christ, he
> does not belong to Christ. [14]because those who are
> led by the Spirit of God are sons of God. [15]For you
> did not receive a spirit that makes you a slave again
> to fear, but you received the Spirit of sonship. And
> by him we cry, "Abba, Father." [16]The Spirit himself

> testifies with our spirit that we are God's children. Rom. 8:9, 14-16

For these reasons we read in Proverbs 3:5-6:

> Trust in the Lord with all your heart and lean not on your own understanding; [6]in all your ways acknowledge him, and he will make your paths straight. Prov. 3:5-6

Because the students believe the lie that God is not a good God, and that He means them harm so He cannot be trusted, and even less so with their lives; they are therefore busy protecting themselves from the Lord, to the point where they seek to appease Him through their works and their sacrifices – always seeking ways to pacify Him to keep Him from harming them. At other times, in their deceit, they portray themselves to be this good and innocent soul who loves the Lord Jesus. The reason for this deceit is to present themselves to God as an offering from a far distance, through some priest, pastor or other, in their service to them. By doing so, they believe they can keep the Lord from touching their lives. This is part of their sacrifice before God.

After understanding the seriousness of the beliefs of king fish, cat and mouse and like beliefs, along with fantasy, I then understood that their hearts were filled with self, leaving no room for the Lord Jesus.

The Lord Jesus is showing me the tremendous need His body, the church, has to be cleansed. The need is beyond anything I could ever dream of. Not in my wildest dreams could I ever dare go into these places where the Lord Jesus has led me. All this is scary to look at, but my Lord has given me faith to stand believing and trusting Him. Where this is leading I do not know, but I choose to trust and follow my Lord Jesus. There is a song that says, "Where He leads I will follow." This I will do to the end with His help. The Lord Jesus is using all this to teach me and to show me the state of the church.

CHAPTER 18

# FULFILLMENT OF THE CALL

'Now get up and stand on your feet. I have appeared to you to appoint you as a servant and as a witness of what you have seen of me and what I will show you. [17]I will rescue you from your own people and from the Gentiles. I am sending you to them [18]to open their eyes and turn them from darkness to light, and from the power of Satan to God, so that they may receive forgiveness of sins and a place among those who are sanctified by faith in me.' Acts 26:16-18

When the beloved Lord Jesus spoke to me through His Word thirty-nine years ago, my state was such that I just could not see myself beyond where I was – timid, self-centered, self-conscious and still very ignorant of the Word of God. In that state, I was not even believing myself to be someone who ought to be in the service of the Lord Jesus, for I saw myself as unworthy. But, because of His great love and determination, He moved circumstances in this life, whereby He left me nowhere to turn or to hide, but only to go forward and embrace the fullness of life in Him, and the call that He has placed on this life. Then, He began to teach me what it means to walk with Him. It was all His doing, for if it was left to me alone I probably would have hidden, especially because of the heavy state of timidity and shame in which I was walking, and that state where I was without an education. Thanks to my Lord for delivering me.

The beloved Lord Jesus then planted His Word in me, and on His Word I have taken my stand. It has become my sure foundation – the rock on which I stand – my life, and with all sincerity of heart, I can say:

> I have been crucified with Christ and I no longer live, but Christ lives in me. The life I live in the body, I live by faith in the Son of God, who loved me and gave himself for me. Gal. 2:20

The gracious, beloved Lord Jesus has fulfilled much of Acts 26:16-18 beginning with, **". . .get up and stand on your feet. . ."** (verse 16a) At the time when He spoke these words to me, I was down on my knees on the floor, and at His command, I jumped to my feet.

Then He said, **"...I have appeared to you to appoint you as a servant and as a witness of what you have seen of me and what I will show you."** (verse 16b) The Lord Jesus has fulfilled all this, as He said He would, for He has since anointed me to be the servant of the living God. He has also made me a witness to the condition of the church, of which I am a part, the state of which He has been showing me for thirty-nine years. He has shown me this through those trips when He sent me to those churches in the USA, Jamaica and Mexico, along with what I have heard and seen through the various radio and TV ministries and read in publications. Yes, I have seen and heard a lot, which has confirmed to me without question, that we, the church, are under thick darkness.

He has also said, **"I will rescue you from your own people..."** (verse 17a) This has also been fulfilled, for the beloved Lord Jesus has separated me from family, race and nationality, and has sent me to Mexico, to a totally different culture, language and people. Today, I do not know the circumstances or whereabouts of those persons who I knew back then, neither am I in touch with former friends nor have I seen anyone from my family. There has been a definite separation. The last time that I saw one of my family members was in 1990, and a separation took place then. This was the very last separation. Since then, I have not laid eyes on even one member of my family. They all thought that I was crazy when I gave up business to go to Mexico, and I do not think they believed, even until today, when I told them that the Lord Jesus had sent me there.

Back to Acts 26:16-18. When the Lord Jesus said to me, **". . .and from the Gentiles. . ."** (verse 17a) indeed, He has separated me to be in the compound in Mexico, and I am not permitted to have a personal relationship with anyone apart from my marital relationship. Neither am I in contact with anyone, other than those few persons with whom I do business, and the students. Apart from going to places within the city on business for the mission, I am not permitted to go anywhere else, unless the Lord Jesus tells me to go, and that is the way it is until today. I see the Gentiles in this context, to be the people of the world, since the Lord Jesus has defined and limited my contact with them.

Whenever the Beloved wants me to go beyond the city limits for whatever reason, He tells me. This has happened in the distant past, but very rarely. In fact, you can count on one hand the number of times this has happened in the last thirty-six years. When I am to go to Jamaica, He gives me clear knowledge of the dates I am to go, and He determines when I am to return, by giving me a specific amount of time I am to be there; and that is the way it has been all these years. Beyond all this, He has called me to the church, and not to the world.

He said, **". . .I am sending you to them [18]to open their eyes and turn them from darkness to light. . ."** (verses 17b-18a) – meaning the church. This is a big order; in fact, too big for my little mind to contemplate. I have therefore let it all go to the beloved Lord Jesus, for only He knows what all this means. Still, this is the call on my life, and that day is coming soon when the eyes of His people will be opened wide for us to see our true state, and therefore be able to see our true need for our Lord and God, and for the abundant life of faith that He, our beloved Lord Jesus brought.

For a long time, I just could not grasp what was being said to me through Acts 26:16-18, for in my mind, I could not connect the church with, "open their eyes and turn them from darkness to light." I had always connected this Scripture only with the beginning of the church, back there in the days of Paul and the other apostles. It was when I began to write these books some twenty-seven years after I was saved, that the Lord Jesus began to open my eyes to see the connection between this Scripture – Acts 26:16-18, and the call on my life – connecting it with the darkness that is over the church. It was only then that my eyes were opened to what the Lord Jesus was saying to me through Acts 26:16-18, and then I began to understand the depth of the darkness that the church is in, using to a great extent the brethren He has placed with me.

On that day, when the Lord Jesus, through His Spirit, comes to open our eyes by removing the darkness from over His church, we are going to be shocked to see the state of darkness that we are in. For He is now opening His Word in a way I have not known before, giving us clear understanding of His intent through many areas of Scriptures, especially in the areas of Salvation and sanctification. At that time, we will then see the tremendous room we have given satan in our lives, and as a result over the church, through our beliefs, which keep us from living and enjoying the abundant life that our beloved Lord Jesus brought. It is that thick darkness that robs us of the reality and the beauty of that life.

The Lord Jesus has been leading me over all these years, and revealing the deep darkness that the church is in. This will be further revealed in the writings that will follow this book. The Lord Jesus has also been preparing me for that big day, when He will begin to open the eyes of His people, and turn them from darkness to light by His blessed Holy Spirit. This is the day I am waiting for, because there are many in the church today, both in the pews and on the pulpits, battling to hold on to the belief that God IS, and especially, is with them at all times. This should not be. Yet, this is common in the church today. This is deep darkness over the church.

This is the day for which the beloved Lord Jesus has been preparing me. It will be the greatest day that the church has ever known since its inception. For on that day, the Lord Jesus will begin the cleansing of the hearts of His people, by the power of His blessed Holy Spirit, from the ways of the sinful nature, the world and therefore from the ways of the devil. Then, the Lord Jesus will fill our hearts with sincere faith towards Him, turning us to Him and to Him alone, to love Him, desire Him, admire Him and to worship Him from pure hearts, which He has given us. For He will purge us of the old ways and purify us to be His holy children, having hearts that are full of faith and love for our God and Lord, not some of the time, but all of the time.

> Sanctify them by the truth; your word is truth.
> John. 17:17

He further said, "**. . .and from the power of Satan to God. . .**" (verse 18a) This will be accomplished on the day that He fulfills His promise to me, when He will begin to turn our hearts back to Him in a way we have not known. We will be turned from darkness to light, and from the power of satan to God, to walk in the abundant life that our Lord Jesus brought.

What this is telling us here, is the Lord Jesus is speaking about the church, His body, which needs to be turned from darkness to light, and from the power of satan to God. This is shocking – at least, to my little mind! Each time I am permitted to examine what the Lord Jesus is saying here, in light of my call, I am shocked. I keep asking myself, how can this be?

But then I remember the angel had said to me, to my surprise, “Turn to God.” In the same way, the Lord Jesus is saying to His body, the church, to turn to Him – our God, Lord and Father.

His call upon this life is for the very last of days, which have been a very long time in coming. But now, the last of days are upon us. I can now see much more clearly, the picture that the beloved Lord Jesus has been painting before me all of these years, and which for a long time, I have been slow to grasp and to understand.

Since the Lord Jesus has put me to write down these accounts, the picture, which He has been painting over these thirty-nine years, is now clearer. The picture now seems to be taking its form – the form which He has chosen for it to take. Although there are a few areas which still have to be completed, the picture is clear enough for me to begin to grasp some of what the almighty Lord and God has been revealing. One thing that stands out clearly in this picture is – the Lord Jesus is coming soon for His church. His will is:

> to make her holy, cleansing her by the washing with water through the word, [27]and to present her to himself as a radiant church, without stain or wrinkle or any other blemish, but holy and blameless. Eph. 5:26-27

Let us not be deceived about this fact. The church must be ready to be presented before the Lord Jesus as a virgin bride. This is the church for which He is coming, and she must be made ready. Everyone who is called by the name of the Lord Jesus, everyone who is His, must open their eyes, ears and heart, and wake up from their slumber, and let Christ shine on them. Do not look forward to the Lord Jesus coming for His bride until she is purified (sanctified), and made ready for the righteous and Holy Groom.

> I am jealous for you with a godly jealousy. I promised you to one husband, to Christ, so that I might present you as a pure virgin to him. 2 Cor. 11:2

This is the church for which the Lord Jesus is coming – a pure and holy church, and nothing less than this will do. Don't be deceived to think otherwise. Therefore, we must be cleansed from the old patterns and ways of ungodliness, such as: the pride of life, lies, deceit, dishonesty, pretense, falsehood, unrighteousness, self-will, self-righteousness, having your own way, rebellion, love for the world and its pleasures, unfaithfulness, willful sinning against our beloved God and Lord, etc.

> Here is a trustworthy saying: If we died with him, we will also live with him; [12]if we endure, we will also reign with him. If we disown him, he will also disown us; [13]if we are faithless, he will remain faithful, for he cannot disown himself. [14]Keep reminding them of these things. Warn them before God against quarreling about words; it is of no value, and only ruins those who listen. [15]Do your best to present yourself to God as one approved, a workman who does not need to be ashamed and who correctly handles the word of truth. 2 Tim. 2:11-15

These are the ways of the sinful nature from which we are saved. The Lord Jesus will be cleansing us from the old patterns and customs of that sinful nature, so that we will no longer live under its influence to sin deliberately against our Lord and God, and so to bring us to that wonderful place, where we will walk uprightly before the Lord Jesus with pure hearts, full of the assurance of faith, and therefore love for our loving God and Lord, **". . .so that they may receive forgiveness of sins and a place among those who are sanctified by faith in me.'"** (verse 18b)

Who could ever imagine that it is the church of our Lord Jesus Christ that needs to receive forgiveness of sins and a place among those who are sanctified by faith? I could never have dreamt this up. Nevertheless, this is just what the Lord Jesus is saying, and for this He has called me, to send me into the church – one who is totally uneducated, and is truly unqualified as far as the natural is concerned for such a task.

Even though the Lord Jesus had imprinted it on my heart, I just did not, and indeed could not understand Acts Chapter 26, verses 16-18 before, in context with the church of today, because I had thought that all of these things that it refers to had already become a part of our lives, meaning the church. But now I can clearly see, because of the condition of the church, how this too is revealing the darkness that is over it. Therefore, the need for its sanctification is to be believed and embraced willingly by each one of us who call ourselves children of the living God and Lord.

The ways of the sinful nature must now be identified, understood and taken seriously by the church, so that the evil/sins thereof can be dealt with through the sanctifying work of the Holy Spirit, to free the body of the Lord Jesus, the church, from its sinful ways.

## SOME OF THE REASONS WHY THE CHURCH IS IN DARKNESS

The principal reason for the darkness the church is in, is the deceptive work of satan that is actively, consistently and continually working against it, which the church is mostly ignorant of.

The following points are results of this work of satan.

1) From the inception of the church, prideful men have tried to reign over the church of our Lord Jesus Christ. And indeed, since the death of the apostles, men have reigned over the church and have brought into it man-made doctrines that have distorted the view of their followers to God's truth – His Word. This has continued to this day.
2) God's Word is not held in high esteem and honored by most Christians and believed to be the infallible Word of God – the Truth, the rule and conduct of faith and everything else in the life of a child of God, by this we must live.
3) As a result, love for God is lukewarm, and in too many cases it is only empty words spoken.
4) The guidance of the Holy Spirit is not sought after, nor embraced by most.
5) Erroneous doctrines that mislead God's people. The result is no sincere submission and obedience nor faithfulness,

from the hearts of many to the Lord Jesus; nor are His Word and will fully embraced, and therefore obeyed.

6) The spirit and soul are not defined and taught by the church because it seems that they are not clearly understood by it. This lack results in much difficulty for God's people.

7) Truth and sincerity of heart are far from the hearts and therefore the lips of many of God's people, therefore having their own way in dishonesty, deceit, pride, falsehood, pretense and self-will, prevail.

8) Most churches do not believe, and therefore do not accept or understand the working of satan against them, neither do most understand the difference between Salvation and Sanctification – being sanctified/the cleansing of the soul, and so satan has a free hand to work havoc in their minds, and in their midst.

9) Because of the lack of faith in the Lord Jesus Christ, psychoanalysis has been given great influence in several churches over God's people. The question is, how could such a theory have such a hold on God's children, when its foundation was laid by an enemy of God? Sigmund Freud was an atheist and a cocaine addict. He is the father of psychoanalysis. His teaching seems to be mostly mental gymnastics to deceive God's people and keep them in a state of false hope, believing that through such mental manipulation they can get the knowledge they need to fix

and change themselves without surrendering to the Lord Jesus Christ. Surrender would then enable them to trust their lives and therefore all their problems to the Lord Jesus – the only One who can fix and change lives. It seems the mission of Freud was to circumvent the work of the Holy Spirit to change the lives of God's people, by having them dependent on this type of analysis, rather than their Lord Jesus. This might be good for the world, but it is definitely not good for God's people. This is darkness over the church.

10) The wickedness, greed and immorality that are common across the church, which satan uses against men and women of God so successfully to bring them down, and therefore to cause discouragement to the body of Christ.

11) Envy, jealousy, competition and resentment are major tools in the hand of the devil, which he uses so destructively to bring division amongst brethren in the church, especially among the leadership.

12) The greed for power; "I deserve"; "I am better than you"; "I should be in that place, not you." Therefore ignorance, pride, arrogance, lack of submission and obedience to authority in the church, are tools the devil loves to use to exalt one and to bring down another and to bring division in the church.

13) There is too much political influence in the church, and it misguides and leads many away from the truth of God's Word.
14) There is too much adultery; supposedly men of God committing adultery with the opposite sex, the same sex, and with young boys and girls.
15) Many souls in the church believe that they are walking in humility, in obedience to the Word of God, and are therefore walking with the Lord Jesus. However, in reality, they are walking in pride, highly exalted in their hearts and minds, which is the way of the devil. The Lord Jesus tells us in His Word that unless we humble ourselves as a little child, we will not see or enter the Kingdom of God. This tells us that when we come to the Lord Jesus, we are to deliberately choose to walk in truth and sincerity, and therefore humility. Without these and a heart of faith, we cannot walk with the Lord Jesus. Humility is a requisite to walk with the Lord Jesus, and pride is required to walk with satan. We have a need to come to knowledge of this truth so that we will be able to choose who we want to walk with, for we are the only ones who can make such a choice.

In a large house there are articles not only of gold
and silver, but also of wood and clay; some are for
noble purposes and some for ignoble. 21If a man

> cleanses himself from the latter, he will be an instrument for noble purposes, made holy, useful to the Master and prepared to do any good work. [22]Flee the evil desires of youth, and pursue righteousness, faith, love and peace, along with those who call on the Lord out of a pure heart. 2 Tim. 2:20-22

As a result of taking a life in the Lord Jesus for granted, ignorance of a true life in Christ, plus other neglects not mentioned here, the church is in darkness, and we cannot live the abundant life that the Lord Jesus brought. Yet for most, they believe that they are living it. These few points that are listed, are barely touching the surface of the problems that the church faces. This is caused by the lack of acknowledging the deceitful forces of satan that are at work against it.

> Finally, be strong in the Lord and in his mighty power. [11]Put on the full armor of God so that you can take your stand against the devil's schemes. [12]For our struggle is not against flesh and blood, but against the rulers, against the authorities, against the powers of this dark world and against the spiritual forces of evil in the heavenly realms. Eph. 6:11-12

> Your eye is the lamp of your body. When your eyes are good, your whole body also is full of light. But when they are bad, your body also is full of darkness. 35See to it, then, that the light within you is not darkness. 36Therefore, if your whole body is full of light, and no part of it dark, it will be completely lighted, as when the light of a lamp shines on you."
> Luke 11:34-36

The Lord Jesus has revealed that there is darkness over His body, the church. These books are written to proclaim this reality to His body, the church, which our Lord declared when He said that no one, and I emphasize, simply no one, is living the abundant life that He, our beloved Lord Jesus brought. As a result of this, darkness covers His body, the church. Since then, He has confirmed and reaffirmed this truth through several visions and revelations, along with placing the church before my eyes for me to see for myself, this state of darkness which He has revealed.

Darkness is a result of, among other things, the very little faith that is being sincerely practiced by some, while others are practicing none at all. Therefore, these souls cannot trust their Lord with their lives or with their problems as they should. This robs them of the light and the spiritual understanding that they should have, which further blinds them to the truth and to that which is truly spiritual, upright and godly. This results in them being more carnal, and therefore having an earthly view and concept of spiritual and heavenly things. This in turn robs them of ever having a genuine trust or love relationship with their Lord and God. Consequently, they will always remain at a distance from their Lord. This is darkness over the church.

In this darkness, reasoning with spiritual things to justify remaining carnally minded, is a way of life, although we still have many other ways of justifying our sins by calling them something other. For in darkness, lies, deceit and falsehood are practiced unawares on an ongoing basis by most. Still, there are those who are aware of doing so, yet deliberately continue in it, because faith is not being practiced, or is not there at all. However, we tend to see nothing wrong with this, as long as we are the ones practicing it, because we are not seeing our own sins for what they are – sin. As a result, they are not being acknowledged. Therefore, there is no repentance, and so dishonesty multiplies and sin reigns and continues to increase, to further separate us from our God and Lord.

> All a man's ways seem innocent to him, but motives are weighed by the Lord. Prov. 16:2

So yes, we go on committing sin as if nothing is happening, while at the same time, we believe ourselves to be innocent, pure and holy. Indeed, many will be very upset if they are told otherwise, simply because darkness does not permit us to see our sins as they truly are – sin against God, and so many continue in them, living fully according to their sinful nature.

This sinning prevents us from moving on in sincere faith, and therefore we are kept at a distance from the Lord Jesus, because when we do not walk in sincere faith before the Lord Jesus, we will therefore be lacking in confidence in our approach to Him. This keeps us always at a distance from Him. That is one of the reasons why verse 18 of Acts 26 speaks of **". . .so that they may receive forgiveness of sins and a place among those who are sanctified by faith in me.'"**

There is a real need in the church to be sanctified, because of the darkness that exists. In this darkness, sanctification is not seen as a necessity for all, and so it is not taught as such. Yet, God's Word declares:

> But we ought always to thank God for you, brothers loved by the Lord, because from the beginning God chose you to be saved through the sanctifying work of the Spirit and through belief in the truth. [14]He called you to this through our gospel, that you might share in the glory of

our Lord Jesus Christ. [15]So then, brothers, stand firm and hold to the teachings we passed on to you, whether by word of mouth or by letter. 2 Thess. 2:13-15

It is God's will that you should be sanctified: that you should avoid sexual immorality; [4]that each of you should learn to control his own body in a way that is holy and honorable, [5]not in passionate lust like the heathen, who do not know God; [6]and that in this matter no one should wrong his brother or take advantage of him. The Lord will punish men for all such sins, as we have already told you and warned you. [7]For God did not call us to be impure, but to live a holy life. [8]Therefore, he who rejects this instruction does not reject man but God, who gives you his Holy Spirit. 1 Thess. 4:3-8

May God himself, the God of peace, sanctify you through and through. May your whole spirit, soul and body be kept blameless at the coming of our Lord Jesus Christ. [24]The one who calls you is faithful and he will do it. 1 Thess. 5:23-24

Sanctify them by the truth; your word is truth. [18]As you sent me into the world, I have sent them into the world. [19]For them I sanctify myself, that they too may be truly sanctified. John 17:17-19

who have been chosen according to the foreknowledge of God the Father, through the sanctifying work of the Spirit, for obedience to Jesus Christ and sprinkling by his blood: Grace and peace be yours in abundance. 1 Peter 1:2

For the message of the cross is foolishness to those who are perishing, but to us who are being saved it is the power of God. [19]For it is written: "I will destroy the wisdom of the wise; the intelligence of the intelligent I will frustrate." 1 Cor. 1:18-19

But God demonstrates his own love for us in this: While we were still sinners, Christ died for us. [9]Since we have now been justified by his blood, how much more shall we be saved from God's wrath through him! [10]For if, when we were God's enemies, we were reconciled to him through the death of his Son, how much more, having been reconciled, shall we be saved through his life! Rom. 5:8-10

Dear friends, now we are children of God, and what we will be has not yet been made known. But we know that when he appears, we shall be like him, for we shall see him as he is. [3]Everyone who has this hope in him purifies himself, just as he is pure. 1 John 3:2-3

Now, brothers, I want to remind you of the gospel I preached to you, which you received and on which you have taken your stand. [2]By this gospel you are saved, if you hold firmly to the word I preached to you. Otherwise, you have believed in vain. 1 Cor. 15:1-2

My dear brothers, take note of this: Everyone should be quick to listen, slow to speak and slow to become angry, [20]for man's anger does not bring about the righteous life that God desires. [21]Therefore, get rid of all moral filth and the evil that is so prevalent and humbly accept the word planted in you, which can save you. [22]Do not merely listen to the word, and so deceive yourselves. Do what it says. [23]Anyone who listens to the word but does not do what it says is like a man who looks at his face in a mirror [24]and, after looking at himself, goes away and immediately forgets what he looks like. [25]But the man who looks intently into the perfect law that gives freedom, and continues to do this, not forgetting what he has heard, but doing it – he will be blessed in what he does. James 1:19-25

Anyone who runs ahead and does not continue in the teaching of Christ does not have God; whoever continues in the teaching has both the Father and the Son. 2 John 1:9

For the grace of God that brings salvation has appeared to all men. [12]It teaches us to say "No" to ungodliness and worldly passions, and to live self-controlled, upright and godly lives in this present age, [13]while we wait for the blessed hope – the glorious appearing of our great God and Savior, Jesus Christ, [14]who gave himself for us to redeem us from all wickedness and to purify for himself a people that are his very own, eager to do what is good. Titus 2:11-14

> Once you were alienated from God and were ene-
> mies in your minds because of your evil behavior.
> [22]But now he has reconciled you by Christ's phys-
> ical body through death to present you holy in his
> sight, without blemish and free from accusation–
> [23]if you continue in your faith, established and firm,
> not moved from the hope held out in the gospel.
> This is the gospel that you heard and that has been
> proclaimed to every creature under heaven, and of
> which I, Paul, have become a servant. Col. 1:21-23

> . . .because of the grace God gave me [16]to be a minister of Christ Jesus to the Gentiles with the priestly duty of proclaiming the gospel of God, so that the Gentiles might become an offering acceptable to God, sanctified by the Holy Spirit. Rom. 15:15-16

Faith enables us to live an upright and godly life. It helps us to take a stand in truth and sincerity, whereby we can stand before our God, confidently trusting Him all the way with our whole heart. God uses faith to purify our hearts, to allow us to have this confidence before Him and to draw close to Him.

> . . .However, when the Son of Man comes, will he find faith on the earth?" Luke 18:8

> When they came to the crowd, a man approached Jesus and knelt before him. [15]"Lord, have mercy on my son," he said. "He has seizures and is suffering greatly. He often falls into the fire or into the water. [16]I brought him to your disciples, but they could not heal him." [17]"O unbelieving and perverse generation," Jesus replied, "how long shall I stay with you? How long shall I put up with you? Bring the boy here to me." [18]Jesus rebuked the demon, and it came out of the boy, and he was healed from that moment. [19]Then the disciples came to Jesus in private and asked, "Why couldn't we drive it out?" [20]He replied, "Because you have so little faith. I tell you the truth, if you have faith as small as a mustard seed, you can say to this mountain, 'Move from here to there' and it will move. Nothing will be impossible for you." Matt. 17:14-20

Like the disciples, we too have a great need for more faith, and by God's inestimable goodness to us, we are going to be given more.

> 'Now get up and stand on your feet. I have appeared to you to appoint you as a servant and as a witness of what you have seen of me and what I will show you. [17]I will rescue you from your own people and

> from the Gentiles. I am sending you to them [18]to open their eyes and turn them from darkness to light, and from the power of Satan to God, so that they may receive forgiveness of sins and a place among those who are sanctified by faith in me.'
> Acts 26:16-18

The Lord Jesus commissioned Paul with these very same words, to go forth and open up and expand the boundaries of the church far and wide – to open their eyes, turning them from darkness to light, and from the power of satan to God, by calling the entire world to repentance. Today, He is using the very same words to call the church to repentance, for the purpose of sanctifying it. This is for its cleansing and its closing.

> "Now I commit you to God and to the word of his grace, which can build you up and give you an inheritance among all those who are sanctified.
> Acts 20:32

Although the gracious and beloved Lord Jesus has fulfilled much of what He had told me He would to in Acts Chapter 26, verses 16-18, the more important parts are yet to be fulfilled. These include the opening of the eyes of His church, turning us from darkness to light, and from the power of satan unto God, so that we may be endowed with the purity that is of faith to live the abundant life that the Lord Jesus brought.

The beloved Lord Jesus has called me for this purpose for the very last of days, as He is preparing to cleanse His body, the church, by His blessed Holy Spirit, in readiness for His coming. He is coming for a holy bride, without spot or wrinkle, and although it is being taught by many that the Lord Jesus can come at any time, He cannot until His body, the church, is prepared and made ready for His holy, majestic appearing.

> Let us rejoice and be glad and give him glory! For the wedding of the Lamb has come, and his bride has made herself ready. [8]Fine linen, bright and clean, was given her to wear." (Fine linen stands for the righteous acts of the saints.) Rev. 19:7-8

The series of writings that follow this will lay out that which the Almighty God and Lord has revealed, for the opening of the eyes of His people, preparing us to be His holy bride, for whom He is coming.

> I am jealous for you with a godly jealousy. I promised you to one husband, to Christ, so that I might present you as a pure virgin to him. [3]But I am afraid

> that just as Eve was deceived by the serpent's cunning, your minds may somehow be led astray from your sincere and pure devotion to Christ.
> 2 Cor. 11:2-3

Obviously, verse 3 of this Scripture has been fulfilled across the church without anyone of us noticing it. This has happened simply because we, the church, have so accepted the status quo that we cannot see beyond the doctrines that blind us. This has allowed us to fall asleep in our beliefs, feeling very comfortable that our doctrine is the right one and "theirs" is wrong, while "they" are saying the same about us. This further allows us to fall into a trance, justified, and no one dares to enter and disturb or interrupt our peace/sleep. If they do, we will be very angry, for we are sure and secure in our beliefs/doctrine.

CHAPTER 19

# SECOND CALL TO ENTER THE SEALED CHAPEL

Today is Friday, April 18th, 2008. A question came to me through an impression in my spirit. The question asked, "What do you want most?" My response was, "To remain my Father's child, always led by You my Lord and my Father, doing Your will according to Your Word in total submission and obedience, being faithful to You, while loving You with all my heart, soul, mind and strength." This is what I want to continue to do above all else. This outshines everything, nothing else comes close to it apart from being home in heaven with my Lord and Father, and the more I examine myself, the more I realize that this is really what I truly want, while I am still here on this earth. "Thank You Lord Jesus for this blessed desire You have blessed me with."

The reason I responded the way I did, is simply because I am finished with wanting my own way and therefore my will. I do not want my will to be done; indeed, I am afraid of my will, because I have seen how destructive my will can be, for it had kept me bound to the ways of the sinful nature and therefore the flesh, the world and the devil. So then, I personally do not want anything to do with my will and ways. This is a sign to me that I am truly finished with the ways of the sinful nature, especially when one considers the beauty and the preciousness of the will and ways of the beloved God and Lord. Once you realize this, you will never again want anything to do with your own will and ways, for they are of the sinful nature. This is the way I want to live and walk before the Lord Jesus every day of my life, and it does not waver or change. Our will and ways tend to lock us into a life of self-importance, self-seeking and self-interest, where emptiness, loneliness and misery are the result, and God is the one who is blamed and accused for it all.

On this Friday, the Lord Jesus told me that I am to enter the chapel the following Tuesday morning at 8:00 a.m. and to remain there for three days. This is four days away, and although I have been waiting so long for this moment to come, here it is, and there are none of the usual expected reactions, emotions or feelings of any kind that one would normally have in the natural. But rather, according to the natural, it is as if nothing was said, for it all took place in my spirit, and remained there steadfast. This is how it has been when the Lord Jesus speaks to me or tells me to do something or to go somewhere. There never is any emotional excitement or reaction in my flesh to these commands; they always seem so low keyed, quiet, gentle and natural, as if they are part of the everyday experience. They therefore seem like nothing outside of the normal is happening. Yet, there are major things taking place in the spirit realm that I cannot get in touch with.

Today is Monday, April 21, 2008, and although I am preparing to enter the chapel tomorrow morning, I still continue to feel as if nothing out of the ordinary is happening, yet knowledge tells me that this could be the greatest moment of my life about to take place, since being blessed with Salvation. But it is too awesome for me to contemplate, and so I won't, for I might become afraid, and I did for a flash of a second; then it disappeared because the Lord rescued me.

The great and loving Almighty, brought back to my mind that I will be meeting with the same God who visited me when I was a child. I remember so well His loving embrace, and later, those gentle, inviting and loving waves that He extended to me as He ascended into the heavens, along with all the other appearances and the many times He has spoken to me: then when He took me to that high mountain and placed me on His bosom and held me there close to His heart. He was so gentle and so tender while pouring out love on me, since love emanates from His person. There was the time He allowed me to follow Him across that mountain and onto the clouds and out there into the blue, where He literally allowed me to enjoy His blessed presence, by playing around His legs as a small child would. Then there was the time after satan had attacked me, and the Lord Jesus appeared in the other corner of the room immediately thereafter. Also, when He, my beloved Lord Jesus, walked alongside the car for eleven hours, as I drove across the desert from the border of Texas, all the way to the border of California. These were major appearances, but there were also several other smaller appearances.

This is the God, Lord and Father I will be going into that room to bow before, and to remain in that posture to honor Him in reverent fear, loving Him, with my whole heart filled with desire for Him, admiring Him every moment, and I pray that He will fill my heart with worship and my mouth with praise to Him – the great, kind, loving and awesome God, Lord and Father that He is. Therefore there is nothing to fear. "Thank You blessed, beloved, holy Father and Lord."

The day for me to enter the Chapel is finally here, and in obedience to my Lord, I approached the sealed door, opened it and entered the room on April 22, 2008. Remember, this room has been sealed for over 12 years since I was anointed there to be the servant of the Living God, and before that for 6 years – a total of 18 years since it has been sealed. When I approached the door of the Chapel, to my amazement, there was no fear, no anxiety, no apprehension, no timidity and no unnatural feeling or response of any kind. Everything seemed so normal, as if nothing out of the ordinary was happening. We unsealed the door and opened it as if this was done every day. I entered the room as normal as if this was something I did on a daily basis. There were no thoughts, no feeling high or low, no emotions or sentiments of any kind. I felt as if nothing was happening out of the ordinary, yet His command was there before me.

I entered the room, and then sat on the floor on a sleeping bag I had brought with me, and suddenly, a sweet peace came within and all around me. I enjoyed it while it lasted.

I looked around at the beauty of the draped walls with their various colors of white and red, blue and gold, and at the Lord's chair covered in purple and decorated in gold around the edges in its place at the head of the table, which measures ten feet long and four feet across. It is covered with a white tablecloth with folds all around it, hanging down to the floor on all sides. The table setting is all in red and gold. The setting before the Lord is all in gold, while all the other settings around the table are in red. The napkins and placemats for the Lord are all white and edged with lace on all sides, while the others around the table are all in red. All the way around the table, right under the white tablecloth on the floor, lays a red cushion band, extending three feet out from under the tablecloth. Sitting on it are small white pillows, placed approximately two and a half feet apart. These are for kneeling. These are not all that are in the room, but I think this is enough to give an understanding to those who are interested.

I thought – how beautiful! Shortly thereafter, that sweet peace left me. Then I said, "I will wait in silence and in hope in my Lord, for He is my strength and my guide." After this, demonic images began to appear in front of me. They were all ugly, but one of them was so ugly, it was unbelievably hard to look at. And no, I was not afraid, for the Lord Jesus kept me from being afraid, as He did at the time of the anointing.

April 23, 2008, the second day in the room. I had a relatively calm morning, but after midday the distraction and the temptation were very heavy, to the point where I could not focus on the Lord Jesus or my purpose for being there, but the Lord Jesus sustained me. This afternoon, there continues to be an unusual discomfort and restlessness that had developed in my body, and a kind of impatience in my mind. Such things I am not accustomed to having. I opposed them, yet I repented, not wanting to take any chance as to why they were there. I further used them to utter a small prayer for those who go through such things on a daily basis. I also had a rough night with very little sleep, along with pain on every side of my body. I lay on my left side and there was pain. I lay on my back and there was pain. I turned on my right side and there was pain, I lay on my stomach and there was pain. I sat up and there was pain.

I believe that the devil was afflicting me in this way, to push me to be discouraged and give up and leave the room in disobedience to the Lord Jesus, to condemn me thereafter. But thanks be to our beloved God and Lord, He sustained me.

On the following day, the Lord Jesus lifted the pain and the discomfort from my body, along with all the afflictions the devil used to torment me with. The devil used such words as: "You are going to be taken up to heaven tonight. Remember you are going up to heaven tonight." He said these sometimes every half-an-hour, while at the same time, having demonic images all around me. All this tells me how much my Father loves me, to have permitted me to be tested in such a way, to prepare me for that which is waiting to confront me in the future.

April 24, 2008, the third day in the room. This day started off as usual with diversions and temptations of all kinds, but not as heavy as they have been on previous days. But the Lord Jesus put a song in my heart alongside the temptations each day. "Thank You beloved Lord Jesus."

Today will be the last day in the room and so we will see what the Lord will do. There is no excitement or emotion of any kind. Everything is very low keyed as if nothing is happening or is going to happen. None of this makes any sense to the mind, but I guess this is how it is supposed to be, so that faith in the living God and Christ will be the overriding factor.

One would think that in such a situation I would be greatly looking forward, with the heart pounding, being anxious about what is to come. But no, I am calm within, as calm as one can be as if nothing is happening, or is going to happen. (After midday, the Lord Jesus removed from my body, another heavy discomfort, along with the pains that had developed. This allowed me to lay down in peace. He also opened His Word to me and gave me two beautiful and profound revelations in it. "Thank You Lord Jesus."

I have waited patiently for thirty-nine years with a low-keyed looking forward for this day to come – and here it is! It is now 12 minutes after 6 p.m. This means the time for the coming of the Lord is hours away, for my three days will be up at 8:00 a.m. in the morning, and there is no sense that anything is happening or is going to happen. This is strange, but I thank the Lord Jesus for this, because I would hate to be anxious and excited. Yet one would think that there would be at least a good feeling about what is going to happen, but in the feeling realm there is nothing, there is not even the slightest feeling or sensation – there is simply no emotion about it. It is as if I have no feeling at all, not even with the demonic images around me, which have been daily since I entered the room. Yet, faith is alive and well in the Lord Jesus and my Father in heaven.

Tonight is the last night in the room. I fell asleep at about 11:00 p.m., and at ten past twelve I awoke to find my body being rocked back and forth from side to side, and from front to back. It felt like an earthquake was taking place, at least I thought so. There were also pointed indentations or impressions being made along both sides of my body – at least, that is how it felt. Before and after this, I had three different experiences of having extremely bright light shining in my face while having my eyes closed. I could not understand how that could be; having my eyes closed made no difference whatsoever. The light shone right through my eyelids, as if my eyes were open. After this I sat up for a while.

By this time it was about 2:00 a.m. and everything seemed to have ended. I thought it was all over, and so I lay down. I had a double sleeping bag on the floor.

At 3:15 a.m., I was laying close to one of the walls with my face turned to it. There was by this time, a very quiet peace all around. Then the precious presence of the beloved Lord came behind me. I could feel His presence against my body, and it seemed as if both of His hands were upon my body, at least that is how it felt, one on my lower back and the other between my shoulder blades. I did not look around, but I calmly said in a very soft voice, "Is that You Papa?" (This is the name given to me to refer to my Lord and Father ever since the day I came home to Him.) And it was. Although He did not answer, He remained there for a moment and then He left. The whole thing was quiet and very low-keyed; it was not the great appearance I had thought would take place.

The Lord Jesus did a mighty work in my mind. He gave me the ability to be able to go over the books and bring them to completion. This did not seem possible before, but now that I have gone over them again, I could see how rough they were and how much they needed to be cleaned up and smoothed out. They needed much work to finish them. Many details were still needed to be completed in all of them, but I did not know or understand how to do such things. But the Lord Jesus knew, and so He gave me that which was necessary to finish them, and without this touch of His, I would not be able to bring them to completion. That day, He gave me the ability to bring them to their conclusion, which I could not have done otherwise. The Lord Jesus also gave me a little more memory, which I desperately needed. Obviously, one of the reasons for His coming was to equip me to be able to finish the books. "Thank You beloved Lord Jesus."

This was definitely not what I had been looking for, especially after the many years of waiting, the elaborate preparations in the room, and the many years that it had been sealed. In addition, I had full knowledge while preparing the room, that it was being prepared for the purpose of the appearance of the Lord Jesus there sometime in the future, and that I would be there before Him. And indeed, the Lord Jesus did come, and I was there before Him, but none of this happened in the way I thought it would. Now I can see that one of the reasons for His coming was about the preparation of me to bring the books to their completion.

The knowledge that someday the Lord would appear, and I would be called to be before Him, was given to me ever since the day I came to the Lord, thirty-nine years ago. All this, plus the many years of waiting, caused me to misguidedly walk in a state of anticipation of a mighty move of God, when He comes to empower this work and get it on its way. But this did not happen. So obviously, the empowering of this work is yet in the future. This appearance was mostly about His books, and through them, His message to His body, the church. The room is still dressed and closed, so there might still be another appearing in the future.

Indeed, when I felt the shaking of my body, at first I thought that this was the beginning of things to come – things are really going to happen in a big way. But when it stopped, and I waited for a long time and nothing else happened, I felt disappointed, and this lead to a feeling of dissatisfaction. All this took place within a moment of time.

It was then that the Holy Spirit quickened me to what was happening within me. This surprised me greatly, because disappointment with what the Lord Jesus does or does not do, are not things I am accustomed to experiencing, and so I quickly knelt in repentance before my Lord. He then showed me the source of the disappointment, which was the expectation that I had held to in my heart over all those years, and although I had died to expectations across the board, I had never seen this in the same context as one would see expectation normally. I only saw it as an anticipation of that which is to come. In that I was deceived, but our God and Lord is faithful. He rescued me that night, for only He knows what that could have led to, because for many souls, unfulfilled expectations have always led to disappointment and a demand. When this is not acknowledged and repented of at this point, it can easily lead to accusation, rebellion and withdrawal, and from then on a difficulty to trust the Lord Jesus again.

When I realized how close I had come to such evil/sin against the beloved Lord Jesus, I was surprised and was very sorry, and so I cried out to the Lord in repentance, to forgive me of this wickedness/sin I had committed against Him. With this done, I committed myself to my Lord, never again to hold any expectation about anything that He will do or will not do, or that He is going to do, now or in the future, not even concerning the things He has promised me. I let them all go to Him, to simply live in trust in Him from day to day in these areas too, for the rest of my life, and with His enabling, this will be so.

After all this happened, I said, "Lord Jesus You do not have to come. You owe me nothing. You have done everything that was needed to be done on my behalf on Calvary's Cross, where You paid the price for my sins and bought me out from under the heavy hand of the devil and sin. You forgave all my sins, You gave me a new spirit, and You redeemed my soul. You gave me Your Word, and through it You revealed Yourself and blessed me with the blessed knowledge of Yourself, Your ways and Your will. You have loved me and given me Your grace to sustain me; You have given me Your Spirit to guide me, teach me and lead me into Your

Truth. You have given me love for You, hope and a bright future in heaven with You, etc. You have done more than enough for me; You don't have to do anymore. Yet, You have and You will, for if You do not I will not be able to walk this road, nor will I be able to make it through all the difficulties ahead of me. I know that I cannot walk this road without You leading me. Thank You, beloved Lord Jesus."

At the same time, a song came into my heart from the Lord Jesus that says, "Lest I forget Gethsemane, lest I forget His agony, lest I forget He died for me, lest I forget His love for me, lead me to Calvary." This is the best I can do with the words of the song, for I do not know the words to this song, other than what I have mentioned. But those of you who know this song, understand the significance of it. It is a hymn.

As I previously stated, at 3:15 a.m. the Beloved appeared, but He did not come in a great and powerful wind that tore the mountain apart and shattered the rocks, neither did He come in an earthquake or a blazing fury of fire. But He did come, with a very gentle, quiet and soft presence. My response to Him was in a very soft and gentle voice, "Papa, is that You?"

After it was all over, I reflected on what I had said to the Lord Jesus, and I thought that it was so very sweet. "Thank You beloved Lord

Jesus for that response." Later, I was reminded of His appearance to Elijah.

> The LORD said, "Go out and stand on the mountain in the presence of the LORD, for the LORD is about to pass by." Then a great and powerful wind tore the mountains apart and shattered the rocks before the LORD, but the LORD was not in the wind. After the wind there was an earthquake, but the LORD was not in the earthquake. [12]After the earthquake came a fire, but the LORD was not in the fire. And after the fire came a gentle whisper. [13]When Elijah heard it, he pulled his cloak over his face and went out and stood at the mouth of the cave. Then a voice said to him, "What are you doing here, Elijah?" 1 Kings 19:11-13

Laying there on the floor, I thought that my greatest blessing that night was the appearance of my Lord, then secondly, was the revelation of the depth of the expectation I had had concerning the coming of the Lord, and how easily that could have led me to accuse my dearly beloved Lord Jesus, and could even have led to rebellion, although I have never done those wicked things against my Lord. Yet I pray that I will never be so arrogant as to say that will never happen to me. Still, I pray that my beloved Lord Jesus will continue to keep me from such evils and wickedness. "Thank You for rescuing me that night, dearest beloved Lord Jesus."

I can clearly see now, why the Lord Jesus came in the way He did. It is because He loves me, and because He chose to reveal my heart in the way He did, to further rescue me from present and future deceit and harm, through the continual sanctifying work of the Holy Spirit. For He is now going to cleanse me of all the evil that was revealed through this experience. That is why He has permitted it to come to the surface, so that I would acknowledge it and repent, so that He could cleanse me of it. "Thank You Lord Jesus."

Today is Monday, April 28, 2008, four days after I left the room. Expectation has its place and purpose, but it should not be applied to the Lord our God, and I will tell you why. Yesterday in the morning, I was awakened with the understanding that to expect of God is to demand of God.

The Lord made it very clear to me then, that we should not expect of God. For instance we should not say: I expect God to answer my prayer, or I expect Him to do this or that for me; or I expect Him to supply my needs and heal me; I expect Him to change me, to deliver me, etc. The Lord Jesus showed me that to expect of Him is to demand of Him, for expectation is a demand.

I did not know this then, and so when I got up and left the room, I checked the dictionary, and among other things, it states that expectation means, "requires as appropriate or rightfully due," and, "require (someone) to fulfill an obligation." I then realized that in reality, to expect anything of God is to demand of God. And for sure, God owes none of us anything, so what could we be demanding from Him? Yet, many of us do, and there I was in the middle of it.

Yes, when we work at a job we should expect to be paid, and we do expect it. If we borrow from the bank or someone, they expect to be paid. If we lend someone our vehicle or tools or anything else, we expect them back. With these few examples, we can easily see that indeed, expectation is in reality, a demand to be paid what is owed to us, or to have the things we have loaned returned to us.

The words/term the Lord gave me to be used in place of expectation is, "to look forward to." In other words, as we pray and make our requests to the Lord Jesus, we can and should look forward to see how the Lord will answer; look forward to see what the Lord's will is in any given matter; look forward to see what the Lord will do with us or for us; look forward to see how the Lord is changing us or what the Lord requires of us; look forward to be going home to heaven to be with my Lord; look forward for the Lord Jesus to fulfill His Word in and through me and look forward to see how the Lord is going to fulfill His Word to me.

We can look forward to the Lord Jesus for all this and more, but we must not look forward for Him to work in us in a prescribed way that is according to our will, ways and understanding. God must do His work the way He does His work, and that is the only way it will ever be done. I know of souls who expect/demand that God do for them that which they deem necessary in the way they want it done, according to their own understanding, will and ways, and if it is not done their way, they murmur and accuse the Lord for not giving them the things that they want. God cannot work in us according to our expectations/demands. That He cannot, and will not do. Everything that God does is done according to His will, and His will alone.

Please be aware that when this revelation came, the books were mostly written, although not finished. The words EXPECT and EXPECTATION had already been used throughout them. I am therefore asking each person who will read these books, to read them with this understanding.

The room in which the Lord Jesus appeared is large. It is twenty-three feet wide by forty feet long. It will now be set apart; maybe for His next appearance, and in the future to be used only for communion, and in those times to worship our dearly beloved God and Father, and the beloved Lord Jesus Christ, when He purifies the hearts of His children to live the abundant life the Lord Jesus brought, so that they walk before Him with a pure heart. Also, I could not have completed any one of the books without the Lord's coming and giving me the further anointing necessary to be able to do so. He has now given me understanding and the additional guidance needed to put the finishing touches on all the books, as He leads me according to His will, to complete them.

In March 2009, the students seemed to have begun to take seriously the state in which they have been living (so I thought), having their hearts filled with many lies of various kinds about God, which the enemy uses to keep them at bay from Him. There they see God as this monster who has wronged them and taken advantage of them throughout their lives from their childhood, and who continues to rob them of life and every good thing that they could have had over the years. To them, He is cruel, unjust, unloving, unforgiving, unmerciful, unkind and on top of that, He hates them, He is vindictive towards them and He rejects them. In their eyes, He is their enemy, and they are His victims. Therefore, they wanted nothing to do with Him, so they have been on the run, trying to escape Him at every point. Yet they are in the church proclaiming, Jesus I love You.

What I am understanding from them now, is all that I have taught them was never received; it was instantly rejected. Indeed, they have closed their ears to any and everything I have taught for over thirty-six years, while pretending that they are receiving it all, in the same way they have rejected God's Word over all their lives. What they are saying to me now, is that for thirty-six years, they saw me as an agent of who they see as this wicked God, who they wanted no part of. In such a state, they see themselves as justified in deceiving me and even provoking, taunting and lying on me – as they have on God – all to discourage me and cause me to give up, so that they would be further justified in their beliefs saying – just as they thought. See, God has abandoned us. According to them, this would let them off the hook, where they would not be the one who renounced their call or their training. Therefore, their state of self-goodness and self-righteousness would remain intact and not be discredited. All of this they have said that they have repented of again and again, only to repeat it. If you do not take responsibility for your beliefs and thoughts, the devil will plant on you what he wants you to believe and think, and you will irresponsibly take them and walk in them and make them yours.

After understanding these things, I thank the Lord Jesus for His precious grace that sustained us all throughout those long years, without which there would be great destruction, and I would have been killed, since getting rid of me was always a priority for them.

They have told me several times, when according to them they have repented, of how they have wanted me dead and out of their way, so that I would not be putting God before them any longer. According to them, getting rid of me would be getting God out of their lives.

Regardless of all that had and was taking place, the beloved Lord Jesus kept our feet to the fire, until He brought all this to a head, to show me the things that He sees in the heart of the church, because without revealing that which is there in the heart, that which satan uses against God's people, the church, it would just go on and on. One would never know what has kept the church in this state of spiritual poverty that it is in. The statement that this makes is: the church seems as if it has no Lord, and this suits the devil's purpose.

This last Sunday, I happened to turn on the TV to a Christian channel, and heard a pastor concluding the service with an altar call. He said that anyone who has marital problems, financial problems, or sicknesses, to come forward for prayer. This call resulted in the entire congregation of several thousand standing up and leaving their seats to come forward. This confirmed to me what the Lord Jesus has been showing me over all these years – the spiritual poverty and therefore the darkness that is over the church.

But does the church want its Lord to reign over it, or is it satisfied with having its own way, going its own way and doing its own thing, all according to its own will? What does the church really want? This question must be answered, so that if it is the Lord Jesus it wants to reign over it, it will then be preparing itself to open its heart through the acknowledgement of its ways, repentance and prayer, and be ready and willing to submit and to yield up its all, to then receive the cleansing that the Lord Jesus is about to bring to it, so that it can then begin to live the abundant life that the Lord Jesus brought.

> 'Now get up and stand on your feet. I have appeared to you to appoint you as a servant and as a witness of what you have seen of me and what I will show you. [17]I will rescue you from your own people and from the Gentiles. I am sending you to them [18]to open their eyes and turn them from darkness to light, and from the power of Satan to God, so that they may receive forgiveness of sins and a place among those who are sanctified by faith in me.' Acts 26:16-18

The students have begun to come to their senses (I think, or could it be I am being deceived again?), but it is a slow process. This is because the hearts are filled to overflowing with evil against their God and Lord – with lies that they have been confirming and reaffirming, which they have held in their hearts against the Lord since their childhood. But our beloved Lord Jesus has extended much grace to them, and He has begun to lead them away from their agreement with satan, to now begin to come into agreement with Him. However, as He does, they continue to let go of it. It would therefore seem that after thirty-six years of working with them, or chopping down branches as revealed through the vision of the jungle, to let the light of the Holy Spirit to shine through, it would appear as if my work has just begun. The conclusion to this matter will be told in later writings.

The Lord Jesus had said to me thirty-nine years ago that He made me a servant and a witness of things He will show me. These are some of the things I am being shown, and continue to be shown.

> "To the angel of the church in Sardis write: These are the words of him who holds the seven spirits of God and the seven stars. I know your deeds; you have a reputation of being alive, but you are dead. [2]Wake up! Strengthen what remains and is about to die, for I have not found your deeds complete in the sight of my God. [3]Remember, therefore, what you have received and heard; obey it, and repent. But if you do not wake up, I will come like a thief,

and you will not know at what time I will come
to you. 4Yet you have a few people in Sardis who
have not soiled their clothes. They will walk with
me, dressed in white, for they are worthy. 5He who
overcomes will, like them, be dressed in white. I
will never blot out his name from the book of life,
but will acknowledge his name before my Father
and his angels. 6He who has an ear, let him hear
what the Spirit says to the churches. Rev. 3:1-6

CPSIA information can be obtained
at www.ICGtesting.com
Printed in the USA
FFHW020339061218
49753470-54216FF